THIRD EDITION

EARNED VALUE
Project Management

QUENTIN W. FLEMING
and JOEL M. KOPPELMAN

PMI
Project Management Institute
Newtown Square, PA

Earned Value Project Management, Third Edition
ISBN: 1-930699-89-1
ISBN 13: 978-1-930699-8-92

Published by: Project Management Institute, Inc.
                 14 Campus Boulevard
                 Newtown Square, Pennsylvania 19073-3299 USA
                 Phone: +1-610-356-4600
                 Fax: +1-610-356-4647
                 E-mail: customercare@pmi.org
                 Internet: www.PMI.org

PMI Publications welcomes corrections and comments on its books. Please feel free to send comments on typographical, formatting, or other errors. Simply make a copy of the relevant page of the book, mark the error, and send it to: Book Editor, PMI Publications, 14 Campus Boulevard, Newtown Square, PA 19073-3299 USA.

To inquire about discounts for resale or educational purposes, please contact the PMI Book Service Center:

PMI Book Service Center
P.O. Box 932683, Atlanta, GA 31193-2683 USA
Phone: 1-866-276-4764 (within the U.S. or Canada) or
+1-770-280-4129 (globally)
Fax: +1-770-280-4113
E-mail: book.orders@pmi.org

10   9   8   7   6

CONTENTS

LIST OF FIGURES

INTRODUCTION

WHEN WE WROTE OUR INITIAL BOOK on Earned Value Project Management in 1996, we had as our primary goal to describe the concept with fundamental principles, which could be applied to all projects in any industry. As we see Earned Value being implemented on more and more projects, we feel that we have accomplished this objective.

Also in our initial edition, we inserted the word "project" into the title. This was deliberate. We wanted to make the point that Earned Value is a technique to better manage projects. It is not intended for use on continuing business processes, operations that have no unique deliverables. Earned Value is for the management of one-time-only projects, and portfolios of projects within an organization.

It has also been our goal to build on the fine work done by the United States Department of Defense (DOD) with Earned Value as a central part of what they previously called the Cost/Schedule Control Systems Criteria (C/SCSC), and now call their Earned Value Management Systems (EVMS). The DOD Pentagon has carefully accumulated actual empirical data on earned value applications, which has transformed the concept into a significant management science.

Since our first edition, we have witnessed the use of simple Earned Value on many projects—including software projects—and we find that particularly exciting. Realistically, Earned Value provides projects with a unique metric called the Cost Performance Index (CPI), and this indicator is the same whether the project represents a long-term, multi-billion-dollar, high-technology project, or a short-term, hundred-thousand-dollar software project. The CPI is a CPI . . . period. It is a solid metric that reflects the true cost performance of any project. Fundamental stuff:

The CPI and other earned value indices provide reliable metrics to compare the performance of one project with all other projects within an organization. Many call this project portfolio management. Earned Value has a key role to play in portfolio management because the data it provides on one project can be compared with all projects within the organization. We have added a new chapter on portfolio management using earned value metrics.

In this third edition, we continue to be aligned with the earned value coverage contained in the Project Management Institute (PMI's) *A Guide to the Project Management Body of Knowledge* (*PMBOK® Guide*), whose third edition was published in 2004. We are also consistent with the *Practice Standard for Earned Value Management*, developed by PMI and its College of Performance Management.

But we have added some important new coverage in this third edition. There is a new chapter covering earned value measurement on project procurements (i.e., the materials, contracts, and subcontracts that projects may issue). With direct labor, it is fairly easy to measure performance, but purchased items always give us a challenge.

We have also taken exception to the inclusion of level of effort (LOE) tasks into the performance measurement baseline. We feel that LOE tasks have no place in a performance baseline and make some specific recommendations on LOE use: quantify LOE and quarantine all LOE tasks.

And perhaps most important, we have continued our earlier theme of suggesting that executives of publicly held companies have a fiduciary duty to their investing stockholders that will require the employment of at least a simple form of Earned Value on all projects that could have a "material" impact on their corporate profits. The Sarbanes-Oxley Act, which was signed into law by the President in 2002, requires full disclosure of all pertinent financial data. We feel that this is a mandate for earned value performance measurement on all significant capital projects.

We want Earned Value to be a tool . . . to help better manage all projects and portfolios of projects within the organization.

QUENTIN W. FLEMING   JOEL M. KOPPELMAN
Tustin, California 92780   Bala Cynwyd, Pennsylvania 19004

1

EARNED VALUE PROJECT MANAGEMENT
. . . AN INTRODUCTION

> *Earned Value Project Management is an invaluable tool in the management of any project. In its simplest form, Earned Value represents nothing more than fundamental project management—managing a project with a resource-loaded schedule. Here, the authors describe the technique in storybook form. It is not a true story . . . but it could be.*

ONCE UPON A TIME, there was a young man who wanted to be a project manager. Don't ask us why.

In school, the young man took the most challenging of technical subjects, and he also liked to manage things. He graduated with a master's degree in a technical discipline and immediately went to work for a small-but-fast-growing hi-tech company. This company was a leader in developing new products for its niche of the market. It had just gone public and its initial public offering of the stock was a huge financial success. The young man knew he had joined the right company. All he wanted was his chance at bat. He wanted to manage his own project.

Weeks went by. Months went by. Months! And he had yet to receive an assignment of any consequence. He was becoming discouraged. He considered updating his resume to start looking around again. If his present employer did not recognize his talents, perhaps others would. He did not have time to waste. This young man was in a hurry.

Then one day, as he was walking down the hall, the Chief Executive came up to him. She inquired as to how he was getting along. Then she remarked: "How would you like an important assignment to manage a new company development project for us?" The young man could hardly get out his enthusiastic acceptance. Then the CEO said: "Okay, if you're interested, call my secretary and get on my calendar for tomorrow." As she was walking away, she commented to him: "This

1

is an extremely important project for our company, and I think you could manage it nicely. See you then."

The young man got little sleep that night. Imagine, his chance to actually manage a project, to be a project manager. He was in the Chief Executive's office a full 30 minutes before she arrived. When they met, she started out by saying: "This is one of the most important potential new products we have in the pipeline, but it needs some innovative thinking, and that's why I think you would be the right person to take this on. I need fresh ideas incorporated into this product."

She outlined her thoughts for the new product, and it was exactly the type of work he had prepared himself to do. She asked him to pull together a half-dozen cross-functional people from within the company and to prepare a project management plan for her review and approval. "If you have any problem getting people released, use my name to break them loose. I don't want stonewalling by anyone. This product is important to our future growth."

Then she closed the meeting by saying: "Time to market is most critical on this project. I know our competition is working on similar products, and I want to be first into the marketplace." The young man got the message, and it was better than he had ever hoped. On his way out, she mentioned another issue: "I would also like you to use a technique I have heard about but can't seem to get started here . . . Earned Value Management Have you ever heard of it?" "Yes, of course, we studied Earned Value in college and I think it would work well on this project" was his reply. "Good, I look forward to seeing your project plan" was her closing remark.

The young man circulated within the company and got the commitment of the right people to do the project planning job. This was a young start-up company, so the impenetrable "stone walls" that were so pervasive in older, more established companies had not yet set in. All he had to do was mention that the big boss was behind this assignment and he got his people. He didn't even have to describe the details of the assignment; they all knew it had a high priority.

PLANNING FOR EARNED VALUE PROJECT MANAGEMENT

The newly formed team met at the project manager's apartment to avoid interruptions and phone calls. "It shouldn't take us very long to put a plan down on paper" was his opening remark. They spent the next few hours conceptualizing and defining the project. After he captured their ideas, the project manager would prepare the final plan for review and approval of the team, and then submittal to the CEO. The project manager wanted everyone to buy into the project plan. They all knew exactly what was required in order to employ earned value performance measurement. It was simply classic project management, "Project Management 101."

First, project team members had to define what constituted the project: 100% of their assumed project scope. For this, they created a Work Breakdown Structure (WBS). Next, they decomposed the project scope into measurable tasks, each with an estimated value, and then assigned responsibility for actual performance of each task to a functional manager within the company. For this, the project team developed a *WBS Dictionary* to record their thoughts. They decided that their project needed 10 units to develop and test, and that each unit would require about the same level of resources to accomplish.

Next, they would take the work conceptualized from the WBS diagram and dictionary, and then prepare a detailed plan and schedule for all the major critical tasks. After a few iterations, they had a "project master schedule" (PMS) that was fully supported by critical path methodology. They did a forward and backward schedule pass to give them assurances that their schedule was, in fact, achievable. From start to completion, the project would take them 18 months to perform.

Lastly, they estimated the resources that would be required to produce these 10 units, which constituted the total project. Each article would cost them $150,000 to produce; thus the total project would require $1.5 million dollars to complete. They charted their requirements as illustrated in Figure 1.1, which they termed their "project management plan." This display would contain the three critical components of any earned value baseline plan: a WBS, a PMS, and a performance display graph. Each element was supported by detailed breakouts. This process is sometimes called detailed "bottom-up planning." The team had done its job, and it was now time for the project manager to take the plan to the CEO for her approval.

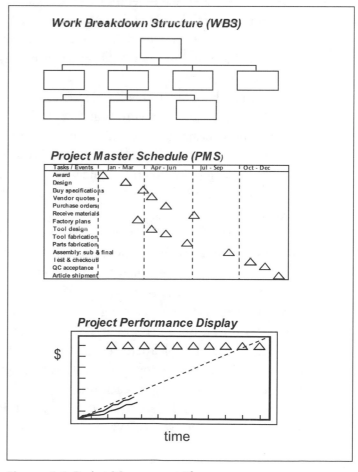

Figure 1.1 *Project Management Plan*

MANAGEMENT'S APPROVAL

The project manager made a copy of the project management plan and gave it to the CEO's secretary so that the CEO could review it prior to their approval meeting. When he was at last able to meet with the CEO, it was obvious that she had thoroughly read the entire plan. Every page was marked up, tabbed, and color-coded. He hoped that she liked what she had read.

The CEO opened the meeting on a positive note: "I want you to know that this is the finest project management plan I have seen as head of this company. I plan to use it as a model for approval of all our future projects." The project manager was off to a good start. She liked it!

Then the CEO went on: "However, you must not have heard parts of my requirements. Time to market is most critical on this project, and you have developed a casual, business-as-usual schedule of 18 months . . . that is completely unacceptable. I need this project completed in not more than 12 months. Can you handle that?" The young man took a deep breath and remarked: "Of course we can." Realistically, he had no clue as to how he would accomplish this, but the message from "on high" was becoming pretty clear.

"Also, you have taken this simple job and gold-plated it at an estimated cost of $1.5 million dollars . . . that also is unacceptable!" The boss was relentless: "The very most I could allocate for this project would be $1.0 million. We are not a big company and I have other commitments. Can you handle that?" The young project manager was beginning to understand why she had become CEO at such an early age . . . she was one tough person to deal with. Without hesitation, the young man accepted the budget dictate.

The CEO realized that she had come down pretty hard on the young man, so she wanted to provide some consoling words before he left: "Again, I want to emphasize that this is the best project plan that I have ever seen in this company, and it will be our role model for others to follow." Her words were some comfort, although the project manager was now starting to worry about what he would say to the other members of his team. Their buy-in was important to him.

As he was about to leave the office, the chief executive added: "I am very pleased that you are going to employ earned value measurement on this project. I would like to review your performance each quarter—at, say, every 3 months into your 12-month, one-million-dollar project!" "She never lets up" was the thought racing through his mind, as well as "What do I now tell the others?"

WELCOME TO THE WORLD OF PROJECT MANAGEMENT

Now, let us stand back from this discussion and try to understand what has taken place. Project team members got together and developed a thorough, comprehensive project plan, with considerable supporting data and schedule metrics, so that they could measure their earned value performance from start to completion. In particular, they scoped 100% of the total assumed project before they would begin to perform, and they created a detailed plan that allowed for the measurement of project performance.

Their supporting bottom-up detail indicated that they needed a full 18 months to complete the project, but the big boss directed them to do it in 12 months. They estimated the cost of the project at $1.5 million, but the big boss quickly cut it down to $1.0 million. What do we call this environment that the young project manager had just experienced for the first time in his professional career? We call it: *"REAL LIFE PROJECT MANAGEMENT!"*

Rarely do we ever get the total time we feel that we need to reasonably do the job. Projects are always in competition with other projects. And the authorized budgets are rarely what we estimate we need to complete any job. We are frequently given what is commonly termed a "management challenge," and we go out and do our best. It matters not if these management challenges are arbitrary, unreasonable, unattainable, unrealistic, or just plain stupid. We, as project managers, must find a way to get it done. Welcome to the wonderful world of project management!

THE FIRST QUARTERLY PROJECT STATUS REVIEW

Three months went by quickly. It was now time for the team to present its performance results to the chief executive and her management committee. This would be an awe-inspiring new experience for the young project team, but the thing that was working in its favor was the fact that team members were performing against a detailed plan, and they knew exactly what they had to do from the go-ahead to completion.

A brief summary indicated the following results: three of the ten units had been scheduled for completion at the three-month point, but only two were accomplished; thus, the team was slightly behind its planned schedule. It had forecast expenditures of $300,000 and had committed $300,000, so the team was right on schedule with its funding profile. Any optimistic person could easily paint a positive picture of this project: "We are right on our cost spending plan; a little behind schedule perhaps, but we are doing well," would be the positive spin put on these results by most practitioners.

However, the chief executive had specifically asked that Earned Value Project Management be employed on this project. That requirement adds a slightly different orientation to project performance data. Earned Value Project Management requires a detailed bottom-up performance plan, and a "three-dimensional" measurement against the baseline plan. Earned Value also requires a periodic forecast of the final expected results, based on actual performance.

In order to employ Earned Value, there must be a plan in place that will allow for continuous measurement of actual performance results. This may sound complicated, but it is not. Earned Value simply requires a focus on the completed physical or intellectual work, together with management's authorized budget for the completed work. We call this the "Earned Value."

In order to employ the earned value concept, a project must measure three dimensions of performance. The first dimension is called the "Planned Value." (Note: the United States Department of Defense (DOD) has been calling this the Budgeted Costs for Work Scheduled (BCWS) for three decades, but we choose to call it by the term "Planned Value.")

To determine Planned Value, the project must ascertain (1) how much physical or intellectual work has been scheduled to be completed as of a point in time, and (2) management's authorized budget for this authorized work. The Planned Value is simply a direct fallout of those detailed tasks specified on the project master schedule (PMS). (Important point: Earned Value requires a baseline master project schedule; or, stated another way, without a master project schedule, one cannot employ Earned Value).

In this case, the master schedule had specified three units to be completed as of the first quarter, and each unit had a budgeted value of $100,000. Thus, the project team could determine that the Planned Value for the first three months of the project was $300,000. (Note: the fact that the team's original estimate for each unit was $150,000 is interesting, at best. Management authorized $100,000 per unit, and management doesn't want to hear about other issues . . . period! Best that team members forget about their original $150,000 estimate.)

Next, project team members will need to measure the second dimension, called "Earned Value" for the same reporting period. To measure Earned Value, they will need to determine (3) how much of the authorized work they actually accomplished, and (4) the amount of management's original budget for the accomplished work. (Note: do not bother with the actual costs at this point because actual costs have nothing to do with creating Earned Value). Their actual performance results: they completed two units each with a value of $100,000, for a total Earned Value of $200,000.

The third dimension that team members need to determine is how much money was spent converting the Planned Value into Earned Value during the measurement period. So they look at the cost ledger and find that they have incurred actual costs of $300,000.

The three dimensions of Earned Value Project Management are now set for the first quarter and expressed in monetary terms, and a performance pattern has emerged for this project:

- The Planned Value was $300,000,
- The Earned Value was $200,000,
- The Actual Cost was $300,000.

The team members now need to analyze their performance results to determine if there have been any schedule or cost variances, which Earned Value Project Management looks at in a slightly different form than does traditional project management.

With Earned Value, a "schedule variance" is defined as the difference between the completed Earned Value less the Planned Value. In this case, team members planned to accomplish $300,000 of work but only did $200,000; thus, they are behind their planned baseline schedule by $100,000. Not so bad until they realize that they only accomplished 67 cents worth for each planned dollar!

Lastly, they need to know if there was a "cost variance." An earned value cost variance is determined by taking the Earned Value accomplished, and subtracting the Actual Costs spent or incurred. Team members spent $300,000 in actual costs to accomplish only $200,000 in Earned Value. Not so good when they realize that for each dollar they spent, they got only 67 cents of value earned! Thus, this project is behind its planned baseline schedule, and overrunning the costs. The negative schedule variance is serious, but the negative cost variance may be non-recoverable!

The team summarizes the results of its earned value performance for presentation to the management committee. It is not exactly a pretty sight, but one of extreme importance in the portrayal of the true status of project performance. This project at the end of the first quarter is performing at only 67% of its planned schedule, and 67% of cost performance. Stated another way, it is overrunning its costs by 50%. Although only at the 20% completion point, by monitoring these three dimensions of earned value data, the project is forecasting a significant final overrun of costs!

The project has already spent $300,000 to complete only $200,000 of work, so it is experiencing a $100,000 overrun of costs. And if the project continues at its present "cost efficiency" rate of earning only 67 cents for each dollar spent, it would need a 50% increased budget to complete the work ($1,000,000 divided by .67 equals $1,500,000). Also, if team members try to get this project back on the 12-month schedule, they will likely have to add additional resources and overtime to do the same authorized work. So the projected costs could equate to about a 100% overrun. (Note: there are scientific studies that reinforce these three forecasting methods.)

Most executives do not like to hear bad news. But this chief executive knows well that bad news does not get better with time; it only gets worse. At issue: bad news known at the 20% point in a project's life cycle gives management an opportunity to take corrective actions and possibly alter the final expected results. Conversely, bad news that is ignored until, perhaps, the 80% completion point severely limits management's opportunities to make the necessary changes to recover performance. Earned value gives management an important "early warning" signal.

These were exactly the kind of performance results that the chief executive wanted to see on this critical project. She wanted the true status—good, bad or ugly. She also knew that she had to take immediate action in order to make additional funds available for this most important project. She made a note to herself to cancel two other projects of lesser importance, to free up funds for this project. This project was important to her company, and it had to be funded to completion.

The CEO now declared: "Thank you for this presentation; it has been most informative. I now know that I was perhaps a little too restrictive in my initial budget authorization to you. I will now authorize a revised budget amount of $1,500,000 to complete this project." "Thank you" was the response from the young project manager. He knew that the team needed at least that amount to complete this project.

"However . . ." The chief executive was not going to let anyone off the hook just yet. "I want you to catch up on the late schedule position and complete this project with all the technical features in another nine months. Can you do that?" The manager's reply: "Yes we can, but that will require an accelerated schedule, and that will likely cost us the full $2,000,000, as we have presented to you."

"Okay, I will authorize this project a total budget of $1,500,000, but ask that you complete it within the 12-month schedule" were the directions from the CEO. "However, as we both well know, to recover this late schedule will likely cost us some additional money, so I will put another half-a-million dollars in my management reserve in case we need it. But it is not your money yet, and we want you back on schedule. Am I making myself clear?" asked the CEO. "Absolutely clear," answered the young project manager, "and we promise to do the best we can for the authorized budget."

"But getting back on schedule is your main performance objective, and the budget goal is simply my challenge to you. Do you understand that the schedule comes first?" was the final comment from the chief executive. "Understood," said the young project manager, who was getting to fully appreciate the delicate role he was playing.

THE FINAL RESULTS

Standing back from this story, we see that this project was likely underbudgeted (at $1,000,000) from the beginning. But based on what was authorized and what the project team was experiencing, the likely final forecast of budget needs was in the statistical range of between a half-million and a full million over the initial ($1,000,000) budget. Both the project manager and the CEO clearly understood this fact. But the CEO was not ready to relax her management challenge to this team. She released an additional half-million dollars to the project, but she asked that they also get back on schedule. Getting back on schedule would cost additional resources, and likely require the full million to achieve. But she was not yet ready to authorize the full amount.

This chief executive knew the benefits of employing Earned Value. She believed the accuracy of data that was being presented by the project team and the final projections of required costs. At the 20% completion point, the team was predicting an overrun of between 50% and 100%, and she was convinced that this would ultimately be the case. In order to fund the completion of this critical company project, she took immediate steps to cancel two other internal company projects of lesser importance. She knew what she had to do in order to free up funds for this high-priority project. Other executives who do not employ Earned Value or do not rely on the performance data often find themselves over-committed in their project portfolios, sometimes experiencing catastrophic results.

The final results were in: this project was completed with all the required technical features, on time within the 12-month schedule. But the final actual costs reached $2,000,000. The new product worked exactly as required, and the additional funds to complete the project were made available by the CEO when she cancelled two other projects of lesser importance.

Life was good at this company. The young project manager's professional career was off to a great start. He performed exactly as desired by senior management. Earned value allowed this company to balance the technical requirements against cost and schedule considerations.

POSTMORTEM: THE VALUE OF EARNED VALUE

Question: Will the use of Earned Value on projects prevent cost overruns?

Answer: Never. Overruns are typically caused by some combination of these three factors:

Management authorization of too low a budget to do the job,
Poor technical performance from the project team, and
Scope creep.

If management authorizes an inadequate budget, the project team performs poorly, or new work is constantly added because the project scope was never properly defined in the first place, Earned Value will not prevent cost growth. Earned value cannot perform a miracle!

What Earned Value will do is provide an "early warning signal" to the project manager, to senior management, and to the customer. It will indicate that the project will likely require so much money to complete, unless actions are taken to change future events. Sometimes project scope will need to be reduced. Sometimes risks will need to be taken. Sometimes additional funds will need to be made available to complete the project.

Earned value project management can help deliver better performance on all projects.

2

EARNED VALUE PROJECT MANAGEMENT
. . . AN OVERVIEW

> *Earned Value is for Projects . . . it is not for*
> *Continuous Business Operations*

MOST PRACTITIONERS OF EARNED VALUE refer to it as "Earned Value Management" or simply EVM. When we wrote our initial book on the subject in 1996, we intentionally inserted the word "project" into the book title. This was done to emphasize an important point not always understood: Earned Value as a technique is effective in the management of projects. But put another way, EVM has very limited utility in the management of continuous business operations. What's the significance of this point? We suggest that you employ Earned Value on your projects, but not on continuing operations.

The latest edition of the *PMBOK® Guide* inserted important new language that distinguishes between an organization's "projects" versus their continuous business "operations."[1] A project is a one-time-only endeavor that has unique work to accomplish and has specific deliverables. You must finish all the deliverables in order to finish the project. Project measurement should, therefore, transcend all arbitrary fiscal periods. Projects are measured from their start to their finish. An example might be a one-time project to establish a new help desk. Until the project is done, the help desk is not operational. Once it is operational, the project is over.

By contrast, a business operation represents continuous work; it does not end, but goes on from one fiscal year through the next fiscal year(s). Guard services, the

---

1 *A Guide to the Project Management Body of Knowledge*—Third Edition, Section 1.2.2.

company cafeteria, and accounting support are typical examples of continuous business operations. Work done in overhead pools is, typically, a continuous operation. The latest *PMBOK® Guide* makes the following important distinction: "Projects are different because the project concludes when its specific objectives have been attained, while operations adopt a new set of objectives and the work continues."[2] Bottom line: Earned Value is recommended to help better manage your projects. Earned Value is not recommended for continuous business operations.

A SIMPLE INDUSTRIAL ENGINEERING CONCEPT GOT SIDETRACKED

The concept of Earned Value has been around for over a hundred years, or perhaps for only four decades, depending on how one determines its beginning. Over the years, it has gone by numerous titles, including factory industrial standards, the value of the work, Earned Value Management, performance measurement, the Planned Value of Work Accomplished (PVWA), the Budgeted Cost of Work Performed (BCWP), the Cost/Schedule Control Systems Criteria (C/SCSC), the Cost Schedule Planning Control Specification (C/SPCS), simply the criteria, PERT/Costs, and numerous other more unsavory titles.

Whatever term has been used over the years, the central focus of Earned Value has been consistent: the accurate measurement of the physical work performed against a baseline plan. Most important, it has provided a reliable prediction of the final costs and schedule requirements for a given project. Earned Value is based on an integrated management approach that provides the best indicator of true cost performance, available with no other project management technique. Earned Value requires that the project's scope be fully defined, and that a bottom-up baseline plan be put in place to integrate the defined scope with the authorized resources in a specified time frame.

In terms of the proponents and opponents of the concept, there appears to be little middle ground. Some individuals feel that the technique provides a valuable tool holding considerable potential, which should be employed in the management of all projects. Others are adamantly opposed to Earned Value, perhaps based on some prior bad experience with it. This group will suggest that the effort required to employ Earned Value far exceeds any utility gained from using the technique. To this camp, we respectfully suggest that they give Earned Value a try in its simplified form, employing only the basics, without all the bureaucratic bells and whistles. They may just find a valuable new tool to help them better manage their projects.

2 Ibid.

We find ourselves generally in the first camp: we do like the benefits of Earned Value. But we also have some definite reservations based on its past employment. It is our feeling that the earned value concept holds considerable promise for broad-based project management applications, but only when employed in a simple, more user-friendly model than has been typically mandated by government agencies in the past. Our reasoning: the requirements to oversee the performance of major new systems being acquired for government agencies on cost-reimbursable-type contracts are vastly different from the more typical needs of most project managers today.

Most project managers commit to performing their projects on a fixed-cost basis, within a finite authorization of company resources. Project management tools must be simple and easy to use, or they will be ignored. Likewise, Earned Value must be made simple or it will be ignored.

A rhetorical question: If the earned value concept is an effective technique . . . why has it not been embraced universally by the project managers of the world? It is our belief that Earned Value has been avoided—sometimes flatly rejected—by project managers, because the technique has been "encased" for the past four decades in countless non-value-added regulations and esoteric interpretations of the requirements. Too often, this has not been project management, but rather bureaucratic dictates carried to the extreme.

For almost thirty years, Earned Value was a part of what was called the Cost/Schedule Control Systems Criteria (C/SCSC). What started out originally as a simple concept used on the factory floor evolved into a sort of exclusive association, in which one had to be specifically trained in the use of a cumbersome new vocabulary in order to be a member of this select group. Most project managers are interested only in completing their projects according to the approved plan, and have neither the time nor the inclination to master a new vernacular. Often, management rightfully rejected the concept in total rather than adopt it in its rigid form. What a shame! For by rejecting this conceptually simple but effective cost-management technique, project managers have missed an opportunity to employ a powerful tool that could complement their other management tools—in particular, scheduling using the critical path method (CPM).

Please note that it is not the purpose of this book to in any way demean what was originally the C/SCSC. As used by the United States government and other governments in the acquisition of their "major system"—where all the risk of all cost growth was on them because they elected to employ a cost-reimbursable or incentive-type contract—C/SCSC was the perfect vehicle, and was demonstrated to be beneficial as a government-required mandate for some three decades.

However, major systems acquisitions by governments likely constitute only a small percentage of the projects of the world. We speculated earlier that less than one percent of the projects in the world fall into the category of "major projects." The overall dollars may be significant on major projects, but the total numbers of such projects are, nevertheless, quite small. But how about the other 99 percent of the projects in the world? With these projects, all risks of cost growth are not necessarily on the owners or the buyers, but rather on the project managers, because they have made fixed-cost commitments to their companies. All the risks of cost growth rest squarely with them. Could these project managers not benefit from a cost-management technique that helps them to achieve what they have personally committed to perform? We believe there is considerable potential in the universal employment of a simplified and user-friendly earned value approach in the management of all projects.

It is now time to take this simple factory management technique called Earned Value, and to employ it as it was originally intended by the industrial engineers over a century ago: to compare their baseline "planned standards" with the "earned standards" to measure schedule performance and, most importantly, to relate these same "earned standards" to the "actual costs" incurred, in order to precisely measure the true cost performance of their projects. We call this three-dimensional performance measurement, or Earned Value Project Management.

THE EARNED VALUE CONCEPT IN A NUTSHELL

There is nothing inherently difficult about the earned value concept. It does not require special training to grasp the fundamentals. In fact, many people use some form of Earned Value in their daily routines and are not even aware they are employing the concept.

For example, most construction-type projects will have someone responsible for performing work that they call cost engineering, which in other industries may be called project controls, management controls, etc. Any time a construction cost engineer takes the time to verify that the physical work was actually accomplished prior to paying a supplier's invoice, that cost engineer is, in effect, utilizing a simple form of Earned Value. He or she is focusing on the critical relationship between the actual costs being expended versus the physical work actually performed. Construction cost engineers focus on the true project performance: what we are getting . . . for what we are spending. That is Earned Value Project Management in a nutshell.

The earned value concept requires creation of a project performance measurement plan—called the Planned Value—which is typically specified by the project's scheduling system. Then, the Earned Value must be measured against the Planned Value, also with use of the project's scheduling system. The physical Earned Value performed is then related to the actual costs spent to accomplish the physical work, providing a measure of the project's true cost performance. It may help if one thinks of Earned Value as representing a resource-loaded scheduling approach.

Earned Value provides project managers with a type of "early warning" buzzer that sounds when faced with impending problems, allowing them to take the necessary corrective actions should the project be spending more money than it is physically accomplishing. Such warning signals become available to management as early as 20 percent into a new project—allowing ample time to take corrective measures to alter unfavorable outcomes.

TRADITIONAL PROJECT COST MANAGEMENT

Probably the best way to understand the earned value concept is to discuss a specific example. We will use the model from the introductory story of the young project manager implementing his one million dollar internal development project covered in Chapter 1.

To illustrate the concept, we will contrast the earned value method with the more traditional approach toward the management of project costs. Under the traditional cost and funding management approach, a new spending plan will be formulated by (or more likely for) the project manager for review and approval by senior management.

Figure 2.1 shows an assumed project cost expenditure plan. It time-phases the $1,000,000 project budget over a scheduled one-year period. The projected expenditures for the first quarter indicate that $300,000 would be required for the first

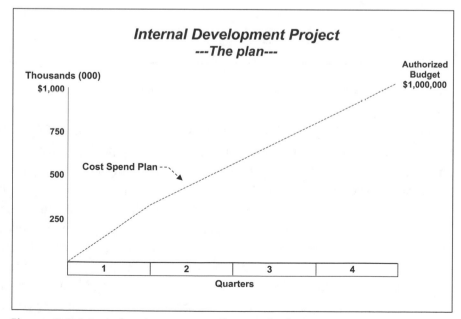

Figure 2.1 *A typical project cost expenditure projection*

quarter. The CEO reviewed the plan and gave her approval for this new, internally funded project. Management would expect the project manager to stay within the quarterly limits of the $1,000,000 total commitment, and to continuously monitor the performance during the life of the 12-month project.

Using a traditional cost management approach, the project manager would, at the end of the first quarter, display the cost performance for the benefit of management, as is illustrated in Figure 2.2. The approved spending plan called for an expenditure of $300,000 for the first quarter and actual results, thus far, show an expenditure of exactly $300,000. One could conclude without further review that the project was performing exactly to its financial plan: $300,000 planned and $300,000

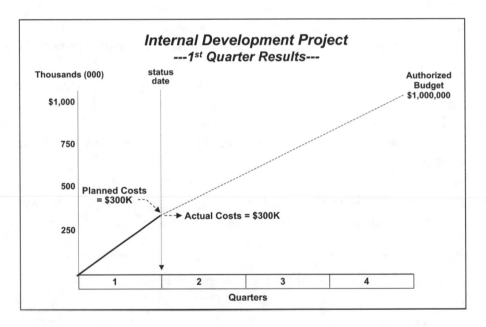

Figure 2.2 *Traditional cost management: plan versus actual costs*

spent. Perfect cost performance. Life is good. A fairly typical, but unfortunately, potentially deceptive approach to understanding project cost performance.

In fact, looking at the data as displayed in Figure 2.2, nobody could really determine the project's true cost performance results. To determine the project's true cost performance, one would need to compare the physical schedule results in the same format as the cost displays. But if the project's financial support people developed their cost displays using one approach—perhaps breaking out the costs by function—and the scheduling people developed their displays using another approach—perhaps reflecting WBS work tasks—the two critical displays of cost and schedule would not relate to each other. It is impossible to relate the true cost and schedule status when these two key functional groups develop their respective plans based on different assumptions. However—and this is an important point—it is a fairly common practice for organizations to have this type of disconnect. Finance will often reflect project costs by a functional organization, and scheduling will often reflect schedules by work breakdown. The two do not match!

An interesting observation: most of the projects in the world today would likely display their cost status for management using a chart similar to that reflected in Figure 2.2. Further, most of the schedule displays being used by projects today will not directly correlate to the cost displays provided by the finance people. Thus, most of the projects today likely are not working to an "integrated" management approach, which allows the project to equate the defined scope with authorized resources, both within the project master schedule. Earned Value Project Management requires an integrated baseline plan that relates the defined scope of work to the budgeted costs, as shown in the project schedule.

Let us now contrast the display in Figure 2.2 with an earned value performance chart, as shown in Figure 2.3. Here the total budget of $1,000,000 will be made up from detailed bottom-up planning, which allows for performance to be measured throughout the life of the project. There are ten milestones to be accomplished, each with a weighted value of $100,000. Once a milestone is completed, the project will earn $100,000.

The amount forecast to be accomplished at the end of the first quarter is now labeled the "Planned Value." Performance through the first quarter called for an accomplishment of three milestones, for a budgeted value of $300,000 of work scheduled. The Planned Value consists of two elements: (1) the work scheduled plus (2) the budget for the work scheduled.

The new three-dimensional project performance measurement that Earned Value provides is introduced in Figure 2.3. This display reflects actual physical Earned Value of only two milestones, representing an Earned Value of $200,000, against the Planned Value of $300,000. The Earned Value also consists of two elements: (1) the scheduled work that was completed and (2) the original budget for the completed work.

We can immediately see that the project is running behind the work it set out to do during the first quarter. It had planned to accomplish $300,000 in work, but had accomplished only $200,000. Therefore, the project can be said to be running a negative $100,000 schedule variance. An earned value schedule variance is defined as the Earned Value ($200,000) less the Planned Value ($300,000), which equals the schedule variance (-$100,000).

Also shown in Figure 2.3 are the Actual Costs of $300,000, an amount greater than the $200,000 Earned Value of physical work performed. Thus, it can be inferred that this project has spent $300,000 in Actual Costs to achieve only $200,000 worth of Earned Value. An earned value cost variance is defined as the Earned Value

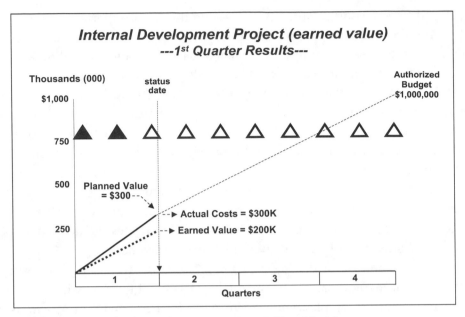

Figure 2.3 *Earned value project management: 3 dimensional*

($200,000) less the Actual Costs ($300,000), which equals the cost variance (-$100,000).

We can also call this actual condition what it is: an "overrun" of costs. This project can be said to be running a negative $100,000 cost variance. The delicate relationships reflected with these actual cost and schedule performance relationships can now be used to predict the final costs and schedule results of the project.

Important point: this project is in trouble. But one could not have discerned that condition using a traditional cost management approach. It is only when Earned Value brings in the three dimensions of performance that we can tell the project is experiencing problems. Such issues need to be addressed immediately by the project manager in order to avoid adverse cost overruns and schedule slippage.

TRADITIONAL COST MANAGEMENT VERSUS EARNED VALUE PROJECT MANAGEMENT

There is an important and fundamental distinction to be made between the data available for management using a traditional cost control approach as compared to the three-dimensional data available when a project employs Earned Value. These critical differences are summarized in Figure 2.4, and focus on variances to the baseline plans.

Using the displays of planned expenditures versus actual expenditures, a project's true cost performance cannot be adequately determined. With a

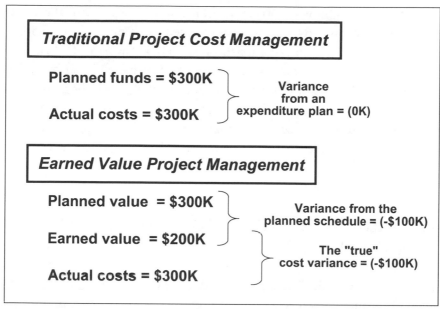

Figure 2.4 *The fundamental differences*

plan-versus-actual costs comparison, there is no way to ascertain how much of the physical work has been accomplished. Such displays merely represent the relationship of what was planned to be spent versus the funds actually spent. Cost performance as displayed at the top of Figure 2.4 indicates perfect results against the original spending plan. The project has spent its allowance. The utility of such displays only has significance as a reflection of whether a project has stayed within the funds authorized by management. Such displays reflect funding performance, not true cost performance. Yet, most projects today typically present their cost performance using similar graphic displays.

In contrast, as shown at the bottom of Figure 2.4, Earned Value Project Management displays three dimensions of data: the Planned Value of the physical work authorized, the Earned Value of the physical work accomplished, and the Actual Costs incurred to accomplish the Earned Value. Thus, under an earned value approach, the two critical variances may be ascertained. The first is the difference between the Planned Value of the work scheduled compared to the Earned Value achieved. As reflected in this chart, the project is experiencing a negative schedule variance of $100,000 from its planned work. Stated another way, one-third of the work originally planned for the project was not accomplished in the time frame being measured. The project management team is clearly behind the planned project schedule. Such variances, when used in conjunction with other scheduling techniques—particularly the critical path method (CPM)—provide invaluable insight into the true schedule status of the project.

Of greater concern, however, is the relationship of the value of the work done, the Earned Value, compared to the funds expended to accomplish the work. A total of $300,000 was expended to accomplish only $200,000 worth of work. Thus, the project has experienced a cost overrun of $100,000 for the work performed to date. This negative cost trend is of critical importance to the project because experience has indicated that such cost overruns do not correct themselves over time; in fact, cost overruns tend to get worse. The actual cost and schedule performance results can also be used independently or jointly to forecast the final results of the project with amazing accuracy.

EARNED VALUE COST AND SCHEDULE PERFORMANCE INDICES: THE SPI AND CPI

Employing the earned value concept allows the project management team to monitor its own performance against a detailed time-phased plan. Exceptions to the plan provide a wealth of reliable information, primarily centered on the cost and schedule efficiency metrics. Two accurate performance indices become available to the

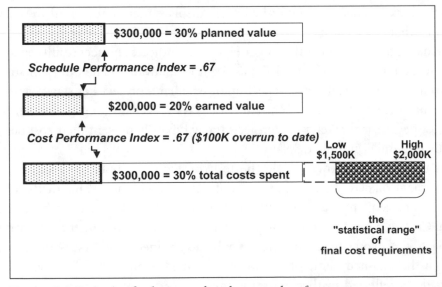

Figure 2.5 *Projecting final costs . . . based on actual performance*

project, as early as the 20-percent point of completion. Such relationships are illustrated in Figure 2.5.

Here, the three primary sets of data, as shown earlier in Figure 2.3, have been converted into a thermometer-type management display reflecting the three dimensions of project performance as of a given point in time. Dimension one—how much project work was scheduled to be accomplished—reveals that the Planned Value was $300,000, or 30 percent. Dimension two—how much work was actually performed—reveals that the Earned Value was $200,000, or 20 percent. Dimension three—how much money was spent to achieve the Earned Value—reveals that $300,000, or 30 percent, was spent.

In this analysis, we are indebted to those in the government who have worked with the C/SCSC concept over the past thirty-plus years, and for the body of knowledge that they have accumulated. These individuals have scientifically demonstrated the utility of these two relationships in assessing the performance of hundreds of projects, large and small, of various contract types, in various project phases, etc. They have developed powerful empirical data.

The first issue to be determined with these actual results: how long will the project take to complete all of the authorized work? The CEO authorized a one-year duration; will that happen? Using earned value metrics, we must determine what schedule-efficiency factor has been achieved for this project after the first quarter results. The project plan called for performance of $300,000 in work after the first quarter; however, only $200,000 in physical Earned Value was actually completed. The project is the equivalent of minus-$100,000 in planned work after the first quarter. At this rate of performance, it will likely take longer than one year to complete the project unless additional resources are immediately added (bringing in more people, using extensive overtime, etc.).

The amount of the Earned Value ($200,000) may be divided by the value of the planned work ($300,000), resulting in a planned schedule performance efficiency factor of only .67. Stated another way, for every dollar of physical work this project had planned to accomplish, only $.67 was completed. This project is said to have achieved a Schedule Performance Index (SPI) efficiency factor of .67. The SPI can be a valuable tool for use in conjunction with a critical path method (CPM) to forecast the expected completion date for the project. The SPI also has utility when used in conjunction with the Cost Performance Index (CPI) to forecast the total funds required to complete the project.

The second issue to be determined: how much money will the project require to complete all of the authorized work? The CEO authorized a fixed amount of $1,000,000 to complete the project; will this happen? To assess the required funds, we must determine the cost efficiency factor after the first quarter. By comparing the amount of physical Earned Value to the dollars actually spent to accomplish that Earned Value, one can determine the cost performance efficiency for a project. When we divide the Earned Value of $200,000 by the actual dollars of $300,000, we can determine that the CPI is .67 for the project. Stated another way, for every project dollar that was spent, only $.67 in physical work was accomplished. This project is said to have achieved a CPI of only .67.

The CPI is a powerful tool to predict the final costs needed to finish a job. The CPI can be used by itself, or in conjunction with the SPI to continuously forecast a statistical range of estimated final costs to complete the project. The SPI and CPI metrics can also be used to compare the performance of a single project to all other projects in an organization. Earned value metrics thus provide powerful tools in the management of a portfolio of projects, by providing accurate and reliable measurements of actual project performance.

USING THE CPI AND SPI TO STATISTICALLY FORECAST A RANGE OF FINAL PROJECT RESULTS

Question: Once a project has established a CPI and SPI pattern based on actual performance through a given measurement period, what is the benefit in knowing these two factors? Answer: Both the cost and schedule performance indices can be used to statistically forecast the final funds required to complete the project. Independent statistical forecasts can be a sort of "sanity check" on the trend and final direction of the project. They can be compared against the optimism that often prevails on projects: "Stay out of our way and let us do our thing." Such forecasts can be developed with the CPI alone, or used with the CPI in conjunction with the SPI.

Assume that, in spite of the negative cost and schedule performance results achieved in the first quarter of the project, the final estimated costs by the project manager are still forecast to be $1,000,000—the amount originally budgeted by the CEO. Would this have been a reasonable forecast? Probably not, unless there were extenuating circumstances that need be considered. A detailed bottom-up estimate to complete all of the remaining tasks is always the more desirable forecasting method. But detailed bottom-up estimates take time to prepare, and actually interfere with performing project work. As an alternative, an earned value statistical forecast can provide an effortless and reliable forecast of final cost requirements.

With earned value data, one can take the total budgeted funds of $1,000,000, divide the amount by the cumulative CPI factor of .67, and quickly, statistically, forecast that about $1,500,000 would be needed to complete the project. This forecasting technique has been demonstrated to represent a reliable indicator of the "low-end or minimum" total required project costs, which many feel is the very best that the project may experience.

A second method to forecast final costs relies on the actual values of both the CPI (.67) times the SPI (.67), and uses the resulting product (.4489) to statistically forecast the maximum funds likely required to complete the job. This method incorporates the cost overrun to date with a behind-schedule condition to produce a more pessimistic statistical forecast. The estimated amount is now something close to $2,000,000, and is considered by many to represent a "high-end" statistical method.

Thus, we can quickly create a statistical range of final cost projections between $1,500,000 and $2,000,000 needed to complete the project, and compare them with the "official" forecast provided by the project manager. The project has already incurred an overrun of $100,000, spending $300,000 to do $200,000 worth of work. The $100,000 spent is typically non-recoverable by the project. Any differences between the project manager's forecast and these statistical estimates should be reconciled with senior management.

Each of these statistical formulas used to forecast final cost and schedule results will be covered in greater detail later in this book.

IN SUMMARY

While the earned value concept was officially introduced to industry four decades ago, most of the applications, thus far, have been largely restricted to the acquisitions of major new systems by agencies of the United States and other governments. For some reason, the technique has not been universally embraced by the countless project managers in the private sector who also strive to perform their work as committed to senior management.

It is the belief of the authors that the resistance to the universal adoption of the earned value concept is not the fault of the technique itself, but rather of the implementation requirements, the terminology employed, and the countless rules and interpretations that have been perceived by many project managers to be overly restrictive. We must find a way to simplify the earned value concept, to reduce it to its bare essentials, if it is to be adopted as a broad-based project management tool for universal applications in all industries. We must find a proper balance between the utility of the earned value technique . . . versus the effort it takes to implement the concept.

That can easily be achieved by getting back to the three-dimensional basics that were used in the industrial factories over a century ago: simply relate the planned standards to the earned standards to the actual costs for accomplishing the work. This book seeks to describe a simple form of Earned Value for use in the management of all projects.

3

THE GENESIS AND EVOLUTION
OF EARNED VALUE

ORIGIN OF EARNED VALUE

In all likelihood, most of us became aware of Earned Value Management when it was a key component of what was then called the Cost/Schedule Control Systems Criteria, or simply the C/SCSC. The C/SCSC constituted thirty-five standards of compliance (called criteria) that were required from management control systems within private industry, to assure consistency in the reporting of performance on major United States government acquisition projects. The criteria were imposed by governmental agencies whenever they underwrote the risks of cost growth; that is, whenever they employed either a cost-reimbursable or incentive-type contract for a new developmental project.

The criteria were first released by the United States Department of Defense (DOD) in December 1967, and were consistently used as the approved method of cost management in the procurement of major new systems. Since then, other United States governmental agencies and several foreign governments have adopted identical or slightly modified performance measurement criteria for application with private industry. Canada, for example, adopted the criteria, but added an additional criterion specifically requiring critical path method (CPM) scheduling on major projects. The C/SCSC were silent on the requirement for CPM, but did emphasize the importance of having a scheduling system.

While the C/SCSC did encompass the concept of Earned Value Management, the C/SCSC had broader applications than simply employing Earned Value. We owe it to ourselves to understand the fundamental differences. Reason: the opportunities for broad-based Earned Value Management exist, but only if the fundamentals can be extracted from within the C/SCSC. Earned Value, as a part of the C/SCSC, was far too demanding and too inflexible for universal project management applications, in the opinion of the authors.

The earned value concept was originally conceived by industrial engineers working in early American factories, by such scientific management practitioners as Frederick W. Taylor, the father of scientific management; Frank and Lillian Gilbreth; Henry Lawrence Gantt; and others. One former United States Air Force general who was involved in the modern implementation of Earned Value over thirty years ago commented:

The earned value concept came to us right off the factory floor, from the industrial engineers who were comparing their **planned standards** with the **earned standards** and **actual costs.** We simply applied this same concept to our one-time-only, non-recurring developmental tasks.[1]

The favorable experience with Earned Value Management, as employed initially on the Minuteman Missile program, eventually led to the issuance of C/SCSC as a formal management doctrine in 1967.

These thirty-five formal management control system standards have led to the development of some rather sophisticated approaches for the monitoring of project performance. They have also provided a means to accurately predict the project's final cost and time requirements based on a project's own performance record as of any given point in time. As early as twenty percent of the way through a new project, the earned value performance results can be used to predict the final required costs within a finite range of values. At the start of a new project, the actual cost efficiency factor (called the earned value cost performance index) has been shown to stabilize, providing data that can be used to predict the final required costs for any given project.

If they were still with us today, the original scientific managers—Taylor, the Gilbreths and Gantt—would all be pleased with the body of scientific knowledge that has been carefully accumulated over the past three decades. In fact, certain professional management societies have incorporated some of these same findings into their professional repositories of information. Of particular significance to those of us working in the profession would likely be the Project Management Institute's landmark document, *A Guide to the Project Management Body of Knowledge (PMBOK® Guide)*. This universally read document describes Earned

---

1 Lt. General Hans Driessnack. In a personal interview (July 3, 1993).

Value in four of its key chapters: Project Integration Management, Project Time Management, Project Cost Management, and Project Risk Management.[2]

EVOLUTION OF THE EARNED VALUE CONCEPT

The earned value concept was conceived over a hundred years ago, sometime in the latter part of the nineteenth century. For purposes of this discussion, we have somewhat arbitrarily divided the evolution of Earned Value into distinct phases so that we can address each stage separately. However, as with any such forced classification, there is overlapping in these divisions.

PHASE 0 — THE FACTORY FLOOR: IN THE LATE 1800S

The earned value concept originally came from the industrial engineers working in the early American factories. For many years, the industrial engineers have done what most corporate executives fail to do even today: they employ a "three-dimensional" approach to assess their performance efficiency for work done in the factory. The industrial engineers measure performance against a baseline called "planned standards," and then measure the "earned standards" achieved against the "actual expenses" incurred to accurately measure the performance in their factories.

The result of this approach is Earned Value Management in its most fundamental form. Perhaps of most significance, the industrial engineers have defined a "cost variance" as representing the difference between the actual costs spent and the earned standards achieved[3]. This basic definition of what constitutes a cost variance is perhaps the litmus test for determining whether or not one is utilizing some form of Earned Value.

PHASE 1 — PERT/COST: 1962–1965

The Program Evaluation Review Technique (PERT) was first introduced to industry as a network scheduling and risk management device by the United States Navy in 1958[4]. PERT's original approach was twofold: to simulate the development planning

---

2 *A Guide to the Project Management Body of Knowledge*—Third Edition, Chapters 4, 6, 7, and 11.

3 Bruno A. Moski, Jr., in *Plant Executives' Deskbook,* (New York: McGraw-Hill Publishing Company, 1951) "Cost Control Fundamentals", page 25.

4 Special Projects Office, Bureau of Ordnance, (Washington, DC: Department of the Navy, 1958). *Project PERT.*

of a new project in the form of a logic flow diagram, and to assess the statistical probability of actually achieving the plan.

As first introduced, PERT placed a strong emphasis on statistical probability, which constituted one of the early difficulties. At the time (in the late 1950s), neither computers nor computer software programs were available to adequately implement the concept. Nevertheless, as a tool, PERT caught the imagination of both management practitioners and academia.

As a scheduling technique, PERT was never as successful as the critical path method (CPM), which came along at about the same time, but in another industry (construction). Two men working with these early concepts described the events at the time:

In 1956, E. I. DuPont de Nemours undertook a thorough investigation of the extent to which a computer might be used to improve the planning and scheduling, rescheduling and progress reporting of the company's engineering programs. A DuPont engineer, Morgan R. Walker, and a Remington-Rand computer expert, James E. Kelley, Jr., worked on the problem, and in late 1957 ran a pilot test of a system using a unique arrow-diagram or network method which came to be known as the Critical Path Method.[5]

Then, around 1962, the advocates of PERT as a scheduling tool chose to take another bold step to expand the concept. Their thinking: if one could accurately simulate the logic of a project taking the form of a network, why not add resources into the network and manage both time and costs? The result was the introduction of "PERT/Costs" in 1962. To accurately describe the environment at the time, since neither the computer hardware nor the computer software programs were available to properly support simple network scheduling, the addition of cost resources into these logic networks merely exacerbated the problem.

Neither the original PERT (which then went by the term "PERT/Time") nor PERT/Costs survived by the mid-1960s. Today, the term "PERT" does live on, but only as a generic title to describe any network scheduling method. In fact, most of the networks today that are called PERT are actually precedence diagram method (PDM) networks, not true PERT networks.

What of importance did survive from the short-lived PERT/Costs experience was the earned value concept. The implementation of PERT/Costs to industry at the time required eleven reporting formats from the contractors. One of these formats included a "cost of work report." Its format contained what was then called the "value of work performed" versus the actual costs:

A comparison of the actual costs accumulated to date and the contract estimate for the work performed to date will show whether the work is being

5 Russell D. Archibald and Richard L. Villoria. 1967. *Network-Based Management Systems (PERT/CPM)*. New York: John Wiley & Sons, Inc., pages 12-13.

performed at a cost which is greater or less than planned.[6]

Thus, Earned Value as a project management tool was initially introduced to modern industry in 1962. As a part of PERT/Cost, however, it would not last long. PERT/Cost had a life span of perhaps three years, but it did leave an exciting legacy: the use of earned value data to monitor the true cost performance during the life of any project.

By the mid-1960s, both PERT/Time and PERT/Cost had all but vanished from the scene. Industry executives and private companies did not take kindly to being told what management techniques they must employ and how they must manage their projects, no matter how beneficial such ideas may have been. The DOD project managers realized that they had to take a more sensitive approach toward private industry; and they did just that with the introduction of the C/SCSC criteria approach.

PHASE 2 — C/SCSC: 1967 TO 1996

The United States Air Force (USAF) took the lead to set standards that would allow it to oversee industry performance, without specifically telling industry what it must do. In 1965, the USAF formed a team called the Cost Schedule Planning and Control Specification (CSPCS) group. Meetings were held by some of the very same people who had been involved in the earlier implementation of PERT/Time and PERT/Cost. By virtue of their PERT experience, they quickly agreed that they would not impose any specific "management control system" on private industry. Rather, they conceived the notion of merely requiring that contractors satisfy broadly defined "criteria" with their existing management control systems. A subtle departure from the PERT experience, but it made all the difference between success and failure for the new approach.

The criteria concept simply required a response from industry to some rather basic questions, but was based on sound project management principles. One individual who was a part of this early process described the answers that he hoped to obtain from industry:

Does the contractor break down the work into short span packages that can be budgeted, scheduled and evaluated? Do they have a cost accumulation system? Do they measure performance against those packages of work . . . and do they then report status and variances to their own internal management? We don't want to tell anyone how to manage[7].

---

6 Office of the Secretary of Defense and National Aeronautics and Space Administration. 1962. *DOD and NASA Guide PERT COST.* Washington, DC, page 17.

7 Lt. Gen. Hans Driessnack. "*How It Started.*" *PMA Newsletter* (March, 1990). Washington, DC: Performance Management Association.

By December 1967, the DOD was ready to formally issue what it then called Cost/Schedule Control Systems Criteria, shortened to simply C/SCSC. The C/SCSC carefully incorporated the earned value concept in the form of thirty-five criteria that were imposed on any private contractor wishing to be chosen for a new major systems contract or subcontract that exceeded established funding thresholds. The DOD imposed these thirty-five criteria on a contractor's management control system any time that a cost or incentive-type contract was used.

Over the three-plus decades since these criteria were put in place, practitioners of the concept have developed a significant amount of scientific knowledge based on the employment of these standards. Much knowledge has been gathered on Earned Value, both scientific and simply empirical. These findings will be covered in our next chapters.

However, there is some bad news: the concept of earned value measurement as a part of the C/SCSC has been largely restricted to the acquisition of major systems by governments. Private industry, with but a few exceptions, did not embrace the full and formal criteria concept.

EARNED VALUE MANAGEMENT AS A PART OF THE C/SCSC PRODUCED MIXED RESULTS

Utilization of the earned value concept within the C/SCSC produced some impressive results. A new body of scientific knowledge based on actual experiences with several hundred projects was developed. However, in other instances, the experience has been less than satisfactory from the perspective of practitioners in private industry. We should candidly discuss these experiences so as to not repeat them in the future.

The C/SCSC went through three decades of bureaucratic evolution that departed from the original (unobtrusive) objectives set forth in 1966, when the criteria were first defined. Esoteric interpretations subsequently led to the development of formalized (rigid) implementation guidelines, surveillance manuals, and implementation checklists containing hundreds of questions (at one point, 174) for use by the practitioners.

The guidance checklists themselves became absolute requirements to impose on contractors' management control systems. In some cases, there were reasonable applications of these checklists. But, in other instances, the implementation rules were arbitrary and perhaps dogmatic.

The criteria checklist questions were intended by their originators to be used as a guideline only, to be exercised with good professional judgment. However, some government practitioners had elevated the checklists and associated questions to a position on a par with the original thirty-five criteria. Contractor personnel understood the importance of having to meet certain oversight standards. But they resented many of the minor peripheral interpretations that were raised to the level of absolute requirements.

By the 1980s, a sort of cultist society of C/SCSC professional practitioners emerged, which did not sit well with many (most) of the project managers in the private sector. Project managers look for simple tools that will assist them in meeting their primary mission of completing their projects on time, within the authorized budget, while achieving all technical objectives.

C/SCSC was a success from a government perspective because it permitted the oversight of contractor performance whenever the risks of cost growth rest squarely with the government. Applications with the government have been consistent and have met the test of time. The original thirty-five criteria have remained consistent and unchanged.

However, Earned Value Management as a part of the original C/SCSC was never accepted or adopted by private industry for use in the management of internal projects. And there were valid reasons for this outright rejection by private industry.

A NEW FOREIGN LANGUAGE EMERGED

Perhaps the single most self-defeating aspect of C/SCSC for project managers in the private sector was the need for them to learn and adopt a new terminology associated with the formal doctrine. Did Earned Value need to be made this complicated? We think not.

For example, instead of calling their plan a "plan," or the "Planned Value," C/SCSC practitioners chose the term "Budgeted Cost for Work Scheduled" (or "BCWS"), or sometimes only "S." Instead of using the term "Earned Value" or "Earned Standards," which would suggest physical accomplishments, the term "Budgeted Cost of Work Performed" (or "BCWP"), or simply "P" was used. Professional project managers do not typically respond to new terms like "S" or "P" words, and they often object to having to learn a new cryptic vocabulary.

Perhaps one of the more interesting and unexplainable phenomena that emerged in the usage of new terminology for C/SCSC was in the deliberate avoidance of ever using the dreaded word "overrun" in discussions. Interestingly, the management of cost overruns was perhaps the primary reason why Earned Value was required on projects in the first place. But, instead of calling an overrun an "overrun," such incomprehensible terms as "OTB"—which stood for "over target baseline"—or "formal reprogramming" or "variance at completion" were substituted for the more unambiguous terms.

The new language, required and unnatural, did not sit well with industry.

PHASE 3 — EARNED VALUE MANAGEMENT (ANSI/EIA 748): 1996 TO THE PRESENT

In spite of the overall impressive results with the use of Earned Value within the C/SCSC, there was concern from both private industry and the United States government, particularly the Department of Defense, that perhaps some changes needed to be made. Earned Value had to be made more "user-friendly" if the concept was to be applied to projects beyond being simply a government-imposed mandate.

On April 18, 1995, in Phoenix, Arizona, at a meeting of the Management Systems Subcommittee of the National Defense Industrial Association (NDIA), this group accepted the task of re-examining and rewriting the DOD's formal earned value criteria. Their objective was to make the criteria more compatible with the needs of private industry.

Over the next few months, members of the NDIA subcommittee met, discussed, and established their own version of the thirty-five cost/schedule control systems criteria. They called the new industry version the "Earned Value Management System" (EVMS) criteria, and it contained just thirty-two criteria, each of them rewritten in a more palatable form. Gone were the ambiguous terms of BCWS and BCWP; in their place were "Planned Value" and "Earned Value." The goal was to make Earned Value a more useful tool for project managers.

On December 14, 1996, the Under Secretary of Defense for Acquisition and Technology accepted the thirty-two industry earned value criteria, verbatim. These thirty-two EVMS criteria were later incorporated into the next revision of the DOD Instruction 5000.2R in early 1997.

The Management Systems Subcommittee of the NDIA was not content to simply have EVM be restricted to the DOD. The NDIA subcommittee then obtained approval for these 32 EVM criteria to be formally issued as an American National Standard Institute/Electronic Industry Association (ANSI/EIA) document. In June 1998, the ANSI/EIA-748-1998 Guide was officially issued to the public.

The significance of these moves does not lie in the revised wording of the criteria, or in the minimal reduction in their number from thirty-five to thirty-two. Rather, the important change was in the attitude of all parties to the process. During 1997, there was a sort of shifting of the Earned Value Management System responsibility from that of a government mandate to the ownership of EVM by private industry. Private industry was adopting the Earned Value Management technique not because it was a government requirement, but because it represented a viable, best-practice tool, which project managers everywhere could use.

Authors' Note: in an Appendix to this book, there is a description of the 32 EVMS criteria and the authors' unofficial description of the meaning of each of the EVM criteria.

IN SUMMARY

Although many positive steps have been taken recently to make the earned value concept more user-friendly, much remains to be done. We now have the opportunity to transfer Earned Value into a widely accepted tool for broad-based project management applications. But we must go back to the basics.

Figure 3.1 shows a chart that depicts the evolution of the earned value concept. It all started in the industrial factories over a hundred years ago. The industrial engineers who conceived this concept used it as a simple management tool. We in private industry should now do likewise.

What we suggest is a return to the original approach, as used by the industrial engineers, but also incorporating the critical success results from applications of the formal C/SCSC and EVMS. Use a simple form of Earned Value to manage all projects within the private sector.

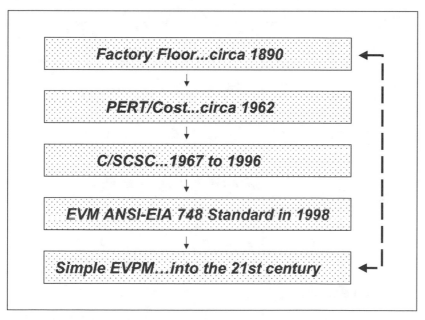

Figure 3.1 *Getting back to earned value basics*

4

THE EARNED VALUE
BODY OF KNOWLEDGE

THIS CHAPTER might well have been entitled: "Ten compelling reasons why Earned Value should be employed on all projects." The empirical data on the actual employment of Earned Value would suggest that it has truly become a "best practice" project management tool. Earned Value provides a project manager with the status of any project . . . available with no other tool.

In a manner somewhat resembling the approach used by the Project Management Institute (PMI) in their careful documentation of the evolution of project management, resulting in their publication of *A Guide to the Project Management Body of Knowledge* (*PMBOK® Guide*), there has been a similar, but less formal, accumulation of data on the subject of Earned Value Management. The authors have elected to call these empirical findings "the earned value body of knowledge."

First we need to candidly address some bad news: most of the data gathered on Earned Value Management has been done by practitioners operating within the United States Department of Defense (DOD). That single fact disappoints many professionals and they often flatly reject the findings by suggesting that: "My project is not a military weapon system."

That fact may be true. Most projects are not within the DOD or even government-sponsored. However, the authors are of the belief that a project is a project. And all projects have similar generic characteristics. Fundamental project management principles apply to any project. For example: scoping the project, scheduling, budgeting, formally authorizing, baselining, monitoring performance, taking corrective actions, etc.; these are all fundamentals that apply to all projects. While the concept of Earned Value began with the industrial engineers in the factories at the turn of the last century, the actual collection of scientific knowledge has centered on its practical applications on projects only over the past three-plus decades.

Since the implementation of Earned Value as an integral part of the Cost/Schedule Control Systems Criteria (C/SCSC) starting in 1967, the criteria concept has been consistently applied to virtually all new major government development projects. There have been no substitutive changes to the earned value criteria for over thirty years. Therefore, the findings and conclusions can reasonably be considered to represent valid empirical project data. These findings have evolved into what is becoming an embryonic earned value management science.

In particular, we would like to acknowledge the outstanding work of performance management personnel within the Office of the Under Secretary of Defense for Acquisitions. These individuals have been responsible for the scientific analyses of several hundred contracts (projects) in which the earned value criteria have been employed.[1] They have formulated some rather sophisticated scientific conclusions based on the consistency, predictability, and reliability of the earned value data. Their findings should not be ignored by anyone managing projects in the private sector. Quite possibly, the project managers in industry may discover a valuable new tool for their use in the management of commercial projects.

The DOD effort has been augmented by studies done at the Air Force Institute of Technology (AFIT) in Dayton, Ohio, which have expanded the empirical conclusions on this evolving management science.[2] It could also be beneficial to review some of these findings to see if they might apply to more universal applications to all projects . . . yes, even in the private sector . . . yes, even on software projects.

Question: Why do the authors feel that the empirical data from DOD projects might be valid for any project? Answer: Because the DOD data contain the results from all types of projects, the GOOD projects, the BAD projects, and the downright UGLY projects! In the commercial sector, when companies "benchmark" their results, they somehow include data from only their GOOD performing projects. The BAD performing projects are somehow missing from their databanks. And any information accumulated on their UGLY performing projects no longer exists; such performance results have been carefully removed. Fact: Management doesn't like to talk about cost overruns, schedule slippages, missing technical features, the number of design changes, testing failures, bugs, undocumented features, and so on!

---

1 In particular, we would like to acknowledge the work of Robert R. Kemps, Gary E. Christle, and Wayne Abba.

2 In particular, Dr. David S. Christensen, USAF retired, now with Southern Utah University.

However, to their credit, the DOD has systematically tracked the performance results on hundreds of projects, good, bad, and otherwise. It does protect the names of the individual companies, and simply uses the data to look for overall trends not associated with any one project or any one company. If you accept the premise that a project is a project, and that they all contain basic characteristics, then what actually happened in the performance of DOD projects may well be compared to other non-government projects.

THE LEGACY OF EARNED VALUE AS IT WAS A PART OF THE C/SCSC

We would like to focus now on what we consider to be the emerging earned value body of knowledge that has been accumulated by individuals working within the DOD Pentagon and the individual branches of the military. Truthfully, the authors have not attempted to reach any type of broad consensus on these ten points. Rather, we have compiled our listing of the issues that we feel have been the most important accomplishments resulting from the employment of Earned Value. To us, these ten findings constitute the beginnings of a valid management science:

1. The employment of a single management control system that provides accurate, consistent, reliable, and timely data to management at all levels, allowing them to oversee the performance of all projects and production work within their enterprise.

One of the primary benefits of employing Earned Value is that it allows for the use of a single management system that can be applied to both projects and production work (batches or lots) within any given organization. The relationship of what work was scheduled versus what work was accomplished provides an accurate indicator of whether one is meeting the time expectations of management. Additionally, the most critical relationship of what work was accomplished versus how much money was spent to accomplish the work provides an accurate reflection of the true cost performance.

Far too often, companies will employ multiple management control systems to monitor various activities. One approach may be used to monitor the work on big projects, another for smaller projects, still another to oversee production work, and so forth. Earned value data is somewhat analogous to measuring the temperature of a human body. If the human body temperature is higher or lower than the standard of 98.6 degrees, the doctor will know to look further. Likewise, earned value performance data exceeding preset thresholds must be explained by management.

Earned value performance data is consistent and can be applied to all projects and production work within the enterprise.

By employing a single management system on all work within an organization, the temptation to try to put a positive spin on negative results can be minimized. Often, companies will allow their various managers to take different interpretations of the same actual results. The project manager, executive management, functional management, chief financial officer, and others will interpret the same performance results to reinforce their own parochial, self-serving positions. Often, one person's interpretation will not match another's interpretation of the same results. Earned Value provides one set of books, one set of reliable metrics, reflecting accurate performance data.

2. A management approach that requires the integration of the "triple constraint": the scope of work, with the schedule commitments, and with the authorized budgets, allowing for the accurate measurement of integrated performance throughout the full life cycle of a project or a production run.

While most management theorists may be quick to express support for any approach that integrates the work to be done with the necessary time and resources, rarely in practice does such integration actually happen. Typically, the contract administrators will define a project one way, the technical staff will implement it another way, and the resource controllers will view the same requirements in still a different way. The scheduling community, not to be outdone, has always had its own unique perspective on what is important, which likely will be at odds with what others have determined to be important. The result: a given project or production effort will often be implemented by the sum of various parochial, self-serving, and sometimes conflicting perspectives. Each function may well measure and report on its own performance in a manner that is in conflict with the way in which other functions are tracking their performance. Whether we like it or not, admit it or not, most projects and production work are defined and then performed in a non-integrated manner.

Starting sometime in the early 1960s, a new concept called the Work Breakdown Structure (WBS) was introduced. The WBS provided an opportunity for all key functions on a given project to view the same project in a like manner, and to speak with a common project language for the first time. Collectively, all functions would have the opportunity to define a given project in a similar manner, which would then relate to other functional perspectives.

With the use of a WBS, key functions would be expected to define and decompose a new project into progressively smaller units, down to the work task level, at which point they would relate the technical work to be done, add the estimated resources, and set the time frame for each task. With the use of a WBS, all critical functions would be expected to work toward an integrated project plan. Performance could then be measured at the lowest task level, allowing the project manager to ascertain how much work has been planned, how much work has been accomplished, and how much money has been spent to accomplish the authorized work. The use of a WBS allowed for performance measurement to take place within an integrated baseline.

Figure 4.1 shows a comparison of the two management approaches just discussed. On the left side is the more traditional functional matrix approach employed by most projects and production work. Here, each of the various functions will take its own peculiar interpretation of project requirements, according to its own unique perspective. This approach allowed (and actually encouraged) projects to be implemented in a non-integrated manner.

By contrast, on the right side of the display is an integrated management approach, required in order to employ Earned Value Management. Each function must work in concert with all other functions on the same defined work, all within the project's WBS. Multi-functional work is defined, authorized, performed, and reported within management control points, typically referred to as "Control Account Plans," or CAPs. Each management control point or CAP will be placed at the lowest element within the WBS. The WBS has thus provided the mechanism for the integration of all project and production work.

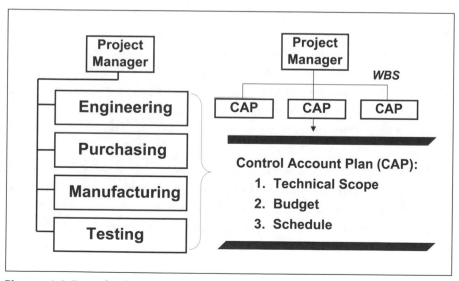

Figure 4.1 *Earned Value requires an Integrated Project Baseline*

3. Scientifically documented empirical evidence collected from over 700 DOD contracts (projects) that have employed Earned Value Management, demonstrating a pattern of consistent and predictable performance history.[3]

Since the mid-1970s, the performance management practitioners within the DOD Pentagon have been empirically tracking the actual results of all contracts (projects) that have employed Earned Value Management as a central component of the C/SCSC. They have documented their findings, analyzed the results, and hypothesized final performance patterns for contracts (projects) that employ Earned Value.

Their findings have been spectacular in that they have demonstrated a pattern of predictable project performance, which can be used to scientifically forecast the future. Figure 4.2 shows the summary displays of these findings. This same chart was initially prepared by DOD practitioners in the early 1980s, with only the number of sample projects changing, from an original 100 projects to well over 700 projects. This chart summarizes these most impressive empirical findings.

The hypothesis of this chart: As early as the 15 percent completion point in a project, the actual performance results (the earned value metrics) will provide an "early warning" indicator to management. Such results can be used to predict the final costs and time requirements within a finite range of values. The results of work accomplished as compared to a given plan can be used to forecast the final project or production results. Their empirical conclusions are simple: If project cost has overrun the work it has accomplished to date, that initial overrun will not likely be recovered on the remaining work. In fact, they conclude that overruns will typically get progressively worse, not better, with the passage of time.

Without attempting to explain the reasons behind these conclusions, they suggest that there is a natural tendency for any project team to provide its best scope definition, planning, scheduling, estimating, etc., for the near-term work. And as the project plans extend into later periods, things like scope, schedule, and budget will be progressively more vague, more imperfect. Thus, later performance trends will likely deteriorate as the project continues through to completion.

4. The development of a metric called the Cost Performance Index (CPI), reflecting that critical relationship between the physical work actually accomplished versus the costs expended to accomplish such work, thereby allowing management to continuously monitor the true cost performance results of any project or production run.

---

3 Chester Paul Beach, Jr., *"A-12 Administrative Inquiry"* citing studies by Gaylord E. Christle, et al, Office of the Under Secretary of Defense for Acquisitions, Washington, D.C., November 28, 1990. This study at the time cited 400 projects from 1977 on, but has since been increased to 700 projects without a change in their findings.

- **GIVEN:**

    Contract more than 15% complete
    1. *Overrun at completion will not be less than overrun to date.*
    2. *Percent overrun at completion will be greater than percent overrun to date.*

- **CONCLUSION:**

    You can't recover!!

- **WHO SAYS:**

    More than 700 major DOD contracts since 1977.

- **WHY:**

    If you underestimated the near, there is no hope that you did better on the far term planning.

Figure 4.2 *The DOD Earned Value Body of Knowledge*

Their empirical findings: As early as the 15- to 20-percent completion point of any project, the cumulative cost performance efficiency factors (Earned Values versus Actual Costs) have been shown to stabilize, and the data provided can be used to predict the final range of costs for any given project. This index is sometimes referred to as the CPI(e), with the "e" representing the cost efficiency.

Note of caution: These same forecasting results are not possible using periodic or incremental performance data. Periodic data has been found to experience wide fluctuations. Periodic performance data thus have limited utility as a long-term trending tool. But periodic data are obviously needed to continuously monitor the most immediate results on a project. In short, use periodic earned value data to monitor current performance status, and cumulative data for predicting final performance results.

Individuals working at the United States Air Force Institute of Technology (AFIT) have been instrumental in extending the scientific knowledge begun in the Pentagon. One significant study provides us with insight into these findings:

Using data from a sample of completed Air Force contracts, Christensen/Payne established that the cumulative CPI did not change by more than 10 percent from the value at the 20-percent contract-completion point.

Based on data from the Defense Acquisition Executive Summary (DAES) database, results indicate that the cumulative CPI is stable from the 20-percent completion point—regardless of contract type, program, or service.

Knowing that the cumulative CPI is important, the government can now conclude that a contractor is in serious trouble when it overruns the budget beyond the 20-percent completion point.[4]

Let us reflect on the significance of these empirical findings. No longer must management wait until all the funds have been spent to determine that additional budget will be needed in order to complete the full scope of a given project. The CPI thus represents the project manager's "early warning signal" and is perhaps the most compelling reason why any project should employ some form of Earned Value. No other project management technique provides these metrics.

By monitoring the cost performance against a detailed project plan, and by relating the value of the work performed against the costs of doing that work, a predictable pattern becomes available to management . . . early in the life cycle of the project. Such patterns can be used by management to both assess the performance to date and predict the final performance results.

The CPI (based on cost efficiency) is determined by simply dividing the value of the work actually performed (the Earned Value) by the Actual Cost it took to accomplish that Earned Value. The use of a cumulative CPI is displayed in Figure 4.3. Perfect cost performance would be 1.0. Conversely, less than 1.0 performance reflects the condition typically called an "overrun" of costs.

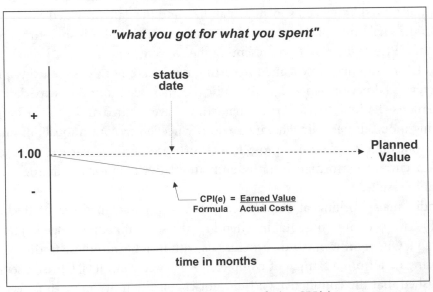

Figure 4.3 *Project performance: watch the cumulative CPI(e)*

4 Major David S. Christensen, PhD, and Captain Scott R. Heise, "Cost Performance Index Stability" from the National Contract Management Association Journal, 25:7-15 (1993), pages 7 and 13.

One more point needs to be made on the utility of the cumulative CPI for universal project management. The preceding findings reflect data produced by major DOD acquisition projects. Major projects will often take months to establish a baseline against which performance can be measured and, thus, the CPI results known.

But what about the typical smaller projects of, perhaps, only one year or less in duration? Such projects can easily be defined and planned with a performance measurement baseline before go-ahead is given by management. Such projects can measure performance from the start of the project. Thus, accurate CPI readings could become available as early as, perhaps, 5 to 10 percent into the life cycle of any project, which is a way of employing a simple form of earned value measurement.

5. The development of a metric called the Schedule Performance Index (SPI), reflecting that important relationship between the physical work actually accomplished against the authorized baseline schedule, thereby allowing management to focus on and manage their schedule time obligations to completion.

One of the more important benefits of employing a performance measurement system is to be able to determine how much of the originally scheduled work has been physically accomplished as of any point in time. The issue is fundamental: Is the project performing on its authorized schedule, ahead of schedule, or behind the planned work? And if there are differences in the schedule performance, what is the value of such work?

Such schedule performance knowledge is particularly powerful for any project when it is compared against the project's critical path position. Both the earned value SPI and critical path method (CPM) indicators, when used in concert, will accurately assess the true schedule position of any project.

Even though the SPI can have little (or no) relationship to the project's critical path, falling behind in accomplishing the work scheduled is one of the first indicators of potential future problems. Project managers do not like to get behind their scheduled work, even though perhaps a more important indicator will be performance against the project's critical path.

The natural tendency when one falls behind the planned work is to add unplanned resources in an attempt to catch up, effectively doing the same work as was planned, but spending more money to accomplish the same effort. Arbitrary decisions to catch up on the planned work, to improve the SPI performance, can cause non-recoverable damage to the project's cost performance. The SPI is a useful schedule monitoring indicator that should be used in conjunction with other scheduling techniques, particularly critical path methodology.

The SPI is determined by dividing the value of the work performed (the Earned Value) by the value of the work planned to be accomplished (the Planned Value) as of any point in time. It is a valuable indicator of schedule performance and also can be used with the CPI to predict the final required project costs.

6. The utility of the cumulative Cost Performance Index (CPI) to statistically forecast the "low-end" range of final required costs at completion.

The cumulative CPI has been scientifically demonstrated to be a stable early indicator of project cost performance. Perhaps its most significant utility is the ability to statistically forecast the final cost requirements for any project.

A statistical forecast of the total, final required funds may be done by simply taking the total project's Budget at Completion (BAC), and dividing this value by the cumulative CPI. This approach assumes that the cost performance results to date will continue to the end of the project. Many consider this to be the "best case" or a "low-end" forecast for a project within a statistical range of final cost estimates.

7. The utility of the cumulative Cost Performance Index (CPI), when used in conjunction with the cumulative Schedule Performance Index (SPI), to statistically forecast the "high-end" range of final required costs at completion.

The combination of the cumulative CPI, when used in conjunction with the cumulative SPI, provides the ability to also statistically forecast the final cost results of a project. Some individuals (with the DOD) consider this technique to represent the "most likely" final forecast, while others feel it represents the "high-end" in the range of statistical possibilities. Either way, it is an important indicator.

The rationale for this combination: If a project is both behind its planned schedule position and is overrunning its initial costs, these two conditions will combine to exacerbate the final results. The use of the CPI alone, or the CPI with the SPI as forecasting tools, will be discussed in detail in a later chapter on forecasting the final cost results.

8. The development of a metric called the To-Complete Performance Index (TCPI) to monitor the remaining effort against specific management financial goals, such goals representing either the original authorized Budget at Completion (BAC), or the project manager's latest Estimate at Completion (EAC).

The remaining (to-go) project work constitutes the only area in which a project manager can influence the final cost results. Costs already spent or committed are effectively "sunk costs"; they are non-recoverable costs. Therefore, it is useful for any project to determine what performance factors will be needed to accomplish the remaining effort, in order to achieve a specific management objective. Such management goals can be variable and can reflect the original project budget; or—if actual results so dictate—can also represent an increased financial goal, reflecting a more realistic and attainable objective.

The TCPI focuses on the remaining project tasks. It is effectively the mirror opposite of the cumulative CPI, in that it reflects what it will take in future performance to recover from a negative actual cost position.

The TCPI takes the work remaining (the total budget less the Earned Value accomplished) and divides that amount by the funds remaining (the latest management financial goal less funds spent) to determine what performance results it will take to meet such goals. The TCPI can be an effective indicator for management at all levels to monitor the remaining project tasks. More will be covered on this subject in a later chapter.

9. The utility of a weekly (or periodic) industrial engineering Cost Performance Index (CPIp) to monitor performance results for production or repetitive-type work.

Although the use of cumulative data has been found to work well to determine the long-term trend or direction of a project, industrial engineers monitoring production work have often used periodic or weekly data to track the cost performance achieved against an established production standard. By breaking

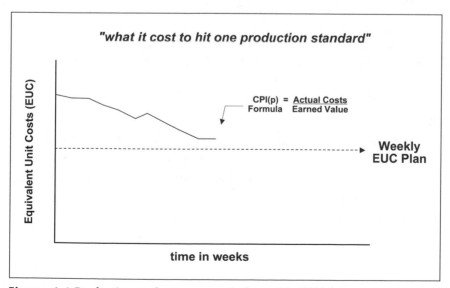

Figure 4.4 *Production performance: watch the weekly CPI(p)*

down a total production effort into detailed subparts (lots or batches), and then establishing a weekly production standard (a Planned Value) for each part, the tracking of production effort has been successfully employed with use of what is called a Cost Performance Index or CPI(p).

The CPI(p) refers to "performance" and the formula is the exact reverse of the more widely used CPI(e). It is determined by dividing the Actual Costs incurred to accomplish the Earned Value by the value of the physical work performed (Earned Value) during the measured or incremental period. Figure 4.4 depicts an example of the CPI(p) plotted weekly against the established "equivalent unit costs" for a given manufactured part, component, or assembly.

Compare the two earned value indices displayed in Figure 4.3, a project cost efficiency CPI(e), with Figure 4.4, a weekly production CPI(p) (which is an industrial standard).

10. The employment of a Management by Exception (MBE) approach, allowing busy executives to focus exclusively on earned value metrics (CPI, SPI, TCPI, EAC)—but only significant exceptions to their authorized plans—thus allowing senior management to effectively control a portfolio of projects or production work within their enterprise.

Lastly—and perhaps the ultimate utility in the use of earned value performance measurement—is that it allows for the employment of the Management by Exception (MBE) principles against established and authorized project or production baseline plans. Executives employing Earned Value need not follow each and every detailed task in order to effectively oversee the performance of all authorized work. Rather, by focusing on only those exceptions to the authorized plans in accordance with specified variance thresholds, management can effectively monitor all critical aspects of performance against their project or production plans.

o o o

These ten items represent to us the more significant findings of the body of knowledge, which has resulted from over three decades in the employment of Earned Value Management. We will use these findings as a basis to suggest a simplified form of the Earned Value, for use with other more established project and production management tools. What we hope to describe is a simple form of Earned Value—Earned Value for the masses—for use on all projects and production work, of any size, in any industry.

5

SCOPE THE PROJECT

THERE IS LIKELY NO SINGLE FACTOR that would contribute more to the success of any new project than starting off with a solid and complete definition of the work to be done, called the project's scope of work. Conversely, there is probably no factor that would contribute more quickly to the demise of any project than to initiate a new effort without having a full understanding of the work to be done.

As Alice learned long ago in *Alice in Wonderland*: If you don't care where you get to, it doesn't matter which way you go.[1] Projects need to know where they are going so they know when they arrive. Projects need to define their scope of work.

Interestingly, the earned value technique cannot be employed on any project unless the project manager has defined the job, the total job, to the greatest extent possible. Reason: Earned Value monitors the physical completion of work, and management's budget for the completed work, which we call the "Earned Value." Such monitoring takes place from as early as possible until all the physical work has been completed. Scope creep, if allowed to happen, would negate the possibility of accurately measuring project performance along the way.

---

1 Lewis Carroll, *Alice's Adventure in Wonderland & Through the Looking Glass*, (London: Bramhall House, 1960), page 88.

UNDERSTANDING THE PROJECT
(WHAT'S IN . . . WHAT'S OUT)

Planning a new project that employs earned value performance measurement is no different than the planning necessary to implement any project. It always helps to know what makes up the project, the whole project, and particularly the outer boundaries of the project. We can think of at least three reasons why this might be important to any project manager.

First, you need to know at the outset when the project is over. You need to know when all of the work that you originally set out to do has been completed. You need to have tangible metrics for any project deemed "Done." You need to know when you may start work on the next project.

Second, you need to know the difference between the agreed-to work and any new work requested of you; that is, whenever someone brings in more work for you to do than you had originally agreed to. For example, if you agree to peel ten bushel baskets of potatoes, and someone brings in an eleventh basket, you will want to ask for some additional compensation (adjustment in the project's budget) for doing that eleventh basket. You may also need some additional time. Unless you had sufficiently defined the scope of work in the first place, you may not be able to tell the difference between basket ten, or eleven, or twelve, etc.

Third—and this is most critical to the earned value performance management concept—you will need to know how much of the entire job has been accomplished . . . at any point in time. The issue is fundamental: If you do not know what constitutes 100 percent of a project, how will you ever know if you are 10 or 20 or 35 percent finished? You must know what constitutes 100 percent of the project scope in order to tell how much of it you have performed during the life of the project. PMI's cranky Olde Curmudgeon wrote about this very issue several years ago:

Failure to define what is a part of the project, as well as what is not, may result in work being performed that was unnecessary to create the product of the project and thus lead to both schedule and budget overruns.[2]

This isn't a new concept. In Chapter 5 of the original 1996 edition of *A Guide to the Project Management Body of Knowledge* (*PMBOK® Guide*), the subject of scope management was nicely addressed. The opening paragraph effectively described the importance for any project of knowing what it has agreed to do, and—perhaps of equal importance—knowing what it has not agreed to do; these are called the project boundaries:

---

2 The Olde Curmudgeon (Dr. Francis M. Webster), "*PM 101*" PM Network, Project Management Institute, Upper Darby, PA, December 1994.

Project Scope Management includes the processes required to ensure that the project includes all the work required, and only the work required, to complete the project successfully. It is primarily concerned with defining and controlling what is or is not included in the project.[3]

One of the key pillars of the earned value concept is that the project manager must know at all times what percentage of the physical work has been accomplished, that is, the percent completed as it relates to the total job. This information is needed in order to compare the physical work done against the actual costs spent to perform that work in the same period being measured. The relationship between the total physical work accomplished as compared to the total dollars spent provides the answer to: "*What did we get for the money we spent?*" For example, if you had spent 30 percent of the project's total budget, but had accomplished only 25 percent of the total project's physical work, what do you call this condition? Answer: *a 20% overrun!*

USE A WORK BREAKDOWN STRUCTURE (WBS) TO SCOPE THE PROJECT

Starting sometime in the early 1960s, there developed a school of thought centered on the belief that project managers needed a new device, a tool similar in utility to the company organizational chart. For years, corporate executives have been using their organizational charts to conceptually define in graphical form: (1) who does what in the company, (2) who is responsible for what, and (3) who reports to whom within the organization.

This notion that project managers needed a special tool led to the introduction of the Work Breakdown Structure (WBS) concept. The WBS is to the project manager what the organizational chart is to the company executive.

The WBS is a tool that is used by the project manager to define a project and to give it cohesiveness so that the project can be managed as a unique one-time effort, a transient unit of work passing through the firm's permanent organization. At any point in time, a given company will have many projects in work, competing with one another for limited company resources. The WBS is the device that integrates the project effort and sets one project apart from all other projects within the same organization.

An important point often missed by some: Although the WBS looks like an organizational chart, it definitely is <u>not</u> an organizational chart. Unfortunately, however, the WBS looks much like an organizational chart. Some people get confused about

---

3 *A Guide to the Project Management Body of Knowledge*, 1996, page 47.

this issue and draw a project organizational chart that they then label as their WBS. This is wrong. The project WBS represents the project work to be done, the deliverable products, both tangible and intellectual. It is not the project's organization chart. However, the WBS can be used to first define the work and then to assign responsibility for conducting the work.

Companies will sometimes go through a reorganization. An important point: A company internal reorganization should never change the project's WBS. A company reorganization may well change who actually performs the specified project work. But a company reorganization should not change the project's WBS.

An example of a typical project WBS is shown in Figure 5.1, representing a diagram for a United States Department of Energy (DOE) project. Note that this is a "product"-oriented hierarchy that progressively breaks out the work elements downward from the top WBS box, called WBS level 1.

The owner of a project will sometimes specify the top three levels of the "Project WBS" to define the desired reporting requirements. Then, the performing project manager will extend the "Contract WBS" down to lower levels to assist in the management of the project by integrating the technical work, costs, and schedule. A key point is that the WBS must reflect the way that the project manager plans to manage the project. Much initial thought must be given to the WBS by both the owner/management and the performing project manager. The WBS should be owned by the sponsor and the project manager, although all parties will have a vested interest in it.

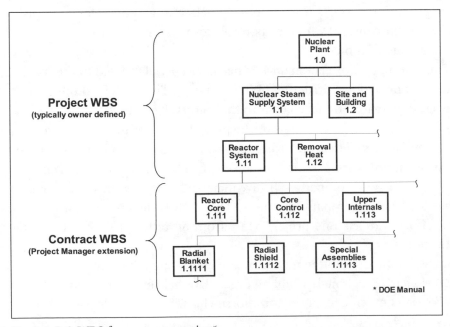

Figure 5.1 *WBS for an energy project**

The emphasis for the WBS must be on the project, the project tasks, and the unique work to be done to accomplish the project objectives, including specification of the project deliverables. Some of the keywords that should be a part of any viable WBS definition: project end items, project deliverables, project tasks and project subtasks.

One of the best definitions of the WBS was published way back in 1976, in which the author was describing what he called at the time a Project Breakdown Structure (PBS). In retrospect, the term PBS is perhaps a more descriptive term than WBS. However, the term WBS stuck, and the earlier term PBS did not:

> The PBS is a graphic portrayal of the project, exploding it in a level-by-level fashion, down to the degree of detail needed for effective planning and control. It must include all deliverable end items . . . and include the major functional tasks that must be performed . . . [4]

The PBS would appear to have its primary focus on the product, whereas the WBS often has its focus on the project's work tasks. Since most of the project managers of the world and the *PMBOK® Guide* use the term WBS, we will do likewise.

From its first edition in 1996, the *PMBOK® Guide* has always provided us with a solid definition of a WBS. However, in the third edition, published in 2004, the *PMBOK® Guide* has given us a modified definition of the WBS, which (to the authors) is the most complete definition of a WBS that we have seen thus far. The Work Breakdown Structure (WBS) is now defined as:

> A deliverable-oriented hierarchy of decomposed project components that organizes and defines the total scope of the project. Each descending level represents an increasingly detailed definition of the project work. The WBS is decomposed into work packages. The deliverable orientation of the hierarchy includes both internal and external deliverables.[5]

By essentially forcing the project team to define its necessary work tasks into progressively greater detail with use of a WBS—including making the important make-or-buy choices—the total scope of the project will then take form.

The WBS in total will define what is to be performed inside and outside of any given project. Returning once again to the wisdom of PMI's cranky Olde Curmudgeon:

---

4 Russell D. Archibald, *Managing High-Technology Programs and Projects*, (New York: John Wiley & Sons, 1976), page 141.
5 *A Guide to the Project Management Body of Knowledge*, Third Edition 2004, Glossary.

A project consists of the sum total of all the elements of the WBS. Conversely, an element that is not contained in the WBS is not a part of the project. Any work that cannot be identified in the WBS requires authorization to proceed, either as a recognized omission or as an approved change order.[6]

At the lowest WBS element, a project will expand the brief task titles into a descriptive narrative that can then evolve into what is referred to as the "WBS dictionary." The WBS dictionary will typically comprise the project's technical statement of work.

The WBS dictionary may also be used to relate the defined work tasks directly to a specific organization responsible for performing the actual work. This summary is sometimes called a project Responsibility Assignment Matrix (RAM).

The project's contractual specialists will also use the WBS dictionary to serve as the basis for creating the contractual Statement of Work (SOW) between the owner/customer and the project manager.

A WORK BREAKDOWN STRUCTURE (WBS) CAN HELP PROJECTS MANAGE SCOPE CREEP

One of the most challenging projects ever was the World War 2 Manhattan Project to develop the Atom Bomb. The Allies had to develop this weapon first, ahead of the enemy Axis, or face the distinct possibility of losing the war. The hero for this effort was a project manager by the name of General Leslie R. Groves. His overall mission was to define and then organize this massive, never-been-done-before undertaking.

Realistically, the Manhattan Project took place some two decades before the project management community was first introduced to the WBS concept. Thus, General Groves was at a disadvantage compared to what his contemporary project managers have in place today: the WBS concept to help define a new project. However, the General likely followed the same processes used by most project management teams today to define their new projects: with use of a WBS.

Figure 5.2 illustrates an imaginary WBS for the Manhattan Project. Level 1 of the WBS always represents the total project. Next, level 2 must reflect the principle subdivision of the total effort: obtaining uranium ore from Africa, developing two types of isotopes, developing the actual bombs, and finally training the flight crews to use this new weapon. The WBS provides an excellent vehicle for achieving a complete definition of project scope. And when a narrative description is added to each WBS element, the WBS Dictionary in essence becomes the project's official Statement of Work (SOW).

6 The Olde Curmudgeon (Dr. Francis M. Webster), "*PM 101*" PM Network, Project Management Institute, Upper Darby, PA, December 1994.

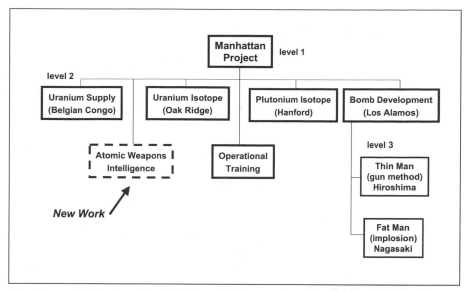

Figure 5.2 *The WBS Dictionary controls a Project Statement of Work*

But the WBS also provides an excellent vehicle for defining the outer limits of one's commitment to a project. This can also be called managing project scope creep. Note in Figure 5.2 the WBS element to the left with the arrow and the notation, "New Work." About one year after General Groves was first designated project manager for the Manhattan Project, he was given additional work responsibilities: that of managing Atomic Weapons Intelligence. This new effort made him responsible for not only developing the new weapon system, but also determining how far along the enemy Axis was in developing its own atomic bomb. The intelligence-gathering function was clearly new work for the Manhattan Project.

Realistically, in the case of the Manhattan Project, the effort was so critical to the war effort that the addition of new work likely did not matter. General Groves essentially had a carte blanche, an unlimited budget. But most projects today operate under a finite amount of funds, and the use of a WBS can help any project maintain the delicate relationship between authorized work and appropriate funding.

By starting out with a complete project definition in the form of a WBS, and with a buy-in to the WBS by all key functional organizations, all projects will have better assurances that the work being done will represent what their customers desire. And if the customer or senior management should ask for more work, or different work, as they often do, the use of the WBS to define project scope will help the project manager make the case for more budget, more time, etc.

SOME SPECIFIC EXAMPLES OF WBS FORMATS

Perhaps the best way to illustrate the utility of the WBS is to review some specific examples. Shown earlier in Figure 5.1 was a WBS for an energy project. This illustrated a product-type breakout, exploding the project from the top down into progressively smaller units.

By way of contrast, another energy project is shown in Figure 5.3, but this time for a construction job. In this case, the WBS reflects the critical phases of the construction effort and the manner in which the project manager plans to implement the effort.

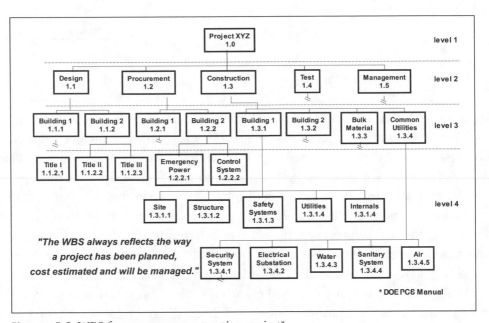

Figure 5.3 *WBS for an energy construction project**

The design work will sometimes be sent to an outside company, as indicated in the box designated "Design 1.1." The project team will procure the high value and/or common materials to achieve a cost savings, as indicated in the "Procurement 1.2" box. The actual construction effort will be contracted with still another firm, as reflected in the "Construction 1.3" box. In this case, the WBS reflects how the major project segments will be managed at level 2: design, procurement, and construction.

Figure 5.3 is a chart taken from the United States Department of Energy's Project Control System (PCS), and a key point is contained in the quote from the PCS Manual, which is shown at the bottom left of Figure 5.3: "The WBS always reflects the way a project has been planned [and] cost estimated, and will be managed." The message here is that the WBS must be owned by the project manager and the project management team, and reflect the way they plan to perform the effort. The WBS should not be the property of any single function, although all functions working on the project should have a say in its formation, and should buy into the final WBS.

Sometimes we see the finance and contracts organizations trying to take control of the project WBS, particularly when there are different sources of funding for the project (federal, state, local, etc.). This is wrong. The funding sources should never influence the composition of the WBS, but it sometimes does. The WBS must ultimately be the exclusive property of the project manager, and should be used to define the project scope of work.

Continuing with specific examples of WBS, the DOD took the lead in the mid-1960s in defining a WBS standard for its industry. This was, frankly, both good and bad for project management. The DOD's WBS document was then called Military Standard 881 (MIL-STD 881) and it described in very specific terms the format in which the WBS was to be used. MIL-STD 881 defined seven specific systems to be managed: aircraft, electronic, missile, ordnance, ship, space, and surface vehicles. Interestingly, at least three of our more prominent project challenges (opportunities) today are missing from this list of seven systems: construction projects, environmental clean-up projects, and software projects.

Figure 5.4 shows an example of just one of the seven specific DOD WBS formats, this one covering an aircraft system. Level 2 of any WBS is most critical because, at level 2, the project manager will usually indicate the approach planned to manage the project. With MIL-STD 881, the particular system would be displayed to the extreme left of level 2, then a series of common elements would be listed, going from

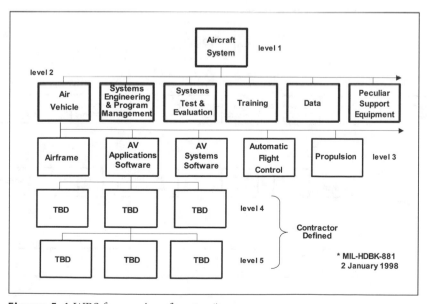

Figure 5.4 *WBS for an aircraft system**

left to right. MIL-STD 881 was very specific in defining the remainder of the authorized elements allowed at WBS level 2: systems engineering-project management, system test and evaluation, training, data, peculiar support equipment, common support equipment, operational site activation, industrial facilities, and spares/repair parts.

There was nothing unreasonable or anti-project management contained in these nine common elements, as precisely specified in the DOD's MIL-STD 881. However, project managers are unique individuals who do not take kindly to being told by anyone how they must define or manage their projects. Considerable friction surfaced over the years between project managers and government buyers when the project managers were told that they must structure their project WBS to conform to the specific breakouts contained in this military standard. The DOD's rigid-standard WBS encroached on the creative territory of project managers, and they resented this intrusion.

We are fortunate now to have the use of relational databases and project management software coding sufficient to make these earlier WBS problems somewhat of a non-issue today. The principles that should guide us are that (1) the WBS belongs to the project manager and (2) the WBS should represent the way the project manager plans to manage the project . . . period.

Figure 5.5 illustrates a simple WBS to build a house. Shown at the left on level 2 are three critical elements of work that will precede the actual physical construction of the house: design plans, a building permit, and a loan. After these critical items are secured, the project manager will divide the project into three distinct categories to

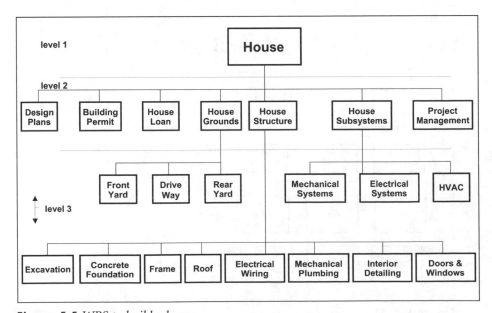

Figure 5.5 *WBS to build a house*

manage as shown at level 2 of the WBS: grounds, structure, and subsystems. All other categories of the project will be lumped into the general category to the extreme right called project management.

Another WBS example is shown in Figure 5.6, this one for a transportation vehicle. Although this might be a commercial venture, the WBS as displayed is consistent with the DOD WBS standard in that level 2 breaks out: vehicle structure, testing, data, and an all-other category called project management.

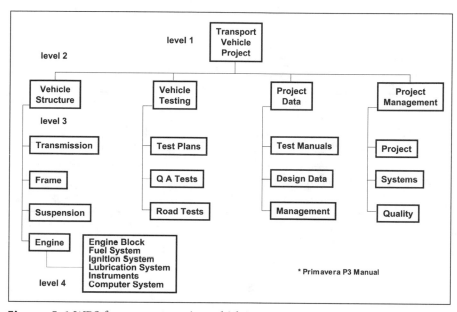

Figure 5.6 *WBS for a transportation vehicle**

The last three illustrations of WBSs are shown in Figures 5.7, 5.8, and 5.9, and represent examples of software projects. Software projects are gaining in importance and would appear to represent a new challenge for project management. As of this writing, there appears to be no universal agreement as to what might constitute an acceptable WBS format for software projects.

MAKE-OR-BUY CHOICES . . .
A CRITICAL PART OF SCOPE DEFINITION

One last point must be made about using a WBS to define a new project. The WBS must reflect the way that the project management team intends to manage the project, which should include the project manager's make-or-buy decisions. Make-or-buy choices typically come after the project has been initially defined, and are an integral part of the project definition process. Stated another way, project scope definition is incomplete

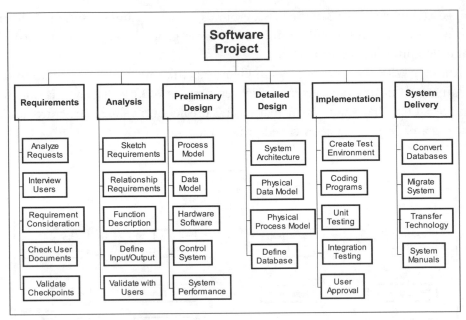

Figure 5.7 *WBS for a software project*

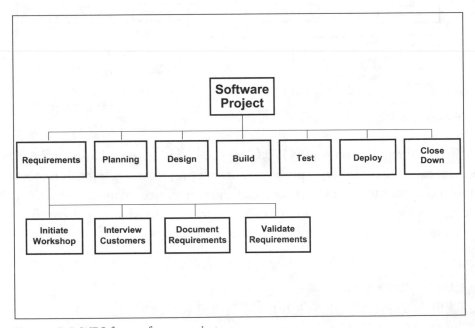

Figure 5.8 *WBS for a software project*

until the determination has been made as to who will be performing the effort: one's own organization (company-made), or procured (bought) from another company.

It does make a difference. Procured project scope creates a legal relationship that, if not handled correctly, can lead to energy-absorbing claim demands, negotiations,

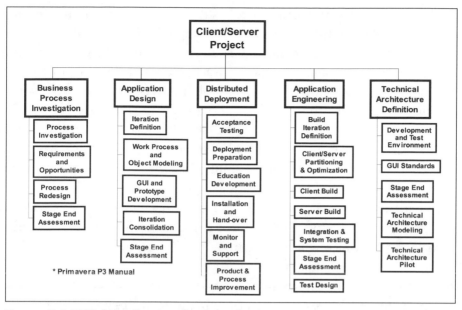

Figure 5.9 *WBS for a client/server software project**

and the claims settlement process. The procurement of project scope is a subject of critical importance to the project manager. Make-or-buy choices should be reflected in the final WBS for a given project.

The WBS at level 2 often reflects the most critical part of the scope definition process. Figure 5.10 shows an illustration of a WBS for a single construction project, but with three distinct management approaches. Each approach needs to be understood because they illustrate the project manager's make-or-buy choices and, hence, the way the project will be managed.

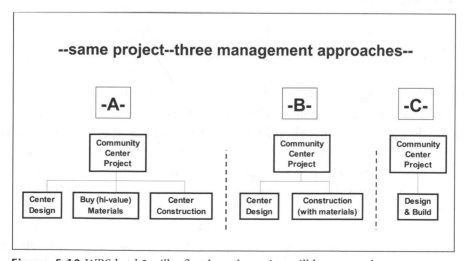

Figure 5.10 *WBS level 2 will reflect how the project will be managed*

To the left side of Figure 5.10 in [-A-] is displayed one approach reflecting the project manager's make-or-buy choices. Under approach [-A-], the design effort will be procured from an external company. The common and/or high-value materials will be purchased by the internal project team, perhaps to achieve a price advantage by the pooling of requirements from multiple projects. Finally, the construction effort will be separately contracted to another firm. This display is similar in approach to the WBS for the energy construction project, as was shown earlier in Figure 5.3. For purposes of simplicity, other important project work has not been displayed in the Figure 5.10 WBS; for example, final site check-out, project management, etc.

Shown in the center [-B-] of Figure 5.10 is a second approach in which the major project effort is divided into only two major parts: the design effort and a construction effort, both of which will be procured. In this case, the construction contract will include the purchase of all materials.

The third approach is shown to the right [-C-], in which case a single design-build contractor will be selected to perform the total design, procurement and construction job on behalf of the owner.

The point of this discussion is that the WBS is a critical tool for the project manager's use to initially define the project, and then to describe to everyone how the project will be managed, also reflecting the make-or-buy determinations. All functions must have a say in the formation of the project WBS and, once approved, should conform to the format of the official WBS.

The WBS is vital in order to achieve an integrated project management approach and to measure project performance during the full life of the project. While all levels of the project WBS are important, level 2 in particular will typically describe the project management approach being implemented.

THE WBS PROVIDES THE FOUNDATION FOR EARNED VALUE

From the beginning, the WBS has always been an integral part of the earned value concept. A hierarchical structure (WBS) defining the project is required in order to integrate the various functions into a common project mission and then to relate the requirements of the project to the company's permanent organizational units.

When the earned value concept was first introduced to industry as a part of the Cost/Schedule Control Systems Criteria in 1967, the DOD mandated 35 management control system standards, or criteria, which had to be met by any firm wanting to contract for a new major government acquisition. Interestingly, the very first of these 35 criteria addressed the issue of defining the project with use of a WBS. This 1967 criterion read:

"Define all authorized work and related resources to meet the requirements of the contract, using the framework of the contract work breakdown structure (WBS)."[7]

In practice, under cost-reimbursable-type contracting, the owner of the project would typically define the first two or three levels of the WBS, representing the way performance was to be monitored and reported during the life of the project. Typically, the project manager and the team would then define the lower levels of the project, extending the WBS to represent the way the work was to be performed. Under fixed-price or lump-sum contracting, where the cost-growth risks rest totally on the project manager, the project management team will define all levels of the WBS, representing how they intend to implement and manage their project.

At the appropriate level of each WBS element, the project will define management control points that initially went by the term "cost account," but more recently have been called "control account." Whatever the term, it is the same concept. The "control account" is a critical point in the WBS, where performance measurement must take place. The control account is also where the integration of scope, schedule, and resources happens, and where the project will measure its performance throughout the duration of the project. The control account is, thus, the fundamental building block for earned value performance measurement. It was defined some three decades ago as:

A management control point at which actual costs may be accumulated and compared to the budgeted cost of work performed . . . a natural control point for cost/schedule planning and control, since it represents the work assigned to one responsible organizational element on one contract work breakdown structure (CWBS) element.[8]

Initially the control account was defined as the intersection point of a single WBS element with a single organizational unit. More recently, with the increasing popularity of integrated multi-functional project teams, the requirement for a single organizational unit has been expanded to represent multi-functional teams. Additionally, while the scheduling of activities may continue to take place deeply within detailed WBS elements, the use of multi-functional project teams has resulted in larger segments of defined work being done within control accounts, at higher levels of the project WBS.

Thus, under the multi-functional project team approach, project management will monitor the performance of fewer management control points — a more logical approach and one which has led to a reduction of some 90% in the total number of management points. A most positive move.

---

7 United States Department of Defense, *Performance Measurement for Selected Acquisitions*, Instruction DOD 7000.2, (Washington, D.C., December 22, 1967).

8 Ibid.

PROJECTS SHOULD USE A
WORK BREAKDOWN STRUCTURE (WBS)

One last issue needs to be carefully emphasized. There is sometimes an organizational conflict between the best interests of the projects, and the best interests (the parochial objectives) of the functions that supply the resources to the projects. Because the functions will frequently support multiple projects at the same time, they may well have other priorities that compete or conflict with the requirements of any given project. Functions typically support multiple projects and employ a matrix form of organization. Individual functions often do not appreciate the importance (to them) of operating within the confines of the project WBS, which perhaps even requires that they relax their functional perspective.

For example, the cost-estimating function will typically have its historical cost data available in great detail, but likely collected and formatted along company functional organizational lines. Unless specifically directed by senior management, individual functions may not see the utility of structuring such data simply to match a given WBS for a single project.

Often, the scheduling function will find a project WBS environment too confining. Scheduling is a critical project function and the people who perform this important role are unique individuals who will often best perform their creative work without restrictions of any sort. However, unless this critical function operates within the overall envelope of the project WBS, the opportunity for the project to integrate its work scope with the costs and schedules will be lost.

From an enterprise standpoint, only if all key project functions perform their work within the framework of the agreed-to project WBS—and, most particularly, the contracting, scheduling, estimating, and budgeting functions—will the project be in a position to adequately integrate its functional work and maximize project performance. Since many (perhaps most) organizations often consist of the sum of their individual projects, the successful performance of each project should be of major consequence to the firm, overshadowing the parochial interests of individual functions. The WBS, if properly defined at the outset, can constitute the mechanism to negotiate functional resources, to set project priorities, and then to measure performance in an integrated fashion throughout the full life cycle of a project.

One final point: We have been attempting to make the case for the use of a WBS for two important purposes: (1) to define all project work down to detailed discrete tasks that can be individually managed, and (2) to integrate the various functional efforts into a common project framework. We can think of no better vehicle to accomplish this objective than a WBS. However, it would be misleading to suggest that the WBS must be used, or that it is the only vehicle to accomplish these goals.

We know of projects that have been successfully performed, which have employed the earned value concept, and which have not used a WBS. But they have substituted another vehicle for the WBS.

A company's organizational structure, if it is stable for the full project duration, may sometimes be used as a WBS substitute to integrate scope, schedule, and costs. In the construction industry, which typically employs a simple form of Earned Value (but does not call it as such), often uses construction historical standards, the Construction Specification Institute (CSI) Codes, or other hierarchical standards as a method to integrate project tasks. Bottom line: the WBS seems to work best . . . but other hierarchical substitutes may, on occasion, be used as a substitute for the WBS.

However, our recommendation is that all projects use the WBS to define, and then implement and control, their work.

IN SUMMARY

We have been attempting to make the case for defining the total project effort before starting to perform the work. Reaching an agreement between the owner and contractor, between the buyer and seller, and between the project and functions, on what constitutes the project scope is important to the success of any project. It is also critical to the employment of the earned value concept.

This discussion reminds us of a remark made by a person who worked in project management. When asked if the projects at his site ever overran their costs, he immediately replied: "We never overrun our project costs . . . all unfinished work gets moved into next year's projects."[9]

Think about this remark for a minute. Question: If one is given a budget to do a certain amount of work, then spends all of the money, but only completes part of the work and moves the unfinished work into next year's projects, what do you call this condition? Answer: An overrun!

Scope management is vital to the effective management of any project. Understanding the scope of a project is perhaps of even greater importance when Earned Value is employed because project performance must be measured throughout the life of the project . . . from implementation until project closeout.

Scope management is likely a project manager's greatest challenge . . . and it is also fundamental to the employment of the Earned Value Management concept. Unless the full scope is properly defined and then managed throughout the life of a project, the ability to meet the objectives of projects will be severely compromised.

---

9 An anonymous quote.

6

PLAN AND SCHEDULE THE PROJECT

IN ITS MOST FUNDAMENTAL FORM, employing Earned Value requires nothing more than managing a project with a good schedule, a schedule with the authorized budget embedded task by task. Earned Value, thus, is managing projects by managing a resource-loaded schedule.

Management will then focus on the authorized work that has been completed, and measure performance by crediting management's official budget for the completed work. Nothing complicated about this. But Earned Value does require a defined measurable baseline made up of all the authorized work, tightly controlled for the duration of the project. The next critical steps after adequately defining the project are to plan and then schedule the work.

UNDERSTANDING THE PROJECT

Previously, we emphasized the importance of completely defining the full scope of any new project, and suggested that this effort is best accomplished using a generally accepted technique called the Work Breakdown Structure (WBS). We recommended that the full project management team collectively define what work it needs to perform . . . including specifying the outer limits of the project's commitment. The WBS is a vehicle that allows for the progressive detailing of project tasks and for the

65

integration of such tasks with various organizational functions; in particular the contracts, estimating, budgeting, and scheduling functions, as well as those line functions that will be performing the defined work.

We refer to the WBS as a generally accepted technique because, while some industries have enthusiastically embraced the WBS as a project management tool, other industries have not. The construction industry, as an example, frequently relies on other methods to define its projects; perhaps most notable is the use of the Construction Specifications Institute's (CSI's) standard codes in lieu of using a WBS. Many construction projects use both.

Of equal importance, by having a clear understanding of what scope of work the project has committed to, project managers have effectively defined what work they have *not* agreed to do. Project managers must be cognizant of the full scope (and the outer boundaries) of the projects that they set out to accomplish. They must be able to discern at what point the project effort has been completed, and know precisely when out-of-scope tasks are being requested. There is nothing wrong with doing out-of-scope work . . . as long as one gets paid something extra for doing the added tasks. This is called managing "scope creep," and such creep must be quickly identified in order to avoid cost and schedule problems.

Once we have an understanding of what we are going to do—once the project is defined—it is time to take the next logical step in the process of implementing a new project that employs the earned value concept: we must formulate a detailed plan, and then schedule all the specified project tasks. The process of planning for any new project is no different with Earned Value. A detailed bottom-up plan is always required.

PLANNING THE PROJECT

Perhaps a good way to start a discussion on project planning is to borrow a quote from Rudyard Kipling, a man who knew nothing about project management . . . or did he? A century ago, this Indian-born Englishman gave us these profound words, which nicely define the key processes of project planning:

"I keep six honest serving men (they taught me all I knew); their names are WHAT and WHY and WHEN and HOW and WHERE and WHO."

Any project manager who could enlist the services of these six honest serving men would be well on the way to defining a viable project plan.

Just what is the project planning process? Well, it all depends on whom you ask. One of the best descriptions of this process was given to us three decades ago by a founding PMI member assigned with the membership number of 007, a PMI Fellow, and a certified PMI Project Management Professional (PMP). We can think of no better description of project planning than that provided by this expert in his book.

He defined the project planning process as requiring ten iterative steps:

1. Define the project scope and identify specific tasks with use of a WBS.
2. Assign responsibility for performance of each of the specific tasks.
3. Identify the interfaces between tasks.
4. Identify the key project milestones.
5. Prepare the master schedule.
6. Prepare the top budget.
7. Prepare detail task schedules.
8. Prepare detail task budgets.
9. Integrate task schedules and budgets with the project master schedule and top budget.
10. Set up the project files.[1]

Now what does all this mean? Well, to us it suggests first that project planning is an iterative process. It must continuously evolve. Planning becomes progressively more definitive with each cycle taken. Each iteration serves to reinforce the viability of the overall plan. The process works best when the full project team is involved, including, if possible, the project's owner or buying customer or senior management. Customer involvement not only brings out good ideas, but also leads to a customer buy-in or approval of the resulting plan. The final project plan should identify specific individuals by name who will be held accountable for the performance of each of the specified project tasks.

We particularly like the mention of the last item, the setting up of project files. All too often, this work is considered to be mundane and is overlooked . . . until the supplier shows up and a team of people must then set out to sift through a multitude of old project documents in an attempt to restore order out of the chaos. Better to start accumulating these critical files early and maintain them throughout the full life cycle of the project.

The one additional step we would like to add to the above list of project planning tasks is that of project "risk management." Risk identification, risk assessment, and risk mitigation planning are of vital importance to completing the project planning process and to the ultimate success of any project.

The risk management process will typically begin with an identification and assessment of the potential risks as envisioned by the project team. They will focus on the known and anticipated risks for the project. Teams will often use the framework of the WBS to display and conduct their initial risk assessment. After the project risks have been identified, they are then normally subjectively quantified as

1 Russell D. Archibald, 1976, *Managing High-Technology Programs and Projects*, New York: John Wiley & Sons, page 141.

to the likelihood (probability) of the risk actually happening and to the impact on (consequences to) the project should such risks materialize.

A risk mitigation plan will begin to take form, often not necessarily eliminating such risks altogether, but hopefully reducing them to acceptable levels. Risk mitigation planning will often impact the planned allocation of project resources and sometimes require added (redundant) tasks to the project. Added resources, task redundancy, and what-if analysis will typically help to bring the project risks down to acceptable levels. Admittedly, we have tried to describe a rather simple form of risk management. Some projects will want to employ more sophisticated approaches to the management of their risks, perhaps using the various software tools available to them.

Additionally, it should be mentioned that today's project managers have available to them the finest array of software tools to help perform these critical tasks. These state-of-the-art tools allow them to plan their new projects quickly, lay out the expected tasks, show the task interrelationships and constraints, expose potential risks, and model various "what if" scenarios. There are numerous planning, scheduling, and critical path method (CPM) software packages available to the general public. The project CPM network serves to reinforce the viability of any new project plan and, if reflected in a formal project master schedule (PMS), will provide assurances that the project will accomplish the project plan to the satisfaction of all vested parties.

SCHEDULING AN EARNED VALUE PROJECT

There is probably no single issue that has greater universal acceptance with project managers than the need for, and the benefits to be gained from, formally scheduling every project. All projects need a schedule to reflect and implement their project plans. Larger projects may have multiple schedules requiring a formal scheduling system. But even the smallest of projects needs to have at least a one-page project master schedule (PMS) to guide it.

The project schedule is likely the best tool available for managing the day-to-day communications on any project. And further, one of the best ways to control a project plan is to monitor performance regularly with the use of a formal scheduling methodology.

In 1967, when the Department of Defense initially released its thirty-five C/SCS Criteria formally implementing Earned Value, three of these criteria specifically dealt with the requirement to employ a formal scheduling system. Earned Value thus relies on the project schedule to provide a framework for allocating the authorized resources; that is, the authorized budgets.

The original 1967 DOD earned value criteria were rewritten by private industry in 1996, but identical requirements for a formal scheduling system were maintained in three of the criteria, as the following quotes describe:

6. Schedule the authorized work in a manner which describes the sequence of work and identifies the significant task interdependencies required to meet the requirements of the program.
7. Identify physical products, milestones, technical performance goals, or other indicators that will be used to measure progress.
23. Identify, at least monthly, the significant differences between both planned and actual schedule performance and planned and actual cost performance, and provide the reasons for the variances in the detail needed by program management.[2]

Question: Are these three criteria unique to the management of only earned value projects? Answer: Absolutely not. These three criteria lay down fundamental scheduling principles that would apply to any project, any industry, anywhere in the world. It is also interesting to note that these same three criteria were incorporated verbatim into the ANSI/EIA-748 industry standard, which applies to the private sector in general.[3]

Since the earned value criteria were initially released, there have been several interpretations as to what may be required from projects in order to comply with these three scheduling criteria. The requirements for a formal scheduling process specified in these criteria can generally be reduced to meeting three obligations, as conceptually displayed in Figure 6.1.

First, all earned value projects must have, at a minimum, a single top-level summary schedule that completely defines the broad parameters of the project. These schedules typically go by the title of "master schedule" or "project master schedule." Such schedules will be the exclusive property of the project manager and issued under the direction of that individual.

All master schedules must be controlled documents, formally issued to all key functions, individuals and suppliers supporting the project. Important note: all the task completion dates as specified on a project master schedule must be respected, and such end dates cannot be altered by anyone other than the project manager. If individual functions or suppliers run late to the specified master schedule dates, such late conditions will not change the required dates contained in the master schedule. While it may be necessary to be late to meeting master schedule dates . . . it is unacceptable to ignore (or re-position) the specified dates in a master schedule.

On a smaller project, there may be only a single one-page master schedule

---

2 United States Department of Defense, *Earned Value Management Implementation Guide*, (Washington, D.C., December 14, 1996.

3 American National Standards Institute/Electronic Industries Alliance, ANSI/EIA-748-1998, *Earned Value Management Systems*, Arlington, VA, May 19, 1998.

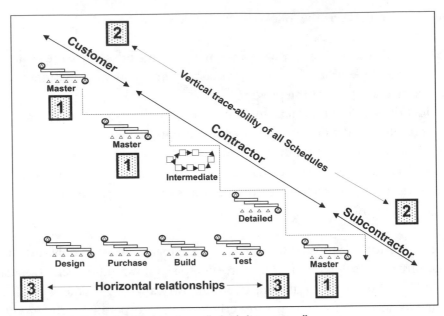

Figure 6.1 *Earned value requires a "scheduling system"*

needed. But as projects increase in size and complexity, with the involvement of possibly the customer, contractor, and subcontractors, the necessity of having a top-controlled schedule to specify the outer time parameters is of critical importance. The requirement for having a master schedule is displayed as items numbered [1] in Figure 6.1, reflecting a master schedule from the buying customer, the performing contractor, and the subordinate subcontractors. All master schedule dates for a given project must be in concert with each other. Any lower-tier intermediate and/or detailed functional schedules would, by definition, be subordinate to the project manager's master schedule.

The second requirement for scheduling earned value projects is that the tasks or milestones described in all subordinate schedules must be in concert with the specific requirements contained in the project master schedule. All the tasks and events depicted on lower-level project schedules must be relatable to the project master schedule; that is, there must be what is called "vertical" traceability [2] going from the lower detailed schedules up to the requirements defined in the top schedule. It may be acceptable to be behind, relative to the requirements of the top schedule. However, it would be unacceptable to not know one's position as it relates to the requirements of the project master schedule. The project manager's master schedule must be supreme; it must be followed on any project.

Vertical traceability simply means that all individuals working on a given project must know when the project manager requires their particular task(s) to be completed and deliverables made, consistent with the project master schedule. For example, on a construction-type job, all project schedules must support the same substantial completion date. On an aircraft development project, all schedules must support the same first flight date, and so forth.

When there are multiple organizational levels involved on any given project—as shown in Figure 6.1, where three separate entities are displayed (the customer, contractor, and subcontractor)—the issue of vertical traceability becomes critical. For example, the buying customer will specify its requirements in the form of a master schedule, which is typically incorporated as an exhibit into the prime contractual document. Then, the performing contractor's master schedule must be issued consistent with the requirements of the customer's master schedule. Further, all subordinate subcontractor schedules must, likewise, be in concert with the requirements contained in the highest-level master schedules. This concept is displayed as item [2] in Figure 6.1.

On projects of major size or complexity, where frequently multiple sites and companies are involved, project managers have gravitated to a more formally controlled scheduling process out of necessity. On such major projects, they will frequently employ some type of a scheduling hierarchy document to pull together the various schedules. Figure 6.2 shows what is called a project "scheduling tree," which is used to vertically link and integrate all project schedules. Each subordinate schedule represents a subproject to the master schedule and, ideally, major project milestones can be linked within each of the respective subordinate schedules.

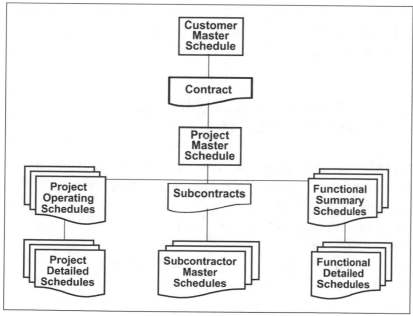

Figure 6.2 *A "Schedule Tree" vertically integrates schedules*

Figure 6.2 reflects the hierarchy of the buying customer, the prime contractor, and the various subcontractors. It also displays the project's peculiar schedules (e.g., test articles) on the left side and the functional organizational (e.g., engineering, procurement) schedules on the right side. The functional schedules for the various departments—for example, engineering—will also contain the tasks necessary to support each project. In the center are listed the various subcontractor schedules. These schedules will also help to prevent an overcommitment of scarce resources.

The third [3] and final requirement of scheduling in an earned value project environment is that there be "horizontal" relationships identified between all dependent project tasks. Simply put, and as shown in the lower left-hand corner of Figure 6.1, the design must be available before materials can be purchased, and the materials must be available before the project deliverable can be built and tested. Relationships and constraints between project tasks must be identified. Most call this requirement critical path methodology.

Interestingly, the creators of the original C/SCSC requirements and the more recent industry EVMS rewrite carefully avoided imposing any requirements for employing a specific scheduling methodology. Rather, they took the approach of merely specifying broad general requirements. Most particularly, they avoided requiring the use of the critical path method (CPM). And yet, we know of no other way to adequately isolate the "horizontal" task relationships and constraints, especially on a complex project, than with use of critical path method scheduling. It is interesting to note that two more recent government initiatives of the early 1990s (to be covered next) were very specific in defining their scheduling requirements. They both required the use of critical path methodology.

GOVERNMENT MANDATES REQUIRING CRITICAL PATH METHODOLOGY

Two (non-DOD) governmental initiatives mandated several years after the initial criteria were released are worthy of mention, because they both imposed rather specific schedule requirements on the private sector when employing the earned value concept. Both required the employment of critical path methodology in the management of earned value projects.

When the United States Department of Energy (DOE) first issued its *Project Control System (PCS)* guidelines document in 1992, it specifically required the use of critical path methodology scheduling as a required technique to be employed on all DOE-funded projects. CPM networks were required to be an integral tool in the management of all DOE projects. This same policy was restated in 2000 with the acquisition of DOE capital assets:

The Department of Energy (DOE) prime contractor's project management system must satisfy the following requirements:

1. The industry standard for project control systems described in American National Standards Institute (ANSI) EIA-748, Earned Value Management Systems, must be implemented on all projects with a total project cost (TPC) greater than $20M for control of project performance during the project execution phase . . .

5. A critical path schedule and a project master schedule must be developed and maintained.[4]

Thus, on projects in excess of $20M (Total Project Cost), the DOE requires both EVM and CPM.

Also of note, when the Canadian Government first released its new earned value management control system guidelines in 1993 for private industry to follow, it required the use of CPM scheduling. The Canadian EVM project guidelines were tailored after the United States DOD C/SCSC, but specifically required that Earned Value Management be used in conjunction with CPM network scheduling.[5]

While the initial DOD 1967 earned value criteria remained silent on which scheduling methodologies had to be employed, these two more recent mandates for governmental project management specifically called for the use of CPM as a required scheduling technique.

EARNED VALUE PROJECT MANAGEMENT REQUIRES A SCHEDULING SYSTEM

In order to implement any form of Earned Value Project Management, two absolute rules have been discussed. First, you must define what it is that you are about to do; that is, you must scope the entire project to the best of your ability. The second requirement deals with the placement of the defined scope into a fixed time frame so that time performance can be measured throughout the life of the project. Some might suggest that these two rules are not unique to Earned Value Project Management, that they are fundamental to all good project management . . . period. We would agree completely with this assertion. Earned Value simply requires that fundamental project management principles be employed.

---

4 U.S. Department of Energy Order, DOE O 413.3, October 13, 2000, *Project Management for the Acquisition of Capital Assets.*

5 Canadian General Standards Board: 1993 "Policy 187-GP-1" (August) *Cost/Schedule Performance Management Standard.*

Just how important is scheduling to the management of earned value applications? We need to understand this issue in order to put earned value implementation on a proper footing.

In 1967, four months prior to the formal release of the DOD's Earned Value C/SCSC, an industrial engineer with the United States Air Force—and one of the early architects of the modern-day earned value applications—aptly described the importance of scheduling in a paper he wrote. He was specifying what was required in order to employ Earned Value, emphasizing the need for a controlled scheduling process. His message to us read:

> As of a given point in time, we need answers to these questions:
> What work is scheduled to have been completed?
> What was the cost estimate for the work scheduled?
> What work has been accomplished?
> What was the cost estimate of the completed work?
> What have our costs been?
> What are the variances?[6]

Items 1) and 2) in the above illustration cover the baseline work scheduled plus the budgeted costs for doing this work. We now call this the "Planned Value."

Items 3) and 4) cover the work actually performed plus the original budgeted costs for doing this work. We now call this the "Earned Value."

Item 5) represents the actual costs incurred in converting the Planned Value baseline into Earned Value. Note that Item 5) has nothing to do with either establishing the Planned Value baseline or in determining the Earned Value accomplished. But Item 5) must be related to the Earned Value thus performed.

It should be clear by now that in order to employ some form of earned value measurement, one must understand the authorized work to be done, and then manage that effort within a tightly controlled time frame; that is, a scheduling environment.

There is one additional earned value criterion that should be mentioned because it requires that a formal scheduling process be in place in order to synchronize: first, the Planned Value of the work scheduled with the Earned Value of the work actually performed; and, second, to relate the Earned Value against the Actual Costs for performing the work. This important criterion reads as follows:

---

6 A. E. Fitzgerald, 1967. "*The Air Force Cost/Schedule Planning and Control System Specification: Experience and Outlook.*" (August 29) From a speech given to the Armed Forces Management Association.

22. At least on a monthly basis, generate the following information at the control account and other levels as necessary for management control using actual cost data from, or reconcilable with, the accounting system:

(1) Comparison of the amount of planned budget and the amount of budget earned for work accomplished. This comparison provides the schedule variance.
(2) Comparison of the amount of the budget earned and the actual (applied where appropriate) direct costs for the same work. This comparison provides the cost variance.[7]

Item number (1) in this criterion requires the synchronization of the Planned Value with the Earned Value in order to isolate any schedule variance from the baseline. The Schedule Variance (SV) formula is thus: "Earned Value less Planned Value."[8] A negative earned value schedule variance simply indicates to project team members that they are falling behind their scheduled baseline work.

Please note that the earned value schedule variance may (often) have no relationship to the project's critical path position. The critical path position is a more important indicator for any project to monitor. Being behind in the work planned for the project will probably cost more to accomplish in a later time frame, but it may not extend the duration or completion date of the project. However, the critical path, if not managed aggressively, could extend the duration of the project and cost dearly in added resources to complete the required work. Both the earned value schedule variances and the project's critical path must be monitored by the project team.

Item number (2) of this criterion is the more serious of the two earned value variances. It is called the "cost variance" and it represents the relationship between the Earned Value accomplished and the Actual Costs it took to generate the Earned Value. The Cost Variance (CV) formula is thus "Earned Value less Actual Costs."[9] A negative cost variance can result in permanent, non-recoverable damage to the project's final cost position.

If a project spends more funds to perform the planned work than it has budgeted, the resulting condition is plainly an overrun. Overruns—even early overruns—have been proven to be non-recoverable by any project. Overruns are rarely (if ever) completely offset by subsequent performance, although many project managers and technical people would dispute this fact. They have a tendency to be optimistic about their ability to recover such losses. However, historical experience

7 United States Department of Defense, *Earned Value Management Implementation Guide*, (Washington, D.C., December 14, 1996.

8 *A Guide to the Project Management Body of Knowledge (PMBOK® Guide)*, 2004, Section 7.3.2.2.

9 Ibid.

suggests that performance in later periods tends to get worse, rather than better, with the passage of time. The reason: planning for later project periods tends to be progressively more vague, less well defined, and, thus, more subject to negative cost performance. The earned value cost variance is a critical indicator for any project team to watch.

THE EARNED VALUE BASELINE VERSUS THE PROJECT'S CRITICAL PATH

In any project that employs Earned Value Management, the project's time-phased performance plan may go by several titles: the Performance Measurement Baseline (PMB), the sum of the Planned Values, the Budget at Completion (BAC), or simply the project baseline. Such baselines will be a reflection of all the work authorized, as delineated in the project master schedule, plus management's budget for the authorized work. Note: management or contingency reserves, if any, will reside outside the PMB—not planned or scheduled, simply a set-aside until needed. A scheduling system is vital to employing earned value measurement.

But there is an important point in respect to performance measurement with Earned Value Management. While a negative "cost" variance is always a serious matter (reflecting, perhaps, a non-recoverable cost overrun), a negative "schedule" variance may or may not be a serious issue. Reason: a negative earned value schedule variance is simply a temporary reflection of falling behind the project's baseline

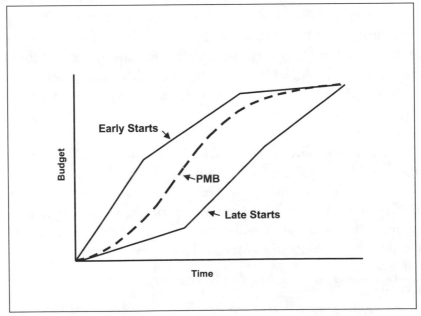

Figure 6.3 *The Performance Measurement Baseline (PMB)*

PMB. The issue we must address is: What does the PMB represent—early starts, late starts, or something else?

To discuss this issue, we need to review Figure 6.3. When creating the initial project baseline, each and every task manager will decide precisely where to place his or her tasks in a time frame consistent with the project master schedule. But there is often wide latitude allowed in the placement of each scheduled task. Some individuals are optimists, others are pessimists, still others . . . who knows?

The issue: Are most of the tasks placed in an "early start" position, with respect to the critical path? Or are most of the tasks placed in a "late start" position, putting each task on or near the critical path? Unfortunately, many of today's project participants do not know the critical path position of their project, having never done the calculations, so the placement of each task merely represents a best guess. These best guesses likely constitute a "most likely" position with respect to the project's critical path(s). Thus, the earned value PMB will likely constitute a time frame set in between the project's earliest starts and latest starts for each and every task.

Subsequently, any negative earned value schedule variances ($SV = EV − PV$) that may result from actual performance must be carefully assessed to determine its true impact on the project's final completion date. A late performing task with considerable positive float may not be serious. But a late task with zero float, or one carrying high risks to the project, can be a very serious matter. It all depends on the placement of each and every task in the PMB. Unfortunately, too many project participants do not know the critical path position of their project.

7

ESTIMATE THE RESOURCES AND AUTHORIZE BUDGETS TO FORM CONTROL ACCOUNT PLANS (CAPS)

ONCE THE TECHNICAL REQUIREMENTS of the project have been properly defined, and all the specified work planned and scheduled, the next logical step in establishing the project's baseline is to forecast how much each task or work package will likely cost. The required resources must be estimated, justified, and then specifically authorized by the project manager in the form of an official project budget. A cost estimate is only an estimate, until it has been specifically authorized by the project manager. Every project needs the specific authorization of scope, schedule and budget by the project manager.

These three initial steps are required in order to employ the earned value concept on a new project. An important point: these three steps are no different than the initial effort required to implement any new project. This is simply following fundamental project management. But these steps are particularly critical to an earned value project because, once the baseline has been put into place, the actual performance against the baseline will need to be measured continuously for the duration of the project.

However, there is one requirement that perhaps distinguishes earned value projects from most other projects. In order for performance measurement to take place during the term of the project, a project baseline needs to be created from detailed bottom-up planning. Performance measurement with Earned Value takes place within management control points that are called "Control Accounts (CA)" or "Control Account Plans (CAPs)." Within each CAP, the work to be done must be aligned with the authorized budget, within a precise time frame specified in the project master schedule.

So that we are all clear on this important matter, let us bring in three precise definitions of what we will be discussing:

Work Package. A deliverable or project work component at the lowest level of each branch of the Work Breakdown Structure. The work package includes the schedule activities and schedule milestones required to complete the work package deliverable or project work component. See also Control Account.

Control Account (CA). (Previously called a Cost Account.) The CA is a management control point where the integration of scope and budget and schedule takes place, and where the measurement of performance will occur. CAs are placed at selected management points of the Work Breakdown Structure. See also Work Package.

Control Account Plan (CAP). (Previously called a Cost Account Plan.) The CAP is a plan for all the work and effort to be performed in a control account. Each CAP has a definable statement of work, schedule, and time-phased budget.[1]

Continuously, on a periodic basis (typically monthly, but sometimes weekly), the project manager will want to make an assessment of how well the project is performing against the authorized baseline. Project performance will be precisely measured employing earned value metrics, normally expressed as a cost or schedule performance variance from the baseline. Such variances will give an "early warning" signal of impending problems and are used to determine whether or not corrective action needs be taken in order to stay within the project's commitment to management.

The process of taking these three initial steps to form an earned value project baseline is conceptually displayed in Figure 7.1. The project baseline must be established, typically in the sequence as shown in the illustration. The project's scope of work must first be defined (Step #1)—often with the use of a WBS—leading to a statement of work, which is then assigned to a functional organization or organizations for performance. The defined scope must next be planned and scheduled (Step #2) down to the detailed work package or task level. Finally (Step #3), the required resources must be estimated and subsequently authorized in the form of official project budgets.

1 A Guide to the Project Management Body of Knowledge (PMBOK® Guide), 2004, Glossary.

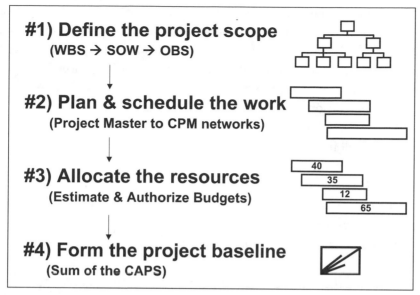

Figure 7.1 *Steps to forming the project baseline*

It should be mentioned that in some organizations, particularly those managing software projects, this conventional sequence is often altered. These organizations will sometimes take Step #1 to define their work, then perform Step #3 to estimate the required resources, and finally take Step #2 to schedule their work. They will change the typical project implementation sequence because they may be constrained by the availability of qualified resources to work on their projects. There is nothing inherently wrong with this approach, as long as the organizations start with Step #1, the project definition process, and end up with an approved project baseline, as in Step #4, displayed in Figure 7.1.

The end objective of taking these three sequential steps, either as Steps #1, #2, #3, or alternately as Steps #1, #3, #2, will be the formation of Step #4, the detailed project baseline. The earned value project baseline is derived from the sum of the "Control Account Plans" (or CAPs). The CAPs provide the measurable performance control points for the earned value projects. The significance of the control account needs to be clearly understood in order to properly utilize the earned value concept. But next we need to emphasize the importance of working with an "integrated" project baseline.

INTEGRATING THE PROJECT SCOPE OF WORK WITH COSTS AND WITH SCHEDULE

One unique aspect of employing the earned value concept is that the technique requires an "integration" of all vital components of the project. What does the term integration actually mean? Simply put, integration in Earned Value means that the technical scope of work, the work authorization, planning, scheduling, estimating, budgeting, cost accumulation—all of these processes—must be aligned with the functions performing the actual work, and all integrated with use of the WBS. This concept was previously described in Figure 4.1, where we discussed the earned value body of knowledge. In that figure, the traditional non-integrated approach was shown on the left side, while an integrated earned value project approach was shown on the right side.

Rarely is the full integration of these diverse activities ever achieved on a typical project. However, an integrated baseline is an absolute requirement with Earned Value Project Management.

When the C/SCS Criteria were first issued in 1967, and later updated by industry in 1996, the requirement for the integration of these processes was clearly mandated in the third criterion, which reads:

> 3. Provide for the integration of the company's planning, scheduling, budgeting, work authorization and cost accumulation processes with each other, and as appropriate, the program work breakdown structure and the program organizational structure.[2]

The integration of an earned value project is achieved with the creation of detailed CAPs, which are the management control points placed at the desired levels of the project's WBS. The CAP is where the management and performance measurement will take place. Within each CAP, the planned tasks will be defined and then assigned to a specific functional organization or organizations for performance.

The cost and schedule and technical performance within each CAP can be summarized and then reported either to the top levels of the project WBS, for the benefit of the project manager, or related to various functional units for the enlightenment of these managers.

CONTROL ACCOUNT PLANS (CAPS)— THE POINTS OF MANAGEMENT CONTROL

At this time, we need to cover what is perhaps the single most important feature distinguishing projects that employ Earned Value from projects that do not. This unique feature is the requirement to develop a detailed, bottom-up performance measurement baseline. The earned value performance baseline is made up from the

---

2 United States Department of Defense, *Earned Value Management Implementation Guide*, (Washington, D.C., December 14, 1996.

individual Control Account Plans, referred to as "CAPs." Originally dubbed Cost Account Plans (or CAPs), industry, in its 1996 update to the DOD C/SCSC, substituted the term "Control Account Plans" for "Cost Account Plan"—a good move since the CAP is a management control point, a subproject in which the performance measurement must take place.

Additionally, and perhaps of greater importance, Earned Value is a technique for accurately relating the money being spent against the physical work accomplished. This delicate relationship determines the cost performance efficiency factor being achieved on the project—the work actually performed by the project for the money actually spent. The cost efficiency factor is particularly critical because poor cost performance is non-recoverable to the project. It has been empirically demonstrated for over three decades that whenever a project costs more money than the value of the physical work accomplished, the subsequent overrun condition does not get corrected. Historically, overruns only get worse, not better, with the passage of time.

Earned Value requires that a detailed bottom-up baseline plan be put in place. The baseline in Earned Value is formed with the creation of self-contained, measurable CAPs. The earned value technique can be employed on projects of any size, from as small as perhaps a few thousand dollars to mega-projects valued in the billions of dollars. The earned value concept is scalable, as long as certain fundamental principles are followed and the performance baseline is formed with use of measurable CAPs.

A little background on the term "Control Account Plan" may be in order. In 1967, when DOD first issued its C/SCSC, it chose to call these measurement units by the term "cost accounts." A cost account was initially defined as the point of intersection of the lowest WBS element with a single functional unit. More recently, with the general acceptance of the concurrent engineering (often called "integrated project teams") concept, the use of a single functional element has been broadened to include all functions working on a single WBS element. The subject of multi-functional teams will be addressed in the next section. Multi-functional project teams have represented an important evolutionary development with Earned Value.

One important point on the use of CAPs: Four elements are necessary for earned value performance measurement. Each CAP must include, at a minimum: (1) a discrete scope of work, typically expressed with work package tasks; (2) a time frame to complete each work package task (i.e., the project schedule); (3) the authorized project resources (i.e., the approved budget). Budgets may be expressed in any measurable form—for example, dollars, hours, units, etc. Lastly, each CAP should have (4) a designated individual to manage the effort, typically called the Control Account Manager or CAM. Most CAMs will have a dual reporting relationship: to the project manager for the project work, and to the functional manager in a CAM's permanent organization.

The CAP is the fundamental building block for performance measurement, and the summation of the CAPs will add up to the total value of the project. The project's master schedule will set the planned time frame for each CAP, and then determine the earned value performance measurement using the same metrics that established the plan.

On smaller projects of only a few thousand dollars in value, there may be only a few CAPs required for the project. However, on larger projects representing millions or even billions of dollars, there will obviously be, out of necessity, more CAPs required. In every case, the project manager must determine the appropriate number of CAPs to be employed, as well as their duration and size.

There are no absolute standards regarding the appropriate size of CAPs. The rule of thumb should be whatever is a manageable number for a given scope of work. What is manageable will likely vary by the type of project being implemented. If the effort covers, for example, state-of-the-art research and development, or routine product testing, or continuous production, or a construction job, what will be considered manageable will likely vary in each case. Also, the amount of procured materials, the subcontracted work, the degree of personal supervision required, and the complexity of the effort will all play into the determination of what constitutes a manageable CAP.

The current trend in most earned value projects would appear to support the employment of lesser numbers and larger-size CAPs. It would also appear to support the use of multi-functional team CAPs, an important subject that will be covered next.

MULTI-FUNCTIONAL TEAM CONTROL ACCOUNT PLANS (CAPS)

The wisdom of earned value projects employing very small and very detailed CAPs—representing the intersection of a single WBS element with a single functional organization—began to be questioned starting sometime in the mid-1980s. On larger, multi-billion-dollar mega-projects, the numbers of individual CAPs often ran into the thousands. This approach was, frankly, both cumbersome and impossible to manage. The amount of energy it took to establish the initial detailed planning, and then to measure performance against hundreds or thousands of detailed CAPs, required more effort than any perceived benefit to management.

Certain individuals working with Earned Value questioned the need for the use of excessive, small, short-span CAPs. Why not combine larger segments of homogeneous work, perhaps representing higher levels of the WBS, and define it as a measurable CAP? As long as one maintained the critical relationship of authorized work to authorized budget, why not measure performance with larger groupings of work, and a lesser number of CAPs?

The integrity of the CAPs had to be maintained. This meant that once a given scope of work was defined for a CAP, and the budgets authorized for the work, the delicate relationship of "defined work to authorized budget" had to be maintained until performance was completed. Indiscriminate transfers of either budget or work, independent of the other between CAPs, would only serve to invalidate performance measurement. All work defined and authorized with a precise budget must remain in concert. Preventing the shifting of work without corresponding funds, or vice versa, is an absolute rule in order to maintain the integrity of performance measurement within CAPs.

In addition to questioning the use of small CAPs, these same practitioners also questioned the necessity of measuring a single function within each CAP. Why not take a given larger segment of homogeneous work, and measure the collective results of all functions performing such work? Would not the performance of the full multi-functional team be a more meaningful measurement than simply the performance of a single function?

Some initial resistance to the use of large, multi-functional CAPs came from government C/SCSC review team directors. Perhaps they were concerned that the necessary discipline would not be present to prevent abuses. However, the DOD subsequently did endorse the use of integrated work-team CAPs in its 1989 supplemental guidance statement document:

> A natural fallout of the work team concept may be the overall reduction in the number of cost accounts with a resultant increase in their size, duration, and resource composition. This will result from grouping organizational elements, WBS elements, or a combination of both into larger, higher-level cost accounts.[3]

This change of policy represented a significant advancement in the use of Earned Value within the DOD. If properly implemented at the beginning of a new project, the use of larger multi-functional work-team CAPs resulted in the elimination of 90 percent of the total number of CAPs required for any project. Thus, with only ten percent of the previous number of CAPs to monitor, management could then focus its attention on the CAPs as a viable management control point, a meaningful sub-project.

An interesting observation: Although the notion of employing larger, multi-functional, integrated cost accounts came from private industry, and was later approved for use by the DOD policy board, it was not implemented on new contracts to any significant degree. Rather, the entire approach was overtaken by other

---

3 United States Department of Defense, *C/SCSC Supplemental Guidance*, Item #4, (July 1989), Washington, D.C.

events of the same period. A new idea came along for the DOD project managers that seemed to incorporate the idea of larger multi-functional CAPs. The new direction was to be called Integrated Project Teams (IPTs), or Integrated Product Development Teams (IPDTs).

A product development management concept called "concurrent engineering" had been in existence for years, and was starting to be noticed in both private industry and in certain quarters within the DOD acquisition community. The concurrent engineering initiative, in fact, overtook the initiative for earned value multi-functional team CAPs. Management gurus were also beginning to coin exciting new terms to describe this phenomenon, like "multi-functional projectization," [4] whatever that term might mean. It sounded a little like the concurrent engineering concept, which was defined as:

> "Concurrent" or "simultaneous" engineering . . . the means of carrying out the engineering process by forming a team whose members come from many disciplines . . . The normal activities of product design and development of manufacturing process are carried out in parallel rather than in a series, reducing the time it takes to perform both tasks.[5]

Some of the military program managers enthusiastically adopted the idea of the use of concurrent engineering, which they were to later call "Integrated Product Development Teams" (or IPDTs). As it did earlier with the initial earned value concept, the Air Force again took the lead and, in 1990, issued the following policy statement urging, or perhaps demanding, the use of multi-functional integrated product development teams:

> Integrated Product Development (IPD) Teams: the integration of all functional disciplines required to manage the definition, development, acquisition, training and support of systems for which we are responsible. The concept has been called "concurrent engineering," "integrated engineering," or "simultaneous engineering" in other organizations. Its principal feature is the merger of several functions in a single organization to ensure that all aspects of design, manufacturing, test, training and support are addressed at all stages of the acquisition cycle, but particularly at the front end.[6]

---

4 Tom Peters, *Liberation Management*, New York, Alfred A. Knopf, 1992, page 13.

5 Bernard N. Slade, *Compressing the Product Development Cycle*, New York, AMACOM Division of the American Management Associations, 1993.

6 Lt. General John M. Loh, USAF Aeronautical Systems Division, Dayton, Ohio, a policy memorandum, *Organizational Alignment to Implement Integrated Product Development*, (March 26, 1990).

Thus, the private industry initiative that urged the use of multi-functional work-team CAPs for earned value applications was quietly made a part of the larger DOD procurement initiative promoting the use of Integrated Product Development Teams (IPDTs). Earned Value benefited from the use of multi-functional CAPs, allowing management to focus on a more meaningful but lesser number of control points. Conversely, the DOD project directors have better accepted, and have adopted, the earned value concept as their own valuable management tool, as a part of their initiative on using IPDTs. This resulted in a win-win situation for all parties in the management process.

We also recommend the employment of Earned Value Project Management with use of multi-functional team CAPs for employment on all projects within the private sector. To us, the integrated project team represents a natural subdivision of projects into meaningful subprojects that align nicely with the project WBS.

Figure 7.2 shows the use of earned value multi-functional team CAPs. Each CAP must incorporate four elements to be viable: a precise scope of work, a schedule, a budget, and a team leader (the CAP manager) to manage the effort.

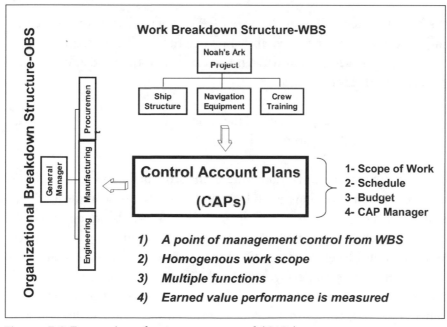

Figure 7.2 *Form points of management control (CAPs)*

ESTIMATES VERSUS BUDGETS . . .
AND MANAGEMENT RESERVES

An opinion: All project managers need some type of "just-in-case" reserves to carry out their challenging work. Such funds are sometimes called contingency budgets, other times management reserves. These values are simply set-aside amounts over and above the allocated budget values that await the misfortunes that too often beset projects . . . they always have and they likely always will. In scheduling, such management reserves will take the form of slack or float, which are time reserves, in addition to the cost reserves.

One important issue facing any project manager: Who should control these monetary or time reserves? Our position: Assuming such values can be uncovered—and this is not always an easy task—the project manager should own and control such contingency funds and schedule float. Why? For this answer, we go to an established authority on the subject of project management who commented on the issue several years back.

It is a natural tendency on the part of every person to provide a certain amount of cushion or reserve in his or her time and cost estimates . . . If approved, then each person will tend to expend all the time and cost available . . . as Parkinson has said:

- The work at hand expands to fill the time available.
- Expenditures will rise to meet the budget.[7]

If a project manager allows more time in the schedule than is needed to perform the tasks, people somehow have a tendency to take all the time authorized—and the excess time will likely cost more money. Also, if more funds are approved than are needed to accomplish the defined work, these funds will somehow typically get spent.

We would now like to make a distinction between an estimate and an authorized budget. Authorizations will typically take the form of an approved budget or an approved schedule. An estimate may well represent the amounts that the person feels will be necessary to accomplish a particular task. However, as we all know, estimates sometimes (always?) contain the estimated value needed to perform a task, PLUS a just-in-case amount to cover contingencies, or expected losses in negotiations, or possibly both.

---

7 Russell D. Archibald, *Managing High-Technology Programs and Projects*, New York: John Wiley & Sons. Quoted from Parkinson, C.N. *Parkinson's Law*, 1957, Boston: Houghton Miffin.

Only the very young and inexperienced would seem to provide true, honest estimates of requirements. Stated another way, there would seem to be a high correlation between gray hairs and estimates that include contingency pads! Project contingencies may be needed, but they must be owned and controlled by the project manager, or else they may well be needlessly consumed.

What most of the more astute project managers have learned to do is to authorize only that which is needed to actually accomplish the work. Any differences are kept locked away by the project manager for the potential problems that will likely happen, but just cannot be predicted in advance.

IN CONCLUSION

In a project that employs the Earned Value Management concept, the project's measurable performance plans will be formed with the creation of CAPs, placed at appropriate levels within the project's WBS. The WBS serves as an integrator of all activities for the project, and allows the defined work in the CAPs to be assigned directly to the functional organizations performing the work.

The formation of CAPs is the last of four implementation planning steps necessary to form an earned value baseline: (1) define the scope, (2) plan and schedule the scope, (3) authorize the necessary resources to form CAPs, and (4) form the project baseline against which performance will be measured through the completion of the project.

What we have been describing is simply fundamental project management, which should be applied to all projects, of any size or complexity, in any industry.

8

ESTABLISH THE EARNED VALUE
PROJECT BASELINE

INTRODUCTION

Some project managers refer to it as their "stake in the ground." Others describe it simply as a "point of reference." Whatever it may be called, all projects need to establish some type of baseline against which performance may be measured during the full life cycle of a project.

This requirement is true for any project. But it is particularly critical for any project that employs the earned value technique. Once under way, project practitioners utilizing Earned Value will need to know precisely how much of the authorized work they have physically accomplished, and management's authorized budget for the completed work, in order to be able to predict how long it will take them to finish the project and how much the total bill is likely to run.

A project baseline is needed in order to determine how much of the planned work has been accomplished as of any point in time. The completed (earned value) work is compared against the work they originally set out to do to assess their planned schedule position. The completed (earned value) work is also compared against the actual consumed resources to reflect their true cost position.

Returning again to the experience gained from the DOD when it first issued the earned value criteria in 1967—and later when these same criteria were rewritten by industry in 1996—the requirement to establish a project measurement baseline has been consistent:

> 8. Establish and maintain a time-phased budget baseline, at the control account level, against which program performance can be measured. Budget for far-term efforts may be held in higher-level accounts until an appropriate time for allocation at the control account level. Initial budgets established for performance measurement will be based on either internal management goals or the external customer negotiated target cost including estimates for authorized but undefinitized work.[1]

The project manager must maintain the authorized baseline, and approve or reject all changes to the baseline. Each change, once approved, must be incorporated into the performance measurement baseline in a timely manner.

The term Control Account Plan (CAP), a management control point, represents the core measurement point for earned value measurement. CAPs are placed at selected elements of the WBS, as determined by the project manager.

Each CAP must contain three discrete elements in order to be viable: (1) a specific scope of work, (2) a time frame for performance, and (3) an approved budget to accomplish the work. Each CAP must have the capability of measuring its Planned Value against the Earned Value, as well as the Earned Value against the Actual Costs. A project's total performance measurement baseline is, therefore, merely the summation of its individual Control Account Plans.

We will need to understand the makeup of the project baseline. Particularly, we should understand how Earned Value is initially planned and then measured within each of the CAPs, and the methods used to accomplish this.

INTEGRATED PRODUCT DEVELOPMENT TEAMS (IPDTS) VERSUS CAPS

In the previous chapter, we described the concurrent engineering concept, or, as it is often called, the Integrated Product Development Team (IPDT) approach. IPDTs have become a very successful project management approach, particularly when new product development is the primary deliverable. A question affecting the earned value baseline: When an organization employs the IPDTs concept, what is the relationship between IPDTs and earned value CAPs? Answer: It all depends. The magnitude of the project will typically determine the project hierarchy.

---

1 United States Department of Defense, *Earned Value Management Implementation Guide*, (Washington, D.C., December 14, 1996.

When an organization uses IPDTs on smaller projects, the IPDTs and CAPs are typically the same. The project forms IPDTs, which are, in effect, CAPs. They are points of management focus where performance measurement takes place. See Figure 8.1. The top part of Figure 8.1 depicts a baseline for a smaller project of perhaps $100,000 in costs. In this arrangement, the designated IPDTs function as earned value CAPs.

On larger projects, of perhaps $100 million or more, the IPDTs effectively become "super CAPs," which are the primary points of project manager focus. These IPDTs will typically have multiple CAPs performing work, subordinate to the IPDT team leader. In this case, the CAPs are effectively subprojects to the IPDT teams. Individual performance will take place within the CAPs, which will roll up to the IPDTs. The hierarchy of a major project is conceptually portrayed in the lower portion of Figure 8.1.

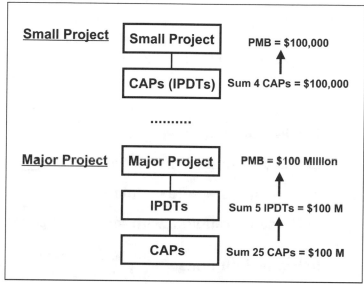

Figure 8.1 *The EVPM hierarchy . . . it all depends*

METHODS USED TO PLAN AND THEN MEASURE EARNED VALUE

Earned Value is dependent upon the project's scheduling system to provide the mechanism for measurement of performance. Stated another way, without a scheduling system in place, earned value performance measurement could not take place. A project scheduling system will, by definition, reflect the project's scope of work, and then place all the defined work tasks into a specific time frame for execution. When one adds resources (management's authorized budget) to the scheduling system and the metrics to plan and consume such resources, the earned value performance plan is in place.

The determination as to which metrics should be used to measure a particular application is a personal judgment issue and will vary by project. We will review the various options available to a project. But it is the job of the project team and the various work package and control account managers to ultimately select the appropriate measurement metrics that best support their particular needs. Planning, measurement, and consistent application are the key to having a successful implementation.

Over the years since Earned Value was introduced to industry, a number of innovative methods have been employed for the measurement of performance. For purposes of summarization, we have grouped these various methods into eight broad generic categories, as displayed in Figure 8.2. We will discuss the pros and cons of each of these measurement methods in order to provide an understanding of each.

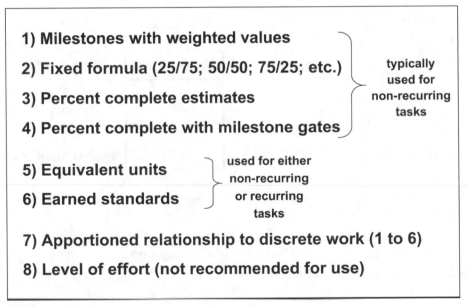

Figure 8.2 *Earned value measurement methods*

Methods 1 through 6, as listed, deal with what is called "discrete" types of performance measurement. Discrete measurement is always the preferred type to use. Method 7 is called an "apportioned" measurement, which means that it has some direct relationship to some discrete base task as shown with items 1 through 6. Method 8 is called level of effort work (LOE), which is <u>not</u> recommended for use by these authors.

1) MILESTONES WITH WEIGHTED VALUES

This method of performance measurement works well and is typically used whenever individual work packages exceed a short duration, perhaps running two, three, or more performance periods (expressed in weeks or months). The longer work packages are converted into multiple measurable milestones to reflect finite divisions of work, preferably one or more milestones in each period being measured. Each designated milestone is assigned a specific budgeted value, which will be earned upon 100% completion of the event. The total work package budget is divided based on a weighted value assigned to each milestone. Once work is underway, values should not be changed.

The weighted milestone method is a preferred method used in performance measurement, but it is also a most difficult method to initially plan and then administer. This approach requires a close working relationship between the work package managers, the scheduling people, and the resource-estimating function, in order to set meaningful milestone values for all planned work. See Figure 8.3, item 1, which displays Milestones with Weighted Values.

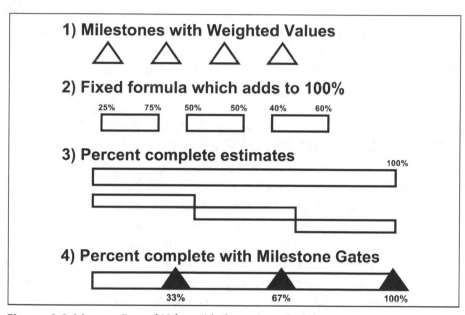

Figure 8.3 *Measure Earned Value with the project schedule*

This approach is sometimes used to authorize interim progress payments to fixed-price sellers under a concept called "Performance Based Payments."

2) FIXED (START/FINISH) FORMULA BY TASK: 25/75; 50/50; 75/25; ETC.

See Figure 8.3, item 2. This approach was most popular in the early years of Earned Value, but its use has somewhat diminished in recent years. Conceptually, it is perhaps the easiest to understand, but it also requires very detailed and short-span work packages to make it work successfully.

We have illustrated only three values for this type of measurement, but, in fact, any distribution that adds up to 100% may be used (10/90; 25/75; 50/50; 40/60; 90/10; etc.).

For example, the 25%/75% method works well when applied to those work packages that are scheduled to start and be completed within the same or two measurement periods. In this scenario, 25% of the budget value is earned when the activity starts, and the other 75% of the budget is earned when the task is completed. Purchased materials often work well with this method: 25% is earned when the materials are defined and ordered, and the final 75% earned when the materials arrive and are consumed.

One important rule to follow when using this method is that the defined tasks not exceed one or two maximum reporting periods, measured either weekly or monthly. You would not want to start a task in January, take credit for 25% of the work, then plan to complete the work in June, five months later. No measurement would have taken place for five months. One or two reporting periods should be the maximum for this method.

3) PERCENT COMPLETE ESTIMATES

To best follow this discussion, see Figure 8.3, item 3, which portrays both a long single task on the top, and a single task subdivided into three discrete tasks, as displayed on the bottom. This discrete measurement method allows for a periodic (weekly or monthly) estimate of the percentage of work completed during the reporting period. Such (subjective) estimates are made by the individual in charge of a given work package. For ease of administration, such estimates are typically expressed as a cumulative value against the full (100%) value of the specified work package.

Typically, such estimates are made on a purely "subjective" basis; that is, one's personal and professional—but unsubstantiated—estimate. Thus, when using this method, if people want to play games with Earned Value by claiming more initial value than they actually have, the subjective percent complete estimate is where it will happen.

Over the years, the percent complete method of estimating performance has received increasingly wide acceptance in private industry. The reason: It is the easiest to administer of all earned value methods. But it is also the method most subject to performance pressures from senior management and others with an individual bias.

There is nothing inherently wrong with the use of subjective estimates of results, as long as the work packages are well defined and senior internal management goes through periodic reviews of status to test the reasonableness of subjective estimates. Many a heated debate has taken place between work package managers and supervisors (sometimes also from their colleagues) when it has been felt that individuals were claiming too much value for their respective work packages. Rarely are such disagreements centered on too little value claimed, except perhaps at year-end bonus time!

If a company is genuinely utilizing the earned value method in the performance of a project, the individual professional integrity of both employees and supervisors will often provide a sort of informal "check and balance" on the accuracy of the periodic estimates. Conversely, if a firm is intent on paying lip service only to Earned Value, periodic subjective estimates can have wide distortions in measuring Earned Value.

To minimize inflated subjective estimates, some firms have developed internal written procedures (operating guidelines) on specific segments of work to more accurately assign percent complete values based on actual work accomplishment. By providing such guidelines to work package managers, some degree of objectivity is thus incorporated into the subjective estimates. Examples of these guidelines may be: planning completed, lines of code released, drawings issued, materials ordered, parts received, tool orders released, and so forth.

Another effective practice, which is sometimes used to buffer excessive optimism when using the percent completion method, is to set a "maximum ceiling" allowed for any work package until it is 100-percent complete. While such percentages will vary from company to company, an 80- to 90-percent ceiling is typical of the values used by many firms. Thus, with an 80-percent ceiling in place, a given work package may earn only up to 80 percent of the manager's subjective estimate until the task is 100-percent complete, at which time the balance of 20 percent may be earned.

4) A COMBINATION OF PERCENT COMPLETE ESTIMATES, WITH MILESTONES USED AS "GATES"

See Figure 8.3, item 4. Private industry has typically embraced the use of percent complete estimates to set earned value measurements, probably because it is easiest to use. The manager of a work package merely assesses the status of the work package, perhaps compares its progress to a personal metric, written or not, and estimates the cumulative value accomplished.

Whatever progress value is selected, the work package manager knows that he/she must defend the estimated value before associates and sometimes before senior management. Personal gaming with the estimates—presenting unduly optimistic assessments—will ultimately come back to haunt the individual work package manager.

If the project manager and company management have genuinely endorsed the earned value concept, the subjective progress estimates by individual work package managers have proven to be quite accurate. In fact, when work package managers' personal reputations are at stake, when they know that management will hold them accountable for accurate earned value assessments, these managers tend to be on the conservative side and often slightly understate performance values to give themselves a cushion for next month's status report.

However, over the years, many of the government's earned value oversight teams have expressed great suspicion of the accuracy of purely subjective work package estimates. Perhaps they have valid reasons. Subjective estimates of earned value performance do work well, but **ONLY** if there is a check and balance in place to challenge the artificial or overly optimistic estimates. It often depends on the degree to which the project managers and senior management have accepted Earned Value as a management tool. If company management employs Earned Value simply because it is a government mandate, the validity of subjective estimates may well be questionable.

As a general rule, government oversight teams encourage the use of objective or tangible milestones for performance measurement. However, the difficulty with weighted milestones is that they require considerable time and energy to put a plan in place. Some feel that an inordinate amount of energy is required to plan a full baseline made up of weighted milestones.

Recently, there has been an evolution in earned value applications that seems to have captured the best of both measurement techniques: the ease of subjective percent complete estimates, used in conjunction with hard tangible milestones. Such milestones are placed intermittently as performance "gates" within long, subjectively measured tasks. Subjective estimates of performance are allowed up to a certain preset value for each milestone. However, subjective percentage complete estimates cannot go beyond a given milestone until certain predefined and tangible criteria have been met.

This method seems to work well in any industry and with any type of project. Thus, the broad universal acceptance of Earned Value may well be the result of finding the right balance between ease of implementation and accurate performance measurement. Subjective estimates with milestones as "gates" may provide that balance.

Three specific examples will be discussed below as we cover the use of Control Account Plans (CAPs) in the private sector.

5) EQUIVALENT COMPLETED UNITS

This measurement method allows for a given Planned Value to be earned for each full unit of work completed, and also for a fractional equivalent of a full unit. The equivalent completed unit approach works well when the project periods are of an extended duration, and it is also used for the management of repetitive work.

Assume that a project represents the construction of ten homes valued at $100,000 per home. The construction cost engineers will have prepared detailed bottom-up estimates for each of the planned homes, subdividing each home into individual cost elements. Assume that the costs covering the site excavation for each unit are estimated to be ten percent of the total value for each house, or $10,000 per home.

At the end of the first month, the project manager may want to quantify the earned value position for the full project. The first month's effort may have consisted of the completion of the excavation of sites for all ten homes. Thus, the Earned Value for the first month would be calculated at $10,000 (for each completed excavation) times ten homes, or $100,000. The measured Earned Value for the full project will be the equivalent of one full home ($100,000), although not one home will have been completed.

The construction industry often uses this approach in making progress payments to suppliers, using a simple but effective form of Earned Value. However, in the construction industry, this method of calculating physical performance is often referred to as a "schedule of values" and rarely as "Earned Value." But, conceptually, it is the earned value method: the relating of actual physical progress to actual costs.

6) EARNED STANDARDS

The use of planned standards to initially set a budget and subsequently to measure the earned performance of repetitive work is perhaps the most sophisticated of all the methods, and requires the most discipline on the part of the participants. It requires the prior establishment of equivalent unit standards for the performance of the tasks to be completed. Historical cost performance data, time and motion studies, setup, teardown, and lost-time factors, etc., are all essential to the process of measuring performance against earned work standards.

This type of work measurement is typically performed by the industrial engineers who originated the earned value concept in the first place. Interestingly, the industrial engineers typically refer to this method as equivalent work measurement rather than earned value. But it is the same concept, earned value, pure and simple.

There is no single method of setting earned value that works best for all types of activity. Probably the best approach for any firm to take is to allow for multiple measurement methods to be used, and the one employed for individual work packages will be based on the collective judgments of the CAP managers working closely with industrial engineers. The use of measuring earned standards is typically limited to repetitive or production-type work.

7) APPORTIONED RELATIONSHIPS TO OTHER DISCRETE WORK PACKAGES (ITEMS 1 TO 6)

Apportioned performance measurement is an acceptable technique with earned value. But it requires a mature organization that has kept historical performance records and understands the relationships of related functions working on common deliverables.

An apportioned task is one that has a direct intrinsic performance relationship to another discrete work package, called a "measurement base" task. Measurement bases for apportioned tasks could be represented by any of the six discrete methods described as items 1 to 6 in Figure 8.2.

One such example of an apportioned measurement relationship might be that of "factory inspection," which typically has a direct performance relationship to the "factory fabrication" labor it is inspecting. However, the inspection budgets would likely be set at a different value (perhaps only five or six percent) of the factory fabrication labor base. When the (apportioned) labor for factory inspection is planned, it is set with a direct alignment to its base work package, the factory fabrication labor. Later, when the earned value for factory fabrication labor is measured at, say, a cumulative 48 percent, the factory inspection work also declares an identical performance value of a cumulative 48 percent.

When the earned value "schedule" position for apportioned tasks is measured, the values used will always reflect the same percentage (Earned Value) as that of its related discrete base. Since the time phasing of the planned value for the inspection will always approximately match that of the fabrication labor, any schedule variances reflected by the fabrication labor, positive or negative, would be similarly reflected with the apportioned factory inspection work. Sometimes apportioned tasks may trail their discrete base tasks by perhaps a single reporting period, and that is acceptable. The apportioned task may start and finish one period later than its direct base task.

However, "cost" relationships for apportioned tasks can be substantially different from their base tasks. A cost variance for the apportioned work package will reflect the difference between the earned value achieved for the base work package and the actual costs incurred for the apportioned work. The cost variance position of the (apportioned) inspection effort may be substantially different from that of the fabrication labor because the inspection work package will relate the same earned value percentage to whatever actual costs the inspection work may have incurred. Thus, if the manager of the inspection work package were to double the number of inspectors from that set in the approved budget, the inspection (apportioned) work package could reflect a negative cost variance, even though the base effort for fabrication labor might be reflecting a different cost variance position.

An apportioned work package will always reflect an identical schedule position to that of its base work package because the Planned Value and Earned Value will be the same for both tasks. However, cost variances may be substantially different for the apportioned work package, because cost variances will reflect the apportioned actual costs, which may be higher or lower than the initial budgeted amounts.

As used in software projects, an apportioned relationship might be "code testing" apportioned to a base called "code design."

8) LEVEL OF EFFORT (LOE) . . . ALWAYS "QUANTIFY" AND "QUARANTINE"

Level of Effort (LOE) activities are those tasks which may be necessary to support a project, but which are more "time" sensitive than "performance" related. Examples of such activities might be the project manager and immediate PM staff, scheduling, budgeting, procurement, contract administration, field engineering, security guards, cooks, bottle washers, helpdesks, etc. LOE tasks sort of resemble indirect work on projects.

Whenever these functions are charged directly to a contract, they normally start at the beginning of the effort and continue for the full term of a project. However, they will generally have no measurable or deliverable outputs. One could almost make the case that these tasks should better be charged into an overhead pool, but that is a different issue.

The problem with LOE work packages is that, whatever budget is authorized in the baseline plan, the planned value automatically becomes the earned value for the project with the passage of time . . . regardless of what physical work does or doesn't take place! LOE tasks "automatically" earn whatever was approved in their plan, up to the full limits of the planned value budget. The earned value always matches the planned value, regardless of whether any physical work was done or not! A dumb concept!

For example, if the Planned Value was approved for ten (10) field engineers, but only two (2) engineers actually worked, the earned value would be shown as ten (10), precisely as approved in the plan. There would always be a zero schedule variance because Earned Value always matches the Planned Value with LOE work packages.

However, since the performance measurement was set at ten, but Actual Costs incurred were for only two, the cost variance for the period would be a positive 500%! Stated another way, the cost performance efficiency factor for field engineering in this period would be a plus-5 times perfect performance. This may seem like an absurd example, but, with LOE tasks, the absurd will happen. Is this performance measurement? We think not. The problem is that LOE work packages tend to distort the discrete measurement in the project, and often mask bad performance that needs management's attention. The only issue is how much LOE distortion is acceptable.

Perhaps a real-life example may help. On a given project to develop a new high-technology vehicle, engineering was behind schedule in the release of its design. The engineering earned value performance was not keeping up with the planned schedule. However, the factory tooling function was reflecting a positive schedule position and was actually underrunning its costs. How could this miracle happen? Engineering was running behind schedule with its design release, but manufacturing was making the tools. Incredible.

A quick review indicated that the engineering tasks were being measured discretely, as was appropriate. However, the tooling function had unilaterally changed its earned value measurement methodology from discrete to level of effort (LOE). It was showing earned value performed, although the delivery of actual tools was running seriously behind schedule. Fortunately, the project's scheduling system independently reflected a disconnect between the positive LOE earned value performance, and the non-availability of factory tooling.

How might you solve the disparity of distortions caused by LOE work? One approach to effectively managing LOE would be to always "quantify" and then to isolate or "quarantine" the LOE work. Let us discuss both approaches.

In every instance where LOE tasks are allowed in the baseline, always understand the extent of the LOE contamination in the baseline. Always "quantify" the value of the LOE in the project's baseline. You do this by dividing the value of your LOE work by the total value of the project baseline (formula: LOE value divided by BAC value).

Project managers are often shocked by the unexpected total of the LOE in their baselines. Excessive LOE is sometimes an indication that the project organization does not accept the earned value concept, and will go along with it only as long as no one measures "my performance." Author's point: If the value of LOE tasks exceeds 5 % to 10 % of the total baseline, the project is not measuring true performance. Rather, it is simply measuring the passage of time. Get rid of the excessive LOE contamination.

How might you live with this condition? In fact, there are often legitimate LOE tasks on any project, like the project manager. But excessive LOE tasks can distort accurate performance measurement. One approach would be to carefully convert all LOE tasks to subjectively measured percent complete estimates. Subjective performance measurement estimates are preferable to allowing LOE distortions.

A second approach to managing LOE is to 'quarantine" all LOE tasks outside the project baseline being measured. Don't bother to measure the LOE tasks, and certainly don't allow LOE actuals to offset discretely measured work. See Figure 8.4 to follow this discussion.

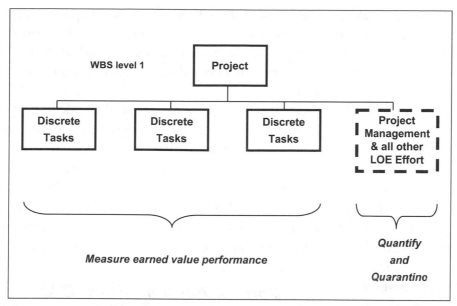

Figure 8.1 *LOE Effort: always Quantify and Quarantine*

All projects should use a Work Breakdown Structure (WBS) to completely define their project scope. Use discrete earned value measurement methods on all effort that has project deliverables; that is, discrete tasks. But any work that has no deliverables, simply quarantine as "Project Management and all other LOE Effort" and place it into an isolated element, as is shown to the extreme right in Figure 8.4. Don't bother to measure LOE; it reflects nothing but the passage of time.

If you allow for LOE tasks in your baseline, and most projects must, a good approach to manage it is first to understand how much LOE you have. Then, either convert it to percent complete discrete measurements, or exclude it altogether from your measurable project baseline.

CONTROL ACCOUNT PLANS (CAP): THE MANAGEABLE SUBPROJECTS OF EVPM

With projects employing Earned Value the point at which performance will be created, monitored and measured is within a generic type of management control cell referred to as a Control Account Plan, or simply the CAP. Since the rewrite of the earned value criteria by industry in 1996, the same designation, CAP, was continued, but the term was changed from Cost Account Plan to Control Account Plan. Both terms were identical in concept, although the title, "Control Account Plan," is likely more representative of the intended purpose of these cells.

CAPs are created by the project manager and team at selected points within the project's Work Breakdown Structure (WBS). This concept was covered earlier and illustrated within Figure 4.1, with the earned value Control Account Plan (CAP) shown on the right side of the display. CAPs are placed at selected levels in a WBS, at levels 2, 3, 4, down to the lowest point where management will want to control a homogenous grouping of work.

The CAP is essentially a subproject, a point of control at which the project manager will focus during the performance of an earned value project. It is that point at which the project's authorized work and resources and time requirements will all be integrated. Within the CAPs, the cost and schedule performance indices will emerge, demonstrating to management where they must take action. The CAP in Earned Value is the fundamental building block that forms the project's measurement baseline. Each CAP will be a self-contained management control cell. In order to be viable, each CAP should contain eight basic elements, as listed in Figure 8.5.

Items 1, 2, and 3, as listed, represent the integration of scope, with schedule and costs. Earned Value requires an integrated baseline. Item 4 requires the designation of someone to be held responsible for the performance of each CAP, typically carrying the unofficial title of Control Account Manager, or CAM. While there

---

Control Account Plan (CAP)

1) **Statement of Work (brief scope description)**

2) **Schedule (start/stop dates for each task)**

3) **Budget (expressed in dollars or hours or units)**

4) **Responsible Person (Control Account Manager)**

5) **Responsible Department (Vice President)**

6) **Type of Effort (non-recurring or recurring)**

7) **Division into discrete work packages**

8) **Method used to measure EV performance:**
   (milestone; formula; % complete; standards; apportioned)

Figure 8.5 *Elements of a Control Account Plan (CAP)*

---

are no absolute rules for what is to be contained in the CAPs, the eight elements listed in Figure 8.5 are fairly typical. At a minimum, each CAP must define the scope, schedule, and costs, and also the person responsible , as indicated by items 1 through 4.

Budgets for CAPs may take any measurable form: dollars, hours, units, standards, etc., any value that can be quantified and subsequently measured. Indirect costs may or may not be included within the various CAP budgets. Some firms hold their project managers responsible for total costs, including indirect costs, while most others hold the project manager accountable for only direct costs, or possibly only direct labor hours.

Indirect costs may or may not be included within each CAP, or simply added to the top project value, perhaps conveniently housed in a separate CAP containing all indirect burdens. The only absolute rule for budgeting is that all project dollars must be accounted for by the project; and whatever items were budgeted to a project to form the Planned Value must also be measured to reflect the actual Earned Value. Some organizations hold their project managers responsible for management of direct costs only, or direct hours only, and have a financial person convert the project metrics into budgeted dollars. The determination of precise project costs will vary from company to company.

Displayed in Figure 8.6 is an example of a sample CAP, which lists four discrete work packages. Each of the four work packages shown has a separate line available to display the Planned Value, the resulting Earned Value, and the Actual Costs.. This is a simple six-month CAP, but it may serve to illustrate certain important points. The four discrete work packages shown use different earned value methods to plan and subsequently measure their performance.

Control Account Plan (CAP)

Work Packages	EV Method	Item	Jan	Feb	Mar	Apr	May	Jun	BAC
1) Work Package #1	Weighted Milestones	Plan	△50	△75	△75	△50	△50		300
		Earn							
		Actual							
2) Work Package #2	Fixed Formula (25/75)	Plan	△25	△75	△25	△75	△25	△75	300
		Earn							
		Actual							
3) Work Package #3	Percentage Complete Estimates	Plan	100	100	100	100	100	100	600
		Earn							
		Actual							
4) Work Package #4	Percent Complete with M/S gates	Plan	100	100 33%△	100	100 67%△	100	100 100%△	600
		Earn							
		Actual							
5) Total CAP	n/a	Plan	275	350	300	325	275	275	1800
		Earn							
		Actual							

Figure 8.6 *A sample Control Account Plan (CAP)*

Work package #1 uses the "weighted value milestone" method. Five milestones are listed, each carrying a discrete value, with the total budget set at 300. The 300 can represent dollars, units, or anything that can be measured. The milestone shown in January must be completed in total before the value of 50 can be earned. Discrete milestones are like an "on/off" switch: each milestone must be 100 percent complete before the value of the milestone can be claimed.

Work package #2 has three tasks, each with a value of 100, the sum having a budget at completion of 300. This work package uses the "fixed formula" of 25%/75% to plan and then measure the performance of each of the one-month-long tasks. When a given task is opened, the earned value is set at 25% and only on total completion of this task can the other 75% be claimed. The fixed formula method works well for short-term tasks, and should not exceed one or two reporting periods.

Work package #3 employs a manager's subjective "percentage complete" estimate to measure earned value performance. This method is the most simple to calculate, but is also the technique that is most potentially subject to "gaming" by a work package manager. Percentage complete estimates work well because they are easy to administer, but they also must be watched closely by management, which must provide "checks" on overly optimistic boasts for earned value performance. Pressures to perform can result in overly optimistic calculations of Earned Value, which may temporarily distort the measurement of performance.

Work package #4 uses the combination of (subjective) "percent complete" estimates combined with (objective) "milestone gates" to keep the performance estimates honest. Here, the responsible work package manager may subjectively estimate the value of work earned up to 200, at which point certain predefined performance criteria must be met before the 200 value can be exceeded. The percent complete estimates with milestone gates incorporate the best of both techniques: ease of administration combined with accurate objective measurement.

One important point needs to be stressed about the relationship of the Planned Value (budget) to the Earned Value. The Planned Value (budget) effectively sets the "ceiling" for the Earned Value that may be claimed for each work package. For example, work package #1 sets the total planned value budget (called the Budget at Completion or BAC) at 300 for the completion of all five milestones. The Earned Value of 300 is the maximum that can be claimed for the completion of these five milestones. Should the completion of these five milestones require the expenditure of 500 or even 1,000 in order to finish, all that can be earned is the total of the planned value budget of 300, nothing more.

CONTROL ACCOUNT PLANS (CAPS) IN THE PRIVATE SECTOR

Some positive trends are occurring within private industry in the use of Earned Value to manage projects. These trends are the result of private industry experimenting, innovating with the technique, and using it in ways that make sense to their primary customers: themselves as project managers. Many project managers have discovered an exciting new tool to help them better manage their work.

As we continue to attend various international conferences—in particular, the Project Management Institute's annual Global Congresses—we find more and more professional papers being delivered on the use of Earned Value to manage projects. But here is an interesting observation: Most of these professional papers describe earned value applications in ways not previously utilized in the more formal, government-mandated applications. Industry has taken hold of Earned Value and is using it to better manage projects, not simply just sending off status reports that are likely never read.

One of the more interesting trends is in the size of the Control Account Plans (CAP), the point at which Earned Value is initially planned and then subsequently measured. The size of earned value CAPs has been on the increase, and this alone will make the concept more viable as a project management tool. The increased size of the control point is the result of two changes in the definition of what constitutes an earned value CAP, which is simply a subproject to be managed.

In the first place, project managers are focusing their attention on larger segments of homogeneous work. They are focusing attention on higher levels of the Work Breakdown Structure (WBS), and thus incorporating greater segments of project scope within each CAP. Additionally, they are including all functions performing this work. Thus, with the use of larger CAPs set at higher levels of the WBS, and the inclusion of all functions supporting the CAP, project management focuses attention on fewer, but more critical, management control points for projects.

In addition, both industry and government are starting to employ a combination of measurement methods to plan the baseline and then measure earned value performance. The use of a combination of (subjective) percent complete estimates, in conjunction with discrete (hard) milestones as measurement gates, provides ease of use with objective measurement.

Three specific examples of earned value applications are worth reviewing because they may well represent the future trend, as the concept shifts from a government-imposed reporting requirement to the private sector, because the project managers have found utility with Earned Value.

CASE 1: A CAP USED ON A HIGH-TECHNOLOGY VEHICLE DEVELOPMENT PROJECT

Shown in Figure 8.7 is an example of a large multi-functional CAP to develop a high-technology project. The period of performance spanned several years in duration. This CAP employed two discrete methods to measure earned value performance. The first two phases, covering the layout design work, employed the CAP manager's (subjective) percent complete estimate, but used it in conjunction with tangible (hard) milestones, each with predefined advancement criteria that served as gates. In the latter phase, the CAP manager used fixed formula tasks (25% to start each task and 75% when completed) for the final effort. The approach worked well! The CAP manager accurately measured performance over a multi-year period.

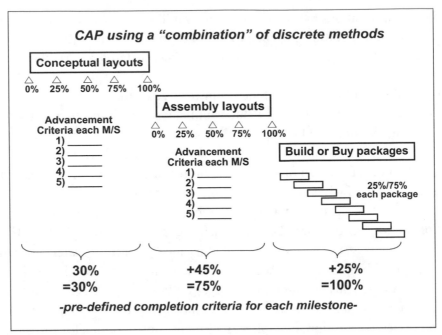

Figure 8.7 *Control Account Plan (CAP) for hi-technology vehicle*

The detailed initial planning was the key to making it work. It took the cooperation of various functions. First, the technical managers had to accept Earned Value as their management tool. The project manager and the chief engineer (sponsors) gave the concept their full endorsement and the other technical managers, including the multi-functional team leaders, followed senior management's example. This major or "super CAP," as illustrated in Figure 8.7, was effectively an amalgamation of several subordinate CAPs, each defined within the framework of the project WBS. The estimating, budgeting, and scheduling functions met with the various technical team leaders to establish their performance plans.

The CAP was separated into three distinct parts, which collectively constituted 100 percent of their total effort. Part one represented the conceptual layout work, and was estimated to be 30 percent of the total design effort. Part two was designated assembly layouts, and represented another 45 percent of the total job. The final phase consisted of a series of small manufacturing build and procurement-buy packages, and represented the final 25 percent of the job.

Parts one and two used the same earned value measurement approach. They both used the CAP manager's subjective estimated percent complete value to set the cumulative earnings each month. However, because each phase constituted a large-dollar-value segment of work, the conceptual phase alone represented 30 percent of the total job; phases one and two would be further subdivided into four performance segments, each measured by specific completion milestone criteria. Milestones would be set up for the four subphases representing the 25-percent, 50-percent, 75-percent, and 100-percent point of completion for the work.

The four specified milestones acted as "sanity-check gates." The CAP manager (subjectively) estimated the earned value position to be anywhere from zero to 25 percent for the initial work in the conceptual phase. However, to get past the 25 percent milestone gate, the CAP had to meet certain pre-specified (very specific) advancement criteria. Such criteria were previously established and approved by management. Once these selected advancement criteria were satisfied, and verified, the estimated performance values could then go beyond the 25 percent milestone.

Illustrated here is a simple but effective way to measure project performance, which incorporates the best of (subjective) manager percent complete estimates with specific (tangible) milestones using pre-defined standards that must be satisfied. This approach still required the oversight of senior management as "checks" on the estimated values in order to challenge excessive percent complete estimates, and to assure that no "gaming" was done in the completion of milestone criteria. This approach worked well in the management of a high-tech vehicle, and similar models can work on any project.

CASE 2: A CAP USED TO MANAGE AN ARCHITECTURAL DESIGN PROJECT

Figure 8.8 shows a second example of a CAP. This one used "weighted milestones" to manage the performance of an architectural design procurement contract in the construction sector. This CAP was used to monitor the performance of a design seller working on a cost-reimbursable-type contract that had a fixed fee, and then to authorize the release of fee payments to the supplier, based on the supplier's performance against specific value milestones.

However, this same approach can work effectively on fixed-price procurements to authorize payments to sellers based on their completed work. Those working on government contracts making progress payments often call these "performance-based payments," but it is simply Earned Value, pure and simple.[2]

Prior to the award of the contract, the project buyer and the contracting seller will jointly agree on the total design effort, and then subdivide the 100 percent contract value into a series of discrete measurable pieces, each piece represented by specific completion requirements. Each milestone will have pre-defined criteria to be achieved in order to be considered complete, and each will be given a fixed performance value, as displayed in Figure 8.8. For simplicity of administration, they often round each milestone to the closest 10 percent value.

This approach is conceptually simple, yet works well. Earned Value does not have to be a complicated process.

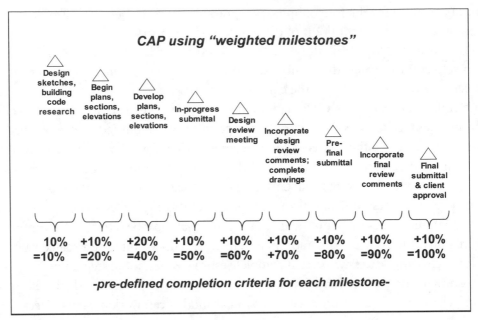

Figure 8.8 *Control Account Plan (CAP) for architectural design work*

CASE 3: A CAP USED ON A SOFTWARE PROJECT

We now approach an area that is perhaps the new frontier for project management: the effective management of software projects. How can one measure the performance of something that cannot be precisely defined or even quantified in total? This is a reasonable question. One possible approach is to define in detail that portion of a new project that is possible to quantify, and leave the remaining undefined work in gross planning packages. In these cases, management will make a preliminary commitment to a new project, until the project can be reasonably quantified.

Figure 8.9 shows a third example of a project employing Earned Value, this one containing six CAPs to manage the performance of a software project. This is the same software project that was defined earlier with the WBS in Figure 5.7. While the total project will be budgeted within the six CAPs as listed, only the first two CAPs will be planned in detail and authorized to begin work. The four remaining CAPs will be subsequently planned in greater detail, but only after the project's requirements have been defined, analyzed, and approved by management.

For both of the two initially defined CAPs, a combination of subjective percent completion estimates will be employed, but with use of specific milestones as gates. In order to be completed, each milestone must meet specific criteria that will be

2 See Federal Acquisition Regulation (FAR) subpart 32.10.

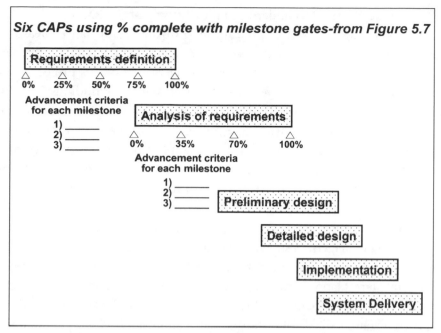

Figure 8.9 *Control Account Plans (CAPs) for a software project*

defined in advance of starting the work. The subjective estimates of percent complete cannot go past any milestone until that milestone is completed.

Note that the first CAP covering "Requirements definition" used four milestone gates at the 25%, 50%, 75%, and 100% points. Compare this with the second CAP covering "Analysis of requirements" that used only three milestones at 35%, 70%, and 100%. It is up to the CAP manager, working closely with the cost estimators, to set reasonable values for each milestone gate. Obviously, the project manager will want to review and approve each CAP prior to authorizing work to commence.

This is an example of a software project employing a simple form of Earned Value, measuring effort that can be defined up to the point at which the total project can be quantified. It is a simple but effective form of Earned Value.

THE PERFORMANCE MEASUREMENT BASELINE (PMB)

Establishing a Performance Measurement Baseline (PMB), a baseline against which performance can be measured, is an essential requirement of Earned Value Project Management. The PMB is the reference point to which a project will relate its actual accomplished work. It will disclose whether the project is keeping up with its planned schedule, and how much work is being accomplished in relation to the monies being spent. While the PMB is critical to the measurement of earned value performance, not all PMBs are alike. We need to understand the anatomy of the PMB.

The primary question: What is the makeup of the Performance Measurement Baseline (PMB) as authorized by management? Answer: It depends on the particular company. What does (senior) company management hold its project managers responsible for in the area of cost performance? Our unofficial findings: The responsibilities of project managers for cost management vary considerably from one company to another, and even from one project to another within the same company. There are no absolute procedures that apply universally to all companies. Project managers are often held accountable for differing levels of cost performance on their projects. Thus, what constitutes a PMB for one project may well be different from the PMB on another project, even within the same company.

To illustrate this point, we have attempted to define a spectrum of cost responsibilities for project managers, as shown in Figure 8.10. This figure begins with the more limited responsibilities as with item #1, where the project manager is charged with controlling only direct labor hours ... period. In many organizations, the project manager will be charged with managing direct labor hours only, thus the project PMB will be composed of purely direct labor hours. While someone in the organization (likely in Finance) will need to convert the direct labor hours into dollars for management reviews, in this situation that is not the responsibility of the project manager.

---

1) Direct Labor Hours (only)

2) Direct Labor Hours (within specific labor categories)

3) Direct Labor Costs (both hours and dollars)

4) Direct Labor in Total (through overhead applications)

5) Materials and Subcontract Costs

6) Other Direct Costs-ODC (e.g. travel)

7) All Project Costs (through General & Administrative)

8) All Project Costs (including profit) = Contract Price

Figure 8.10 *Composition of Performance Measurement Baseline*

With each additional step, moving from # 1 through # 8, the responsibilities of the project managers for cost control are broadened, and they are held accountable for managing additional categories of costs, as with overheads (indirect costs), materials, other direct costs—yes, even profits. Total accountability for all profit and loss of a given project is shown in item #8.

Many project managers will have limited responsibility managing all categories of project costs; thus, their performance baselines will be represented by the lower numbers, as illustrated in Figure 8.10. Other project managers will be charged with greater roles. However, in order to track earned value performance, we must understand precisely what management expects them to control.

Perhaps a few specific examples will help illustrate the point. We will display two examples of a Performance Measurement Baseline (PMB), one for a simple project, as in Figure 8.11, and another for a complex project, as shown in Figure 8.12.

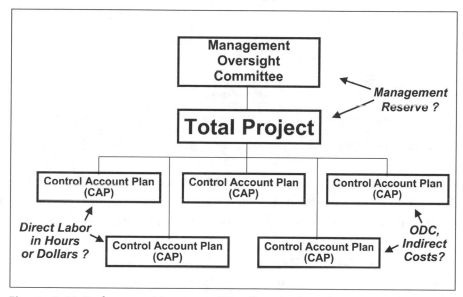

Figure 8.11 *Performance Measurement Baseline: simple project*

The majority of projects in existence today likely employ a simple baseline, as illustrated in Figure 8.11. Here, the project manager has divided the project into five points of management control—five subprojects, represented by the five Control Account Plans (CAPs) listed in the figure.

Each CAP will contain a specific amount of work to be accomplished, an authorized budget to accomplish the work, and a time frame for completing the work. Each CAP may be simply comprised of direct labor hours, as in item #1 from Figure 8.10, or hours within labor categories, as per item #2, and so forth. The PMB for this simple project will be composed of whatever categories of costs management expects the project manager to control. These CAPs may also include other direct cost items (ODC); for example, materials, subcontracts, travel, and even indirect costs. It is always a good practice to isolate direct labor items from materials and ODC.

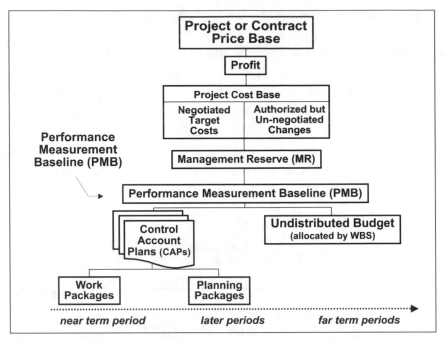

Figure 8.12 *Performance Measurement Baseline: complex project*

What about a category of costs called Management Reserves (MR)? Again, there are no universal rules for us to follow. In some cases, senior management will allow the project manager to have and control MR. In other cases, senior management will want to control the MR. Our preference is that if the project manager owns MR, it be placed in a separate CAP strictly controlled by the project manager. MR should never be left in the various functional CAPs where it likely will be consumed.

To illustrate the PMB for a more complex type of project, quite often representing an external company contract performed for a profit, refer to Figure 8.12. Here, the project is progressively subdivided into various categories of costs beginning with the total project or contract price base. After dedication of the anticipated profits by the chief financial officer, the project manager is left with the project cost base.

The project cost base is the value that the project manager has to manage for the project. It will include all categories of both direct and indirect project costs, even though the indirect costs will be beyond the immediate control of the project manager. Nevertheless, the project cost base must provide for all project costs, except for any forecasted profits.

One important issue that always exists for project managers is the necessary division of the authorized project cost base into two distinct parts: (1) those firm project costs that have been negotiated, and (2) any soft changes that have been authorized but not yet negotiated. In order to keep the project cost baseline consistent with a changing environment, the performance measurement baseline (PMB) must include both the negotiated scope and also that effort which is recognized as a legitimate change, but the exact value of which has not been settled. Deciding precisely what value to budget for the authorized but unnegotiated work is always a challenge for the project manager. However, all authorized changes must be included in the project's performance baseline in order to maintain the integrity of the work being measured.

The PMB is displayed at the center of Figure 8.12, and is central to the earned value management process. Within the PMB will be housed two categories of budgets: the allocated budgets taking the form of Control Account Plans (CAPs), and the undistributed budgets for the far-term periods, often representing authorized but unnegotiated changes.

While long-term undistributed budgets will reside at a higher summary planning level, such budgets need to be allocated to a specific element of the project WBS. Until undistributed budgets move into definitive CAPs, they may or may not be assigned to specific organizations for performance. However, all budgets within the PMB must be identifiable to a specific WBS element and properly time-phased in order to maintain the integrity of the PMB.

The CAPs comprising the PMB will be represented by two distinct categories: detailed work packages for the short-term effort, and gross planning packages for the distant work. There are no absolute rules for making the distinction between what constitutes a work package versus a planning package, or even undistributed budgets. These somewhat general categories will vary by project and by company.

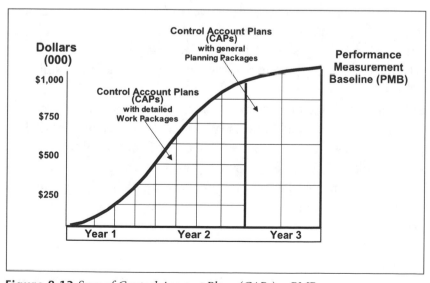

Figure 8.13 *Sum of Control Account Plans (CAPs) = PMB*

However, by employing the "rolling wave" planning concept, projects with a duration of up to three years may well plan all of their CAPs down to the work package level. Other projects exceeding perhaps three years in duration may define their short-term effort in definitive work packages, but leave their out-year tasks in higher-level planning packages until they approach the period of performance. Projects with less than a five-year duration may have no use for undistributed budgets, except to temporarily house any authorized but not yet negotiated changes in scope.

Once the performance measurement baseline has been established, based on individual CAPs, the next appropriate action is to time-phase the baseline to form a total project performance curve, as displayed in Figure 8.13. In this display, we have illustrated a project baseline of sufficient duration to warrant the use of both definitive work packages for the short-term (years 1 and 2), and planning packages for the long-term effort (year 3).

MAINTAINING THE PROJECT BASELINE: MANAGING CHANGES IN SCOPE

A wise person is alleged to have once said: "There are three certainties in life: taxes, death, and changes to project scope." That wise individual must have worked on projects similar to ones we have all enjoyed.

It is always frustrating to work hard to establish a project baseline, to have all parties agree on the baseline, and then to watch the changes begin. Likely, it would not be wise to eliminate all changes, even if we could. Changes to project scope often result from a desire to make improvements in the final product deliverables. But if we cannot eliminate changes altogether, then at least we must strive to control the changes. Changes should represent what we intend to do, and not simply what we are unable to avoid.

Setting a firm baseline in place based on an agreed-to scope of work is likely a key initial action required by all project teams. Closely aligned to this task is the need for the project manager to have in place some type of change control procedure that will allow the project to approve or to reject proposed changes based on a deliberate determination by the team. Changes in work scope should not inadvertently happen because someone failed to prevent them. Rather, scope changes should only result when specifically approved by the person authorized to make changes . . . the project manager. Bottom line: project managers need to have enough clout to say "no" to proposed changes.

In order to manage changes effectively, a project needs to keep track of all pressures to change direction, deliberately or inadvertently. Controlling a baseline requires both information and an information retrieval system. Each action that alters or potentially alters the approved baseline needs to be carefully tracked so that the project manager can make a conscious decision to approve or reject each change.

Figure 8.14 shows a simple baseline change control log. The first line item on such a log would be the initial approved project baseline value. The next lines are reserved for the change traffic, to be listed in chronological order as they occur. Each change or potential change should be listed as it surfaces as a line item on the log.

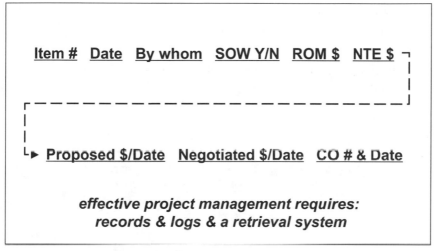

Figure 8.14 *EVM requires baseline control*

As each potential change develops, the information will need to be systematically added to the log as it becomes available. For example, the rough order-of-magnitude (ROM) dollars need to be estimated and logged, and the authorized not-to-exceed (NTE) dollars need to be shown, leading ultimately to a negotiated amount and issuance of the resulting change order (CO).

Effective project management requires that records and logs be kept and that some type of information retrieval system be put in place and maintained. Any of the automated spread sheets or simple databases can facilitate this critical task for the project.

IN CONCLUSION

Creating a detailed, bottom-up project plan is necessary in order to employ the earned value concept. Such plans need to be built upon detailed and individually measurable Control Account Plans (CAPs), the sum of which will form a project's time-phased Performance Measurement Baseline (PMB). The measurement of project performance takes place not at the top project level, but rather within each of the detailed subordinate CAPs. Each CAP (or subproject) must be measurable at all times: the amount of work planned (the Planned Value), the amount of authorized work accomplished and authorized budget (the Earned Value), and the resources consumed (Actual Costs) in converting the Planned Value into Earned Value.

Likely, most PMBs are set on a monthly incremental basis. However, it is becoming increasingly popular to measure the performance of direct labor hours on a weekly incremental basis. If management desires weekly performance measurement, such metrics must be incorporated at the time the PMB is initially set, not as an afterthought. Tangible weekly measurement metrics must be specified to allow for weekly oversight.

Managing all changes to the project scope as they occur is essential to maintaining the approved project baseline, and necessary to employ the earned value concept.

9

EMPLOY EARNED VALUE
IN PROJECT PROCUREMENTS

PROJECT PROCUREMENTS ARE UNIQUE

Question: How important is the management of procurements to the success or failure of a particular project? Answer: It all depends on what is being purchased by the project. Projects are unique, and sometimes their required procurements can also be unique.

Realistically, there are often extremes. Some projects may have zero things to buy. Everything that is accomplished on these projects may be done using company resources: the company's own people, facilities, capital equipment, etc. Other projects may well procure a few items, but such buys are limited to commercial commodities that are readily available from retail stores or on the Internet. Procurements on these projects are routine and low-risk. The only risk is one of timing. All procured articles must be available to the project in time to support the master schedule.

However, at the other extreme are projects that may buy as much as 75 to 95% of their project scope from other firms. Often, these procurements require the development of something new, something that does not presently exist. Projects in this category, that buy most of their scope from external sources, include the development of new systems and items acquired for the government—whether they be new weapons systems, environmental clean-up, information systems, whatever. Construction projects often buy most of their work from other firms. Information technology projects to create a new management system, ERP, MRP, etc. are normally handled by outside firms under some type of a procurement arrangement.

Information technology (IT) work has become increasingly important to organizations, and sometimes most of this work is done by an in-house staff. However, increasingly, the IT effort today is handled with corporate "outsourcing" strategies—a deliberate policy of procurement. Sometimes the IT outsourcing companies elect later to "offshore" much of the work—also a deliberate procurement decision. And when the off-shoring results in the creation of "virtual teams" to produce something new, the measurement of project performance can become quite challenging. Earned Value, in these cases, may well have an important role in the managing of IT projects, as well as the outsourcing, off-shoring and virtual teaming.

The point we are making: Each project must be assessed on a case-by-case basis by the project manager. If the procurement of scope carries with it significant risks in terms of dollars, complexities, and long durations, it may well be beneficial to the project to employ Earned Value on these buy items. The workers on each project must decide this for themselves.

However, there is an important difference in the measurement of performance of the external buy items as contrasted with the internal direct labor, and we need to fully understand this distinction.

LABOR VERSUS PROCUREMENTS . . . THERE ARE FUNDAMENTAL DIFFERENCES

Measuring the earned value performance of internal direct labor is typically quite easy. Most companies have in place some type of a labor reporting system that is generally effective, particularly when compared to the way most firms track the status of their procurements. Direct labor reporting is usually done on a weekly basis. It doesn't matter whether day one is a Saturday or a Sunday or a Monday; seven calendar days later, the actual books will close and the results will be known. Project participants will know how many labor hours have been expended and how much money has been spent, and can determine the actual hourly rates. Everything about direct labor is normally done on a weekly basis. Thus, earned value measurement is fairly easy.

Remember the rule: In order to employ Earned Value on any project, the organization must have the ability to accurately measure three independent dimensions: 1) Planned Value (authorized work plus authorized budget; 2) Earned Value (authorized work *completed* plus authorized budget); and 3) Actual Costs to accomplish Earned Value. These three dimensions are displayed in Figure 9.1. The primary focus is on the Earned Value. The formula is very basic: Earned Value less Planned Value gives us the schedule variance. Similarly, Earned Value less Actual

Costs provides the cost variance. It is relatively easy to measure the three earned value dimensions on direct labor.

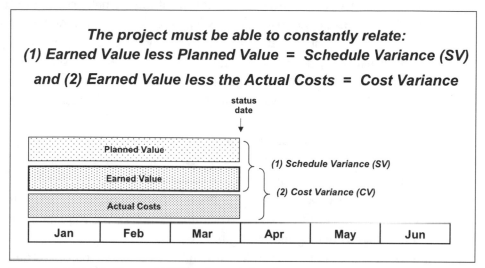

Figure 9.1 *The challenge of EVPM: determining the CV and SV*

However, this is not the case with the purchased items. The tangible performance milestones necessary to plan and then measure Earned Value often span several accounting periods, and are frequently performed by different functions. With procurements, it is difficult to synchronize the three dimensions of Earned Value.

Let us trace some key events that accompany procurements on projects, and note the various functions that perform the work.

1. The project manager must define the items to be procured. This is usually done by conducting a make-or-buy analysis, typically under the direction of the project manager or staff.
2. The engineering or design organization must define the technical requirements of the purchases. This results in a procurement specification.
3. The project manager or staff must request a procurement by issuing a formal Purchase Requisition.
4. A formal order to buy must be given by the buyer, who issues a Purchase Order.
5. The purchased items must be received, inspected, and accepted, or the purchased services verified. This consists of taking physical possession of the commodities and/or verifying the satisfactory completion of services. Various functions perform this work.
6. Payment must be made for the purchased goods. The Accounts Payable organization must issue a check to the seller, and the costs must be recorded on the accounting ledger.

Each of these milestones represents a necessary task in the procurement process. In particular, the Actual Costs must be determined and related to the measured Earned Value. Earned Value measured versus the resulting Actual Cost figures are needed in order to determine the cost efficiency. Without knowing the Actual Costs, one cannot determine the cost efficiency and thus employ the earned value concept.

However, these necessary procurement milestones may take place weeks or even months apart, and often are done by different functions. Question: How do you measure Planned Value and Earned Value, and determine Actual Costs for these procured items? Answer: You must separate the work into distinct physical tasks, then plan, schedule, add a budget for each task, and measure the actual performance for each task. To further complicate the process, the Actual Costs on the books often may not represent the Earned Value being measured. In these cases, you may need to "estimate" the relatable actual-procurement costs because the sellers may not have been fully paid; or sometimes they have been overpaid for their services. Managing material costs is not as easy as managing direct labor costs.

Question for each project to answer: Is it worth the extra effort to employ Earned Value on the procured work? Yes, if the procured items carry high risks, challenging complexities, new technologies, and are vital to the success of the project. Probably no, if the project is simply buying routine materials or services. Each project must carefully assess its needs. Earned value measurement may not be warranted in all cases.

ISSUE: PROCUREMENT "COST ACTUALS" OFTEN NEED TO BE "ESTIMATED"

The third critical dimension in the measurement of Earned Value is the Actual Costs. But with the purchased items, as contrasted with direct labor, the actual costs on the accounting books may or may not accurately reflect the work being measured.

What is so difficult in tracking the Actual Costs of the purchased items? We suggest you refer to Figure 9.2 to follow this discussion. Shown at the top of the figure are the three dimensions of Earned Value. As of any point in time in the life cycle of a project, the three dimensions of Earned Value must be measured.

The relationship between the Planned value and Earned value provides the schedule variance (SV). Even with the procured work, these two relationships are fairly easy to determine. Both Planned Value and Earned Value can be readily measured using the project's scheduling system. The six key functions of procurement, as listed above, can be planned and then earned by updates to the project's master schedule.

But by contrast, the project's earned value cost variance (CV) consists of the relationship between the Earned Value achieved, less the Actual Costs consumed to

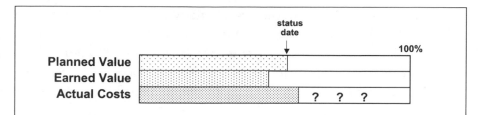

Figure 9.2 *Sometimes you must "estimate" the actual costs*

accomplish the work. The cost variance (CV) is particularly important because poor cost performance is normally non-recoverable by the project. If one overruns the costs for completed work, these represent sunk costs. They are not likely to be offset and recovered by performance on later tasks. Thus negative cost variances are critical to track. However, in order to determine the cost variance, one must know how much money has been spent to accomplish the Earned Value. One must have accurate cost actuals.

Let us discuss the issue of Actual Costs for procurements from two extremes: Actual costs can sometimes be overstated on the accounting books; at other times, they can be understated. In these instances, selected procurement costs may need to be "estimated" by the project in order to match the Earned Value being measured.

A word of caution: We are not suggesting that the procurement Actual Costs on the accounting books be adjusted or manipulated; rather, temporarily "estimated" to allow for an accurate presentation of procurement cost status to management.

PROCUREMENT ACTUAL COSTS MAY SOMETIMES BE OVERSTATED (MUST ESTIMATE DOWNWARD)

In the construction industry, it is not unusual for the owner to authorize some type of an "advance" or "mobilization payment" to assist the performing contractor of a new project. The purpose and payback timing of such payments must be determined in order to synchronize the physical earned value performance with the actual recorded costs. If such advance payments were to be used strictly for the mobilization of construction forces, and such work might take place within a short time period being measured, then a separate task labeled "mobilization" effort may be sufficient. This task may be planned, performed, and the Actual Costs incurred during a single time frame. The three relationships of Earned Value would thus be synchronized.

If, however, the advanced payment is to be used partially for site mobilization and partly to aid the constructor with its initial cash flow, then the two activities must be divided into two separate work tasks in order to relate the payments to the physical work being measured. This would be particularly true if the cash-flow credits were to extend over several months before repayment of funds to the owner. Two work packages must be established and measured separately: (1) contractor mobilization, perhaps a one-month task, and (2) cash-flow advance, perhaps allocated and recovered over a longer duration, such as six months.

Another condition of (temporary) overpayment may occur whenever the project purchases common materials, some of which may be immediately consumed by the project, and some of which may be put into the project inventory for later use. Sometimes these stored materials will be transferred to other projects, in which case a "borrow-and-payback" accounting process must take place.

It is not uncommon to buy materials for multiple projects but, for administrative convenience, to charge the costs to (and store the materials with) the largest single project. However, such practices can distort the measurement of cost performance on a given project. Solution: The surplus or inventoried materials must be placed into separate work packages so that both the performance and Actual Costs may be accurately reported against the proper project.

PROCUREMENT ACTUAL COSTS MAY SOMETIMES BE UNDERSTATED (MUST ESTIMATE UPWARD)

Sometimes the very opposite condition may occur with the procured items. Earned value performance for procurements may be accurately monitored and properly claimed, but the Actual Costs for accomplishing the work may not yet be fully recorded on the project's accounting ledger. Performance results will be distorted. How can this happen?

Many projects are initiated with a significant amount of the workforce comprised of both company and non-company personnel, often called "purchased labor." These purchased professionals go from project to project to help work the peak labor loads. They are treated as regular company employees, and their work is most often directed by internal company supervision. A planned value performance baseline is set for all direct labor, company and purchased labor, and their work is earned in a normal fashion.

However, sometimes missing in the equation are the Actual Costs for the purchased labor to compare against the Earned Value being credited. The result can be a distorted cost efficiency rate, which often masks problems that need to be addressed by management. How does this happen? Often it is a combination of factors, including the late submission of invoices by the purchased labor firm, the slow processing of invoices, and late payment of invoices by accounting. In these cases, the Actual Costs for the purchased labor must be estimated in order to accurately match the Earned Value credited.

Let's now discuss another example of distortions that can occur with seller progress payments. Again we will use the construction industry as an example, because the construction industry seems to monitor its suppliers' performance about as well as any industry. Whether the job is fixed-price or cost-reimbursable, in order for a supplier to receive progress payments for construction work, the supplier must demonstrate that it has physically performed the work. Sounds a little like Earned Value, and it is, but the cost engineers in the construction industry typically do not refer to it as such.

In construction, the performing seller must define the job in the form of detailed subtasks, with a budget value assigned to each task, and the sum of which totaling the costs of the contract. This is typically called a "schedule of values." In order to be paid for the work, the supplier must carefully estimate the value of the work accomplished for each task. The supplier determines the percentage complete, and give the Earned Value for each task.

Assume that the total construction job has a contract value of $1,000,000. After the first month, the supplier may estimate by individual task that the total job is ten percent (or $100,000) complete. If the project manager agrees with this estimate, a check for $100,000 will be requested, less what is called a "retention" or a "withhold." Retentions or withholds will vary by contract, but are typically in the range of 5% to 20% of the requested progress payment. Such withholds are held and not released until the job is fully completed. In this example, a check for $100,000 less approximately 10% may be issued, so that the accounting ledger will reflect a net value of only $90,000.

If the project were measuring its earned value performance, it might claim $100,000 in Earned Value, but will have only $90,000 in Actual Costs on the accounting ledger. Cost performance would, thus, incorrectly reflect a positive 1.1 CPI when, in fact, performance should only be 1.0. Eventually, when the retention is subsequently paid to the supplier, the inflated cost performance will return to its correct position. In the meantime, however, the overvalued performance of the contracted work at a CPI of 1.1 may well serve to mask poor performance of other critical areas that may need the attention of the project manager.

It may be a cumbersome process to have to "estimate" the actual costs of procurements. But, if earned value credit is claimed, it is important to make sure that the related Actual Costs being reported match the work claimed. To do otherwise is to present to management a positive cost position that may be distorted.

SIX STEPS TO EMPLOYING EARNED VALUE ON PROJECT PROCUREMENTS

The decision of whether and how to employ Earned Value Management on the procured items can be an important one for any project. In some cases, the procured work will be absolutely critical to the very success of the project—in which case Earned Value may be warranted. But in other cases, what the project buys may simply be routine commodities, in which case the detailed planning and oversight required for earned value measurement might not be warranted. Each project's practitioners must decide this issue for themselves.

If project practitioners elect to employ Earned Value on their procurements, they must understand that it will require more effort to employ the concept on buy items than on in-house direct labor. More detailed planning and oversight will be required. And to compound the difficulty, "turf-wars" will sometimes break out between the procurement organization (the buyers who will have exclusive procurement authority) and the other line organizations (such as engineering and the project office) that

---

1) Continue scope definition to include make or buy analysis,
    then compile a "Listing of Procurements"

2) Place all procurements into three generic categories

3) Determine an earned value method for each procurement

4) Time phase a project procurement baseline

5) Measure actual earned value performance, estimate actual costs

6) Forecast final costs (EAC) based on earned value performance

---

Figure 9.3 *Six Steps to Employing Earned Value on Procurements*

will not. "I am in charge" conflicts sometimes arise between functions that should be working in concert.

Assuming that the project practitioners have elected to employ Earned Value on all or some of the procurement work, how best to accommodate this with the least amount of effort? The authors recommend that projects employ a simple six-step process, as displayed in Figure 9.3. We will want to understand each of these necessary six steps.

STEP 1: CONTINUE THE SCOPE DEFINITION PROCESS TO INCLUDE A "MAKE-OR-BUY ANALYSIS," AND THEN COMPILE A LISTING OF ALL THE WORK TO BE PROCURED

All projects will need to define what work will be done. This is called the scope definition process. But, in addition to defining what will be done, it is often a good practice to go one step further and specify who will be doing the work. This is particularly important when some of the most critical project work will be done by an outside organization under a legally enforceable contract.

Procurement relationships are typically non-forgiving, in that you must correctly specify what you want to buy, or pay for costly changes. The project needs to compile a complete listing of the anticipated buy work. This is typically done by conducting a make-or-buy analysis. The end product will be a listing of all the procured items for the project.

STEP 2: PLACE ALL DEFINED PROCUREMENTS INTO THREE GENERIC CATEGORIES

Although all procurements share a common factor—they all represent scope that will be procured from outside organizations—not all procurements are the same. Most of the items bought by the project will be routine, commercially available from suppliers. These articles are typically called "COTS": commercial off-the-shelf items. But other buys may require the creation of something new, something that does not presently exist. These few procurements may well carry the same or even higher risks than the performance of the entire project. Certain procurements can be key to the success or failure of a project.

In such cases, it may be advisable to follow the practice employed by some firms of placing the items to be purchased into distinct generic groupings. Why? Because the project must manage its procured items differently, depending on their complexity and the risks associated with each unique procurement.

Some organizations have found it advisable to place the listing of procured items into three distinct categories, as described below, going from the highest-risk procurements down to the routine purchases:

1. Major (high risk) complexity procurements, the purchase of something that does not exist, tailored to the project's unique specification. These would be considered critical subprojects.
2. Minor (low risk) complexity procurements will often represent large monetary values, but the commodities exist and will conform to the seller's existing product specification.
   (Note: Minor product tailoring—such as unique nametags or special color schemes—would not add risks to the procurement, and thus would not change their classification. However, major alterations to a seller's existing product—perhaps requiring a product redesign and perhaps new product testing—would likely place them into a Category (1) procurement).
3. Routine buys of COTS (Commercial Off-The-Shelf) commodities or purchased services.[1]

The Category (1) items will typically represent only a few procurements on any project. But the very success of the overall project may be dependent on the performance of these few critical subprojects. Thus, they must be managed well if the project is to succeed. Typically, these items will represent the creation of something new to the project's specifications. They may represent a new component requiring a new design and testing, a major new information technology system, new subsystems, major subportions of the project, etc. Earned Value will likely be warranted on all of the Category (1) procurements. These items will be few in number, but high in both risks and costs.

Category (2) buys can also represent big-budget items and long-term commitments by the project. But the risks of failure are relatively minimal because the deliverable products exit. These are items that have been developed by the sellers to the seller's own product specifications. Some examples: electrical generators, radar systems, transportation vehicles, and crane rentals. Since these items are typically high value and are consumed by the project upon delivery, earned value measurement is likely also warranted. Meeting schedule performance of these items is very important.

The Category (3) buys are often a nuisance to manage because there are so many detailed items to order, track, receive and inspect. The risks: These articles must also be available to support the project schedule. However, Earned Value Management

---

1 Quentin W. Fleming, *Project Procurement Management: contracting, subcontracting, teaming,* (Tustin, California: FMC Press, 2003) page 14.

may or may not add to the control of such items. Most companies have in place a type of material requirements planning system (MRP) that may be adequate to control these articles. Earned value measurement may not be beneficial to employ on this category of buy items.

What we are suggesting is that projects follow Pareto's 80/20 rule when employing Earned Value on the procurement work. Category (1) buys represent high risks and big budgets, and Category (2) items will be large, discrete, and easy to track. Together, Category (1) and (2) might represent only 10 to 20% of the items to be bought, but perhaps 80 to 90% or more of the procurement budget. By contrast, Category (3) buys would likely constitute perhaps 80% or more of the procured units, but only 20% or less of the budget dollars. Our suggestion: Employ Vilfredo Pareto's 80/20 method and apply Earned Value to only the big-budget, high-risk items. Let the company's existing MRP or material control system manage the Category (3) buys. Timing is all-important. Our suggested approach is illustrated in Figure 9.4.

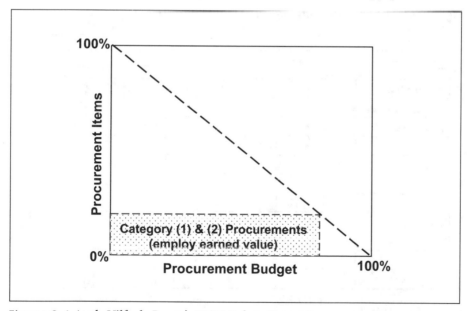

Figure 9.4 *Apply Vilfredo Pareto's 80/20 Rule to Procurements*

STEP 3: DETERMINE THE APPROPRIATE EARNED VALUE METRIC FOR EACH TYPE OF PROCUREMENT

Once the buy items have been listed and categorized, a management decision can then be made as to how best to plan and subsequently measure the physical performance of each category; that is, how to covert the Planned Values into Earned Value. There are numerous possibilities available that were discussed in the last chapter.

Category (1) Major (high-risk) Complexity Procurements

- **Weighted Milestones**
- **Percent Complete Estimates with Milestone Gates**
- **Schedule of Values, or CPM Network with Resources**
- **Full ANSI Std 748 Flow-Down**

Category (2) Minor (low-risk) Complexity Buys

- **Weighted Milestones**
- **Percent Complete Estimates with Milestone Gates**
- **Fixed Formula**
- **Performance Based Payments (FAR Subpart 32.10)**

Category (3) Routine COTS or Purchased services

- **Percent Complete Estimates**
- **Percent Complete Estimates with Milestone Gates**
- **Apportioned to a Direct Base**

Figure 9.5 *Place Procurements into Three Generic Categories*

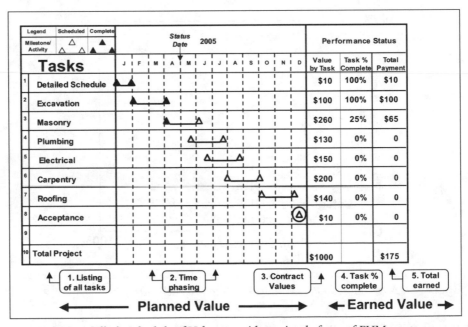

Figure 9.6 *A Seller's Schedule of Values provides a simple form of EVM*

Figure 9.5 displays the three broad generic procurement categories, followed by a listing of the possible methods available to measure performance.

With Category (1) or (2) procurements, either weighted milestones or percent complete estimates with milestone gates will work well. With Category (1) procurements, the construction industry will often require a resource-loaded critical path method (CPM) network that can be quickly summarized to display a time-phased "schedule of values." An example of a seller schedule of values is shown in Figure 9.6.[2] The seller's Planned Values would be represented by items 1, 2, and 3. Performance updates (Earned Value) to support progress payments would be reflected in items 4 and 5.

On major government-sponsored projects and selected critical procurements that would warrant the full and formal earned value measurement, the project buyer may require EVM in accordance with ANSI/EIA Standard 748. The Federal Acquisition Regulation (FAR) is expected to provide the appropriate solicitation and contract clauses for requiring the full employment of ANSI/EIA Standard 748, sometime in 2005.

Category (2) procurements are listed in the center of Figure 9.5. Since this category is often represented by high-value discrete line items, they are easily tracked individually. Many companies use the fixed-formula method on these articles. Often they will plan for 25% of the budget to be earned when an order is placed, and the other 75% earned when the components are delivered and accepted. Actual Costs must be estimated.

On fixed-price orders with multiple deliveries, the Federal Acquisition Regulation (FAR) has created what is called "Performance Based Payments" under FAR subpart 32.10. Here, the buyer and seller must agree on performance measurement metrics that, when completed, will trigger a payment to the seller. The sum of the payments must add up to the value of the purchase order. Interestingly, FAR subpart 32.10 represents earned value measurement in its finest form. However, at no place in the solicitation or contract clauses does the term "Earned Value" appear. We find that interesting.

Category (3) procurements are listed at the bottom of Figure 9.5. Should the project elect to employ Earned Value on this category, three methods, as shown, are recommended. A manager in charge of production can estimate the percentage completion value of these bulk parts each month. Or, the use of milestone gates can also be employed to lend objectivity to the estimates. Finally, some firms with good historical performance records may elect to use an apportioned relationship of these purchased materials to a base account to measure the earned value performance. Fabrication or manufacturing labor against bulk purchased parts is sometimes used as the measurement base.

STEP 4: TIME-PHASE A PROJECT PROCUREMENT BASELINE

Once all procurements are placed into three generic categories and a decision made on what items and what methods will be used to measure performance, the procurements must then be time-phased to form a procurement baseline. Performance of

---

2 Ibid, page 212.

the buy items will be measured only on a monthly basis. Weekly earned value measurement may be available to measure direct labor, but not for procurements.

The one exception to monthly measurement of performance may occur with "purchased labor" employees. If a given firm has a direct labor management system that will allow for purchased labor to be incorporated, then this category of purchases may be planned and earned on a weekly basis. However, the Actual Costs will need to be "estimated," as previously mentioned, and invoices and payments are slow to be processed.

STEP 5: MEASURE THE ACTUAL EARNED VALUE PERFORMANCE, AND ESTIMATE THE ACTUAL COSTS

Earned Value will need to be measured on the procured items on a monthly basis. As with direct labor, the focus will be on the Earned Value achieved. Variances from both the schedule and costs will need to be highlighted.

One of the (legitimate) criticisms of Earned Value over the years has been that the contractor and subcontractor data being presented is often old, one or two months later than the comparable internal project data. This is often the case when actual cost data from the suppliers is required to reflect current status. The availability of actual cost data from major suppliers (Category (1) and (2) procurements) will often pace the presentation of key supplier performance. This practice does not need to be the case.

The near-real-time measurement of seller performance can be achieved rather easily by a focus on the high-risk, high-dollar value procurements, represented by Category (1) and (2) procurements. Their Planned Value and Earned Value can be monitored with use of any of the methods listed in Figure 9.5. And if the project "estimates" the related Actual Costs, near-real-time cost performance can be presented.

STEP 6: FORECAST THE FINAL EXPECTED COSTS (EAC) BASED ON EARNED VALUE PERFORMANCE

The primary purpose of employing Earned Value on any project is likely to get an early warning indication whenever the costs are likely to exceed the authorized budget—early enough to work the problem. Executive management and project management are entitled to know how much money it will take to complete a given project. This is called the Estimate at Completion (EAC).

Project procurements can sometimes have a major impact on final EAC costs. It all depends on the magnitude of the procurements and the inherent risks. Let's discuss the procurement EAC process by generic category, starting with the easy category: the COTS or routine buys.

Category (3) COTS procurements may represent most of the procurements, but there is nothing complicated about them. Either a company material requirements planning (MRP) system or a manager's estimate should accurately quantify the final costs for this category of buys. Budgets are established for these items based on two variables: an assumed quantity (usage) and an assumed cost (price). At the point at which orders are placed for these items, it is usually known whether or not the budget is adequate to do the job. Thus, if the costs being paid for the articles increases over budget, or more units are being consumed, it is known and an accurate forecast of final costs can be made.

Category (2) buys are perhaps the easiest to forecast an EAC, because they will be few in number and, typically, large in value. These items can be tracked individually by the project's buyers, who can set the Planned Value and Earned Value, and accurately estimate the Actual Costs.

Now, let us discuss the real challenge: Category (1) major complexity procurements. These buys usually carry the highest risks because the seller is creating a new product to the buyer's unique specification. Sometimes the final deliverable product may not work for a variety of reasons. The seller may not have performed well, in which case it must keep trying until it gets things right. Depending on the contract type, cost-reimbursable or fixed-price, seller performance can have a big impact on project costs. Defective products from one seller can sometimes impact the performance of other sellers. With Category (1) procurements, a simple form of Earned Value may be warranted, as illustrated in Figure 9.6.

Major complexity Category (1) procurements can experience cost growth for a number of reasons. Each of these procurements, and they will be few in number, must be individually monitored and a forecast made of final EAC costs. Assuming that the Earned Value has been properly measured, and actual costs accurately estimated, a Cost Performance Index (CPI) may be available for each of these buys. Likely the most accurate assessment of EAC costs would be to take the total budget for each Category (1) buy and divide it by the seller's cumulative CPI. This approach would provide a reasonably accurate EAC to forecast the final required costs for the procured items.

Procurement cost projections must be incorporated into the total project EAC.

LESSONS LEARNED: PERFORM A PRICE AND USAGE VARIANCE ANALYSIS

After the project is complete, it is often a good and effective practice to stand back and ask yourself: "What happened?" Did we perform according to our plan, or were we off? With regard to the purchased items, and sometimes also direct labor, it is often a good practice to conduct what is called a price and usage variance analysis.

Background: When the earned value criteria were rewritten by private industry in 1996—it later became ANSI-EIA Standard 748—an important process was dropped from the compliance requirements. No longer were contractors required to perform a price and usage variance analysis on the items bought. The reasoning behind this change escapes us. How can you get progressively smarter in the future if you do not take the time to fully understand how well or poorly you performed in the past? We call this "lessons learned."

A price and usage variance analysis is most often applied against materials that are purchased for the project. But this same analysis can also apply to direct labor budget results. Anytime a budget is established based on an assumed price (the costs per unit or the per hour labor rate) times the assumed usage (the number of planned units or estimated labor hours), this type of analysis will work.

What the price/usage analysis does is compare the original "basis of estimate" (which set the budget) with the actual performance results. Let's take a specific example. Assume that a budget is issued for $120. Actual results come in at $192. What happened?

If the budget was set at $120 for procured material items, the basis for setting the $120 budget may have been an assumed quantity of 10 units at $12 per unit. Later, when the item was bought and the work done, the actual results came in at $192, an overrun of $72. What happened? Did we consume more than the budget for 10 units allowed, or did the actual purchase unit price go up? Or, as is most often the case,

---

Budget: $120. (Budget assumption: 10 units x $12./unit)

Actuals: $192. (Issue: what caused - $72. overrun?)

Price Variance Formula:

Budget Price – Actual Price x Actual Quantity

= Price Variance = ($12 - $16) x 12 = - $48 (changes in price)

Usage Variance Formula:

Budget Quantity – Actual Quantity x Budget Price

= Usage Variance = (10 – 12) x $12 = - $24 (changes in usage)

Figure 9.7 *Price and Usage Variance Analysis*

were there changes to both the units consumed and the prices we paid? Unless we understand precisely what happened, how can we improve our performance the next time we bid on similar work? We need to conduct a price/usage variance analysis.

The formula for a price/usage analysis is simple and is illustrated in Figure 9.7. You must first determine if you spent more money per unit than was planned, then determine if you used more units than were provided for in the budget. Most often it is a combination of both factors, but one factor may be the primary cause and you should know this. In this illustration, the $72 overrun was primarily caused by an increase in the unit purchase price. But the increased quantity also contributed to the overrun.

As a result of the price/usage analysis, we now know that two-thirds of the overrun was caused by an increase in purchase price, and one-third was caused by increased usage. With this knowledge, hopefully, we can establish a better budget the next time we propose the costs of similar work.

Also, as was mentioned earlier, this same type of analysis can be useful when reviewing what happened on direct labor budgets. Sometimes, the basis for setting the budget estimate assumes junior labor rates, but then senior people are put on the job. A price/usage variance analysis may help set a better labor budget the next time around.

10

MONITOR PERFORMANCE AGAINST
THE EARNED VALUE BASELINE

A BASELINE ALLOWING FOR THE MEASUREMENT of earned value performance must be established by the project. Such baselines will be formed from detailed subprojects, which are typically called Control Account Plans, or CAPs. Earned Value CAPs are simply the points chosen by the project for management control. The sum of these sub-projects, or CAPs, will add to the total project baseline. Management reserves and profits, if any, are left outside the performance measurement baseline (PMB).

In Figure 10.1, we have illustrated a project with only five CAPs, as listed across the bottom. As projects increase in size, more CAPs will be added, allowing for adequate control. Question: What's the proper number of CAPs for a given project? Answer: It all depends on a given project's size, duration, complexity, and associated risks. There are no absolute guidelines as to the proper size of CAPs. Each project must determine its own proper span of management control. However, a lesser number of CAPs seems to work best.

Complex projects requiring a large number of CAPs may elect to group their CAPs into logical project teams, sometimes called integrated product development teams (IPDTs), which are typically relatable to the project's WBS. Performance measurement will still take place within each CAP, but summarized for management oversight into higher-level teams. A typical project manager employing Earned Value will first look at the top project summary, then drill down to look at results by WBS,

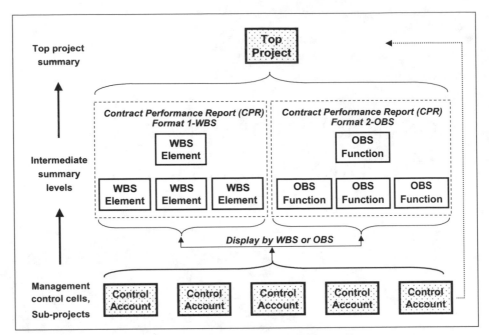

Figure 10.1 *An Earned Value Baseline equals the sum of all CAPs*

then down to individual CAPs that may be experiencing problems.

Sometimes it will be desirable to summarize the CAP performance by both the Work Breakdown Structure (WBS) and the functional Organizational Breakdown Structure (OBS), or both, as illustrated in Figure 10.1. Some management teams like to track project performance by both project deliverables (WBS) and the functional organizations (OBS). Four of the formal earned value criteria require a summary of performance by both the WBS and OBS.[1] However, that is more detail than the authors usually recommend for most projects. One summary of CAPs, by WBS, is generally sufficient for most projects.

To be viable, each earned value CAP must integrate three elements: (1) a defined scope of work typically expressed in the form of work tasks; (2) a time frame to start and finish each task—that is, the schedule; and (3) an authorized budget. Each control account plan will be performed and measured separately, and the sum of all CAPs will constitute the total project baseline. Earned value performance measurement focuses on exceptions to the baseline. The earned value concept exemplifies "management by exception."

Management will want to assess the long-term trends in project performance and take the necessary actions to maintain their planned course. Earned Value is a sort of strategic trend indicator, providing answers to a number of questions. For example: If the project were to continue at the present rate of performance, where

---

1 See earned value criteria numbers 5, 17, 18, and 25 as summarized in the Appendix to this book.

would it end up? Based on the detailed plans and performance results, how much money will be needed to complete the total project? How long will it take to complete all of the work for the total project?

The purpose of earned value measurement is to discern the long-term performance direction of the project and—based on actual physical performance—to be able to forecast as early as 20% complete what the ultimate cost and schedule requirements will be. It provides a sort of *50,000-foot observation platform* for busy executives to monitor the long-term direction of their projects. Somewhat analogous to "critical path management" and the "float" positions, earned value metrics provide reliable indices to determine how much money and how much time it will likely take to finish the total job.

BEFORE GIVING APPROVAL: VERIFY THE VIABILITY OF THE PROJECT BASELINE

The authorized budgets to accomplish the authorized work must be achievable. Stated another way, it would be pointless to authorize budgets that are impossible to meet, and then to track performance against the impossible targets.

Prior to giving official approval of the baseline, one important issue for any project manager to determine is how viable the proposed baseline is. Some proposed project baselines may be flawed: accidentally, unintentionally, but sometimes deliberately. If the proposed project baseline is not realistic, not achievable for whatever reason, it would be pointless to authorize it and then attempt to measure performance against it. Suggestion: first verify that the proposed baseline is doable.

One fundamental problem with project baselines can be that the authorized budget is simply too low to accomplish the authorized work. Severe competition for new business will sometimes result in inadequate budgets to accomplish the required work. Whenever this condition occurs, there is the temptation to create what is called a "front-loaded" project baseline. Management at all levels should take care to avoid giving approval to a front-loaded baseline. We need to understand this issue.

Figure 10.2 illustrates an example of a front-loaded baseline. The top section displays a listing of all the work to be done task-by-task, while the bottom shows a distribution of the authorized budget to accomplish this same work. It would appear, at first glance, that there is a serious mismatch between the phasing of the authorized work, and the phasing of the authorized budget. The distribution of budget is skewed to the left of the physical work. Accidentally or intentionally, the budget is loaded in the front part of the project.

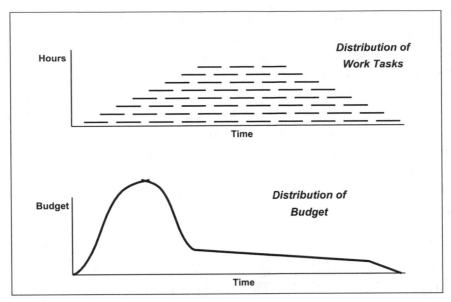

Figure 10.2 *Danger: "Front-Loaded" Baselines*

Performing organizations, when short of adequate budget, will sometimes place adequate budget in the short term, and then set inadequate budgets in the long-term, hoping that changes in scope will bring them fresh additional budgets. Watch for this condition.

This type of assessment can be made at the total level on a small project, or with larger projects by examining the individual CAPs, project teams, or WBS elements. Message for project managers: Always take care to verify that there is a proper phasing of the required work versus the authorized budgets. You do not want to track performance against unrealistic targets. Executive management and the paying customers have a right to know the full truth. Project managers have an obligation to report the full truth.

ESTABLISH VARIANCE THRESHOLDS TO FOCUS ON "EXCEPTIONS" TO THE PLAN

An earned value project baseline must be created from the bottom up, based on the sum of detailed control account plans (CAPs). But employing the management-by-exception concept does not require that each and every CAP be strictly monitored by someone throughout the life of the project. Rather, the project manager and the project team will want to focus their attention on only meaningful exceptions to baseline plans.

Thus, the project must define what constitutes "meaningful" deviations from their plans. They will want to rely on a computer buzzer to go off whenever acceptable tolerances have been breached. Each project must, therefore, define what constitutes acceptable performance levels in order to avoid being inundated with data. These tolerances are called variance thresholds. A performance variance threshold is simply the point of unacceptable deviation from the authorized plan; that is, management by exception.

Such variances will usually focus on at least three segments of project performance, as illustrated in Figure 10.3. For example, items (1) and (2) will be used to monitor incremental short-term performance as set by the project manager. Such increments will certainly represent monthly performance; but sometimes weekly, and, in extreme cases, daily performance. The frequency of project status reviews will normally determine what constitutes the proper increment to track. Incremental variances are reflective of immediate past performance and will typically incur wide deviations, a "good week", a "bad week," etc.

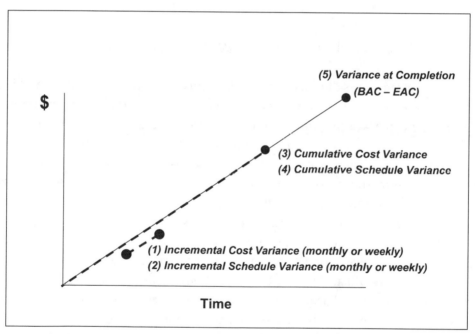

Figure 10.3 *Thresholds for Variance Analysis (plus or minus values)*

Items (3) and (4) will reflect the cumulative cost or schedule performance position and will be more stable indicators, reflecting the long-term direction of the project. The cumulative positions are needed in order to forecast the final cost results on the project.

Lastly, item (5) represents the bottom line. These critical deviations will reflect the differences between what management has authorized in the form of a total project budget, versus what it might require to complete all of the project work. These variances are most significant and constitute why we employ earned value on projects. As early as possible—at the 20% completion point—we want a projection of how much the project is likely to cost, so that management can take immediate action on the remaining effort.

There are no absolute guidelines for setting variance thresholds. Each project must experiment and determine its own variance levels. Thresholds can be expressed in percentage values (e.g., a 5% variance level) or in absolute numerical values (e.g., $10,000 increments). Sometimes projects will set positive variance thresholds at twice the value of negative variances simply because they want to focus their attention on what is going wrong, rather than right, with the project.

It is not uncommon for the initial variance settings to be too tight, thus inundating the project team with too much data, much of it of little significance. No problem. Variance levels can easily be relaxed for the next measured period. Experiment.

INDIRECT (OVERHEAD) COSTS VARIANCE ANALYSIS

There are two categories of costs that a project must deal with: direct costs and indirect costs. Direct costs are relatively easy to identify and control, as they are typically initiated by people working directly on the project. These costs generally represent direct labor costs, travel costs, purchased materials, computer equipment, etc.

The second category of costs is not so easy, not so obvious. These are called "indirect" or, sometimes, "overhead" or "burden" costs. These are also legitimate costs, but ones that cannot be identified against any given project or contract. These costs are accumulated in organizational pools (engineering, manufacturing, offsite, etc.), then allocated back to projects based on established methodology, typically distributed as a percentage of direct charging labor. Some organizations with significant procurement effort will accumulate the costs of buying items and allocate such costs over the procured items. The indirect allocation processes will vary depending on the industry involved, but must be defined and consistently applied.

How significant are these indirect costs? Such costs will vary by industry, from as little as perhaps 15% allocated over direct labor to as much as 300% in certain industries where there are huge investments required in capital equipment and machinery. The aerospace and defense industry is an example of an industry where indirect burdens can be in the 200% to 300% range.

The significance of these costs is profound in the management of project costs: direct costs can be controlled by the project manager, whereas indirect costs cannot be controlled by the project manager. While the project manager may be held responsible for controlling all project costs, indirect costs are beyond the capability of any project manager to control.

Indirect costs can only be controlled by executive management, several pay grades above most project managers. Question: What can project managers do to protect their best interests and not be blamed for conditions beyond their control? Answer: Keep accurate records of the relationship of "controllable" direct labor, versus the "uncontrollable" indirect costs. If indirect costs become excessive and exceed or overrun the budget, the project manager must delicately remind senior management that it was their job to keep indirect costs under control. Easy for us to say!

There are two approaches to budgeting indirect costs on projects, and these will vary by company. To follow this discussion, we suggest that you review Figures 8.11 and 8.12. Both are examples of projects made up of the sum of Control Account Plans (CAP). The issue: Where do you place the indirect cost budgets? Some firms follow the practice of allocating indirect cost burdens into each CAP, thus holding each CAP manager responsible for the results of indirect cost performance.

Another approach, and one practiced by many firms, is to place indirect costs into a separate CAP, perhaps entitled "Indirect costs." This approach makes the analysis of cost results a little less complicated. The budget is established based on the approved relationship of direct labor to indirect burdens, perhaps set at a rate of 100%. If costs go up, it results in an overrun of project costs. Should indirect costs go down, as they sometimes do, the project has a windfall.

What happens in real life? If indirect costs underrun, such costs are taken back by the project manager or senior management. If indirect costs go up over the budget, executive management has been known to suggest: "Can't you help us with OUR problem, perhaps use a little less direct labor on this job?"

The management of indirect costs is a necessary part of project management. That's why project managers are paid these outrageously high salaries! (Just kidding.)

To help with the analysis of indirect costs, there are project management software packages on the market to analyze and help control costs by category, including indirect costs. If the project manager is responsible for all project costs, including the impossible (indirect costs), they must keep track of the variances between the original budgeted baseline and the actual results experienced.

DISPLAYS FOR MANAGEMENT OVERSIGHT

Management needs to be continuously apprised of how well, or how poorly, each project is performing. Because Earned Value requires a detailed bottom-up baseline, actual performance can be tracked at various levels of a project. At a minimum, an earned value project will be monitored at the top summary level, and within each of the detailed Control Account Plans (CAPs), which will aggregate to the top project level. As projects increase in size and complexity, management will often find it advisable to monitor and manage summary levels—for example, integrated project teams—which will typically relate to the project's WBS.

While Earned Value provides a wealth of reliable data to track, there are likely no better indicators as to the health of a project than the two common efficiency indices, called the Schedule Performance Index (SPI) and the Cost Performance Index (CPI). These two indices can represent either incremental project performance, or a cumulative position reflecting more stable, long-term directions for a project.

Figure 10.4 displays cumulative SPI and CPI curves. Also shown across the top of the chart are three major project milestones that can be compared against the earned value curves. This chart can represent any level of interest to management: the top project, individual CAPs, project development teams, WBS, or functional OBS displays.

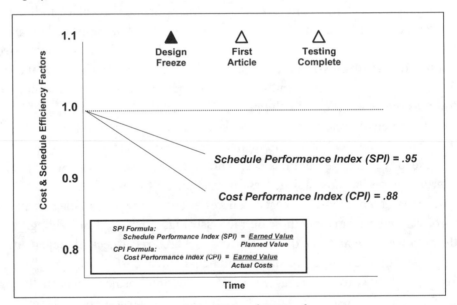

Figure 10.4 *Tracking the cumulative CPI and SPI Performance*

The interesting aspect of tracking the cumulative SPI and cumulative CPI is the ultimate direction each curve will take. At some point in time, all SPI curves will level off, then make their way back up to ultimately touch the 1.0 line when all the authorized work has been completed. Although the project may be late compared to the original baseline plan, at the completion of the project there will be no schedule variance. The formula for the SPI: Earned Value divided by the Planned Value.[2]

By contrast, the CPI curve is much more important, and more permanent. The CPI typically does not fully recover to the 1.0 line after performance reaches about

2 Project Management Institute: *PMBOK® Guide*, Third Edition, page 174.

20% complete. The reason: If the project spends more than the budgeted amount for a given segment of work, such variance represents an overrun of costs. Rarely, if ever, are overruns recovered by subsequent performance. Cost overruns usually represent permanent losses. The formula for the CPI: Earned Value divided by Actual Costs.[3]

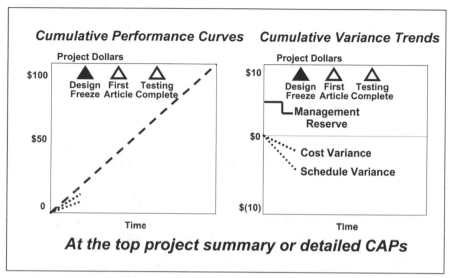

Figure 10.5 *Side-by-side displays to monitor performance*

Now let us review a different earned value display, likely one of the more popular of all displays, as illustrated in Figure 10.5. These charts are often referred to as side-by-side displays, and actually represent two separate data charts.

Both charts display data over a common time scale across the bottom. Both track the same major milestones across the top. However, the vertical scales and data displayed are different on both charts. The left chart reflects cumulative performance data for the total project, while the right chart focuses on the resulting variances from performance.

Also of interest to management is the level of management reserve still available to the project. In this case, management reserve is shown in the right chart and there is still sufficient management reserve to cover the negative cost position.

Variance thresholds as discussed above come into play with management displays. Once these variances have been refined to the point at which they reflect only critical issues facing the project, management can focus their valuable time on only the critical issues.

Each project manager must decide what type of management displays work best for the team. Displays can be easily modified to reflect whatever is deemed important to the project, which may change from the start to the finish of a particular project.

3 Ibid, page 173.

THE MEANING OF AN EARNED VALUE SCHEDULE VARIANCE (SV)

One more item needs to be mentioned when discussing the monitoring of performance. It sometimes comes as a surprise to many that an earned value negative "schedule variance" may not necessarily constitute a serious scheduling issue to a project. Rather, the earned value schedule variance simply reflects a variance from the approved baseline. Such deviations may or may not be critical to the project. You do not want to waste valuable resources, overtime and added people, if the negative schedule variances are not critical to completing the project on time.

As was pointed out earlier in Chapter 6 and was illustrated in Figure 6.3, being ahead of, or behind, schedule often depends on where each task was placed in the baseline. Likely, most earned value baselines reflect simply a best guess, perhaps the most likely position for each task. The time placement of each task may have little relationship to the project's critical path. Unfortunately, some projects, perhaps many projects, have little understanding of their true critical path position.

A negative schedule variance in Earned Value simply means that the project has fallen behind in accomplishing its scheduled work, the Planned Value. The formula is: Earned Value (EV) less Planned Value (PV) equals a schedule variance (SV). As a general rule, management at all levels dislikes being behind schedule, no matter how critical the schedule variance may be. It is sometimes an emotional issue resulting in a decree such as: "everyone on overtime" or "bring in more people for this job!"

It is sometimes misleading to look at an earned value schedule position alone and rely on it to provide the project's schedule position. Projects need other scheduling tools with measurement metrics to discern their true schedule position. Earned value metrics alone will not portray an accurate assessment of schedule status.

A little history is in order. In the mid-1980s, the Department of Defense (DOD) commissioned the prestigious consulting firm of Arthur D. Little to study the earned value concept and to report back on its findings. This firm described the meaning of earned value schedule variances about as well as any that we have heard. We will thus quote a couple of sentences from its final report to the DOD, inserting the term "earned value" ahead of "C/SCSC," as it was then called:

> An earned value (C/SCSC) schedule variance is stated in terms of dollars of work, and must be analyzed in conjunction with other schedule information, such as provided by networks, Gantt charts, and line-of-balance.

By itself, the earned value (C/SCSC) schedule variance reveals no "critical path" information, and may be misleading because unfavorable accomplishments in some areas can be offset by favorable accomplishments in others.[4]

Whenever a project is employing Earned Value and it experiences a negative schedule condition, it should understand the true meaning of this condition. All that the earned value negative schedule variance indicates is that the project has fallen behind in accomplishing its planned work; that is, it is running a schedule position of less than 1.0, as depicted in Figure 10.6. Recommendation: Those tasks hat are late to the original baseline plan should be carefully assessed to determine two issues.

Issue One: Are any of the late tasks on the project's critical path, or on the near-critical paths, so as to potentially delay the final completion of the project? If so, overtime and/or additional resources may be warranted.

Issue Two: Are the late tasks considered to be high risks to the project; that is, do they constitute a risk of not meeting project objectives? If so, overtime and/or additional resources may be warranted.

If, however, these late-to-the-baseline plan tasks are determined to have a positive schedule float position (slack) and are not felt to represent high risks to the project, then added resources should not be authorized. The reason: Any added resources will have a permanent negative impact on the cost efficiency rate, and produce no positive critical path schedule results. The critical path will determine the earliest time that the project can be completed. Unless there are compelling reasons, additional resources should not be spent merely because the project is experiencing a negative schedule variance.

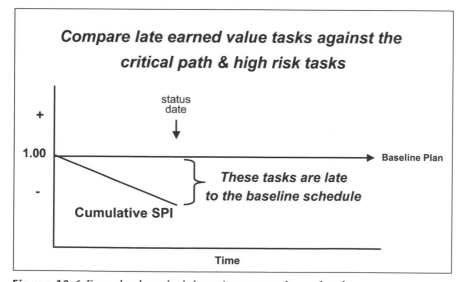

Figure 10.6 *Earned value schedule variances must be analyzed*

4 Arthur D. Little, White paper prepared for the Office of the Assistant Secretary of Defense, Comptroller, 10 July, 1986.

11

FORECASTING THE FINAL COST
AND SCHEDULE RESULTS

THERE ARE NUMEROUS REASONS why organizations are beginning to employ at least a simple form of Earned Value to help them better manage their projects. Earned Value requires that projects work to a fully defined and "integrated" baseline, meaning that the defined scope of work must relate to the authorized resources, which are then locked into a time frame for performance. We know of no other technique that fully integrates the project's scope with costs and schedules, thus providing an accurate measurement of performance.

But perhaps the single most compelling justification for employing Earned Value is that it enables the project manager to be able to "statistically" forecast the (probable) final cost and schedule results on the project . . . from as early as the 20-percent completion point. With Earned Value, the project does not have to wait until it is 70- or 80% spent to know that it has a cost problem. The 70% point is too late to alter the project's final course. Earned Value gives a project manager an "early warning" signal in time to take corrective action, in time to influence the final results by taking aggressive actions . . . now!

Figure 11.1 displays an example of what we are describing. This project has been defined and a total budget (BAC) authorized for the work. The project has completed only 20% of its work but is off to a bad start. Performance has not kept up with its scheduled plan, and it is spending more money to perform the completed work than management has budgeted. It is both behind schedule and experiencing an overrun. With an earned value baseline in place, the project can quickly forecast how much it will need in added resources and time to complete the total project. Earned Value predicts the final performance results by providing a statistical range of values, in time to take aggressive management actions should the forecasts be unacceptable.

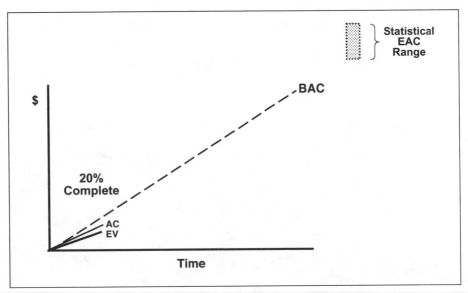

Figure 11.1 *Cost risks can be managed . . . with an "early warning"*

Such early forecasts have been proven to be extremely reliable using earned value data. They are based on a combination of two factors: (1) the implementation of a detailed bottom-up performance plan, and then (2) the subsequent actual measurement of performance against the project plan. These two factors have been shown to provide accurate statistical forecasts.

Two performance indices resulting from Earned Value are needed to forecast the project's final cost and schedule results. The first and most valuable is called the Cost Performance Index (CPI), which represents that delicate relationship between the value of the work physically completed and/or in-process, as related to the Actual Costs incurred for doing such work. If one spends more money than one physically performs, such performance results in an "overrun."

The second index needed to forecast final results is the Schedule Performance Index (SPI), which measures the work accomplished against the baseline plan. These two indices can be used independently or in conjunction to statistically predict the final results quickly and accurately.

THREE FACTORS DETERMINE THE FINAL PROJECT RESULTS

While the earned value performance indices can be most useful in predicting the final results on any project, the benefits from these indices are dependent on three critical factors. Each of these factors deserves some discussion because they can influence the utility of the performance indices in predicting the final cost and schedule results.

Factor #1: The quality of the project's baseline plan

Not all project plans are created equal. Some individuals and companies are quite good at developing their project plans. Others are not. Some people consistently "fire first" and "aim later." The quality of project plans will vary and will influence the final project results.

The competitive environment under which a given project plan may be implemented will often influence or bias the project manager's strategy. Competition sometimes results in risk-taking by the creators of the plans, and will incorporate varying degrees of uncertainty into the final baseline plans. Project plans are often different depending upon the amount of competition present when management gives its final approval. Earned Value will measure performance to the baseline plan, whether the plan is realistic or ambitious or impossible to meet.

The quickest way to experience "scope creep" is to not adequately define the initial project scope. The surest way to "overrun" project costs is to underbudget the project. The best way to assure a schedule slip is to mandate a completion date that is impossible to achieve. Earned Value accurately measures project performance, but must assume that scope definition is adequate, and that the project has been given an achievable budget and a realistic schedule.

Factor #2: Actual performance against the approved baseline plan

Once the project plan has been approved and implemented, another important variable comes into play. This variable is the actual performance results against the authorized plan. Is the project's performance meeting, exceeding, or falling behind the approved project plan? Such performance factors can be quantified and monitored for the duration of the project.

Both the cost performance index (CPI) and the schedule performance index (SPI) efficiency factors can be watched for trends, and also used to statistically forecast the final results for any project employing Earned Value.

Factor #3: Management's determination to influence the final results

A third factor is also most critical and can often influence the project's final results.

If project management closely tracks the earned value performance trends and does not like, or cannot accept, the final forecast results, to what extent will management take aggressive actions on the remaining work to alter the final outcome?

Final forecast results are not necessarily preordained. Final project results can often be altered, but only when aggressive management actions are taken . . . early. The critical variables are several. To what extent will project performance data be monitored and the data believed by management? What actions will be authorized to alter the management approach on the remaining project tasks? And, finally, if the project's final forecasts are unacceptable, to what extent will all discretionary (non-critical) work be eliminated, budgets reduced, risks taken, and so forth, in order to bring the final projected results down to acceptable levels?

Aggressive project management actions, if taken quickly, can often alter the final projected outcome for the project.

THE PROJECT MANAGERS "OFFICIAL" ESTIMATE AT COMPLETION (EAC)

When individuals accept the responsibility for all aspects of project performance, including the technical quality, costs and schedule performance, they, in effect, put their careers on the line. If things go well, management knows precisely whom to credit. If things go poorly, management also knows precisely whom to blame. Thus, when it comes to forecasting the final cost results on any project, the person holding the job title of "project manager" should have a major say as to the value of the final forecast, called the "estimate at completion" (EAC).

How do projects typically estimate their final costs? The *PMBOK® Guide* describes this process about as well as any book we have read, so we will paraphrase its suggested approach.[1] Most projects, when it becomes apparent that they are going to exceed management's authorized budget, will take their total costs for the work performed, and prepare a new detailed estimate to complete (ETC) all of the remaining work. The formula is thus: Cumulative Actual Costs plus a new ETC. This forecast is likely the most reliable because it builds on the actual experience of the project for the work performed to date.

However, here's a question: What's wrong with this approach? Answer: Preparing the ETC is a royal pain in the neck! Preparing a new ETC is <u>non-project work</u>. The very people who are performing on the project, who are often frustrated because they are running behind their initial schedule, must stop doing real project work and prepare a new baseline plan called the ETC. Rightfully, most project professionals resent

---

1 Project Management Institute: *PMBOK® Guide*, Third Edition, page 175.

(perhaps hate) doing an ETC. And to add insult to injury, there is never a budget to cover "ETC preparation." Management is often sympathetic, but merely offers: "What's the big deal, you've got all night and this weekend to prepare a new ETC."

Whenever a project commits to employing even a simple form of Earned Value, the project team will want to focus on the actual results against their baseline plan. They will look for exceptions to the plan and monitor the schedule variances and cost variances, as displayed in Figure 11.2. Perfect schedule performance can be quantified as 1.0: For every dollar of work planned, they get a dollar of Earned Value. For every dollar spent, they get a dollar of Earned Value, thus also achieving a perfect cost performance of 1.0. The focus is on the Earned Value achieved versus the schedule plan and the actual costs. These same baseline variances can be converted into efficiency factors taking the form of the CPI and SPI, which can be used to forecast the final project results.

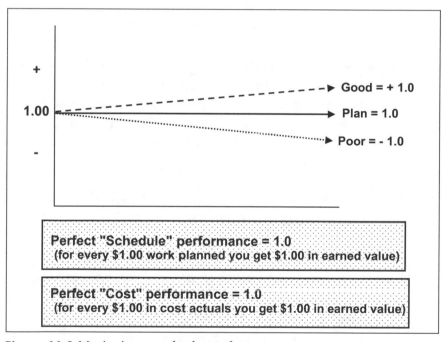

Figure 11.2 *Monitoring earned value performance*

By employing Earned Value, any project can develop an independent range of statistical EACs in a matter of seconds. The range of statistical EACs can then be compared against the project manager's latest official EAC, or even used in lieu of the project manager's EAC, should management have sufficient confidence in the earned value process in place. In the latter case, the project can then avoid the undesirable necessity of stopping real project work to prepare a new, detailed ETC.

And if the forecast value is undesirable or unacceptable to management, actions can be taken immediately to bring the projected final costs down to acceptable levels.

EARNED VALUE METHODS TO INDEPENDENTLY
FORECAST A "RANGE" OF FINAL EACS

Earned Value Management allows any project to continuously monitor its cost (CPI) and schedule (SPI) efficiency rates, reflecting actual performance trends. These efficiency indices can also be used to statistically forecast the expected final position on a continuous basis. Projects that elect not to employ Earned Value miss this opportunity to precisely quantify their actual performance.

Over the years, a number of formulas have evolved to statistically forecast the final estimated costs at completion (EAC) on any project employing Earned Value. By last count, there were close to twenty distinct formulas available to predict the final cost position.

However, in this discussion we will limit ourselves to suggesting just three of the more accepted formulas, as are portrayed in Figure 11.3. These three formulas will provide the project with a "best case," a "most likely case," and a "worst case" scenario. These three independent EACs can be quickly compared against the project manager's "official EAC" to assess whether or not the project might be experiencing a cost problem.

One important point to understand: By preparing a range of EACs, we are not trying to pick a final forecast number for the project. That task rightfully belongs to the project manager and is typically done with a bottom-up ETC as previously

---

- **The Project Manager's "Official Estimate"**
  (Actual costs + a new "bottom-up" ETC

  * * *

  EVPM independent statistical EAC comparisons:

  1) Low-end over-run to date... the "best case"
  (Mathematical EAC formula)

  2) Middle range EAC... the "most likely case"
  (Cumulative CPI EAC formula)

  3) High-end range EAC... the "worst case"
  (Cumulative CPI x SPI EAC formula)

Figure 11.3 *Forecasting a Range of Estimates at Completion*

described, rather than with a statistical forecast. We are simply attempting to assess whether or not the project may have a cost problem that needs management's immediate attention.

The processes of statistically forecasting a range of final cost estimates will center on setting three variables for a project, as of any given point in time:

1. **Determine the total of actual costs incurred to date.**
2. **Determine the value of the Work Remaining (WR).** By definition, this is considered to be the budgeted value for the uncompleted work. This is typically expressed as the total Budget At Completion (BAC), less the Earned Value already accomplished, which equals the WR.
3. **Divide the Work Remaining (WR) by some performance factor (pf).** For example: 1.0, or the cumulative CPI, or the CPI times SPI.

With use of these three variables, any project can statistically forecast the estimated final costs to complete the project.

> ### SPECIAL ISSUE: MANAGEMENT RESERVE (MR) OR CONTINGENCY RESERVE (CR)

One important issue needs to be mentioned for any project that may have management reserves (MR) or contingency reserves (CR): What do you do with MR and/or CR when making a statistical EAC forecast? For many projects, this may be a non-issue because management will not allow MR or CR. However, if there are MR or CR funds available to the project manager, they must be considered while making a final statistical cost projection. We must give instructions to the spreadsheet about what to do with MR or CR.

One of three scenarios can impact MR or CR funds when projecting a statistical EAC:

1. The final EAC forecast can <u>exclude</u> the full value of the remaining MR or CR funds, based on the assumption that these funds will not be consumed by the project; or
2. The remaining MR or CR can be <u>divided</u> by the negative performance efficiency factor (the CPI or the CPI times SPI), which will increase the final projected costs; or
3. The MR or CR can simply be <u>added</u> to the calculated EAC at its full 1.0 value, based on the assumption that these funds will be consumed, but at their full budgeted value.

Because the allocation of MR or CR typically goes for specific, well defined tasks at the time the budget is released, we would tend to support the third scenario. We would add the full value of MR or CR to the EAC and expect a 1.0 consumption rate.

The assumed use of MR or CR funds should be a judgment call by the project manager.

SPECIAL ISSUE: LEVEL OF EFFORT (LOE) TASKS

If you haven't gotten the message yet, the authors dislike Level of Effort (LOE) measurement. Our reason: LOE tasks measure the passage of time, period. They do not measure performance of work. Because the measurement of LOE tasks is set on "autopilot"—with Planned Value automatically becoming Earned Value with the passage of time, regardless of whether any work was done—LOE can seriously distort project performance measurement.

In Chapter 8, we suggested that all LOE work be "quantified" and "quarantined." This approach was displayed in Figure 8.4. With respect to forecasting the final costs for LOE, we do have a suggestion.

Take the quarantined LOE tasks off of autopilot. Do not measure LOE work by assuming that Planned Value becomes Earned Value with the passage of time. Rather, our recommendation is to convert all LOE tasks to subjective percent complete estimates as displayed in Figure 8.3, with item 3. While subjective percent complete estimates are not the best measurement possible, they are far better than the distortions resulting from PV becoming EV automatically.

1. The "Mathematical" or "Overrun-to-Date" Estimate at Completion

The first of the three forecasting techniques to be discussed goes by a couple of titles in industry: the "*Mathematical EAC*" or "*Overrun-to-Date EAC.*" This EAC method is depicted in Figure 11.4, and it has two formulas that are also displayed in the two boxes across the bottom. The easiest formula to use is simply: Math EAC = Actual Costs, plus the BAC, less the Earned Value. However, in order to compare the three statistical EAC methods using a similar format, we have also provided the formula on the left: Actual Costs plus the Work Remaining (BAC − EV), divided by a 1.0 performance factor (pf). Both formulas will provide the same result.

In this scenario, the performance factor for the remaining work is 1.0, which means it assumes that all future work, starting now, will be done precisely at the full budgeted rate. An ambitious goal. This EAC formula is not widely accepted in government quarters and has actually been referred to as "useless." However, we like it and it is frequently used within private industry for a couple of valid reasons.

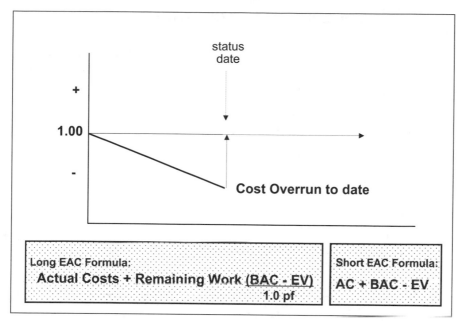

Figure 11.4 *The "Mathematical" or "Overrun-to-Date" EAC*

First reason to use this formula: the Mathematical or Overrun-to-Date EAC is often the first indication announcing to the project manager and executive management that they may have a cost problem on their project. As we discussed earlier in Chapter 1, if a project spends $300,000 to accomplish only $200,000 of budgeted work, the project has experienced a "cost overrun" for the initial work that it has performed. Management deserves to know this fact.

Second reason to use this formula: the Mathematical EAC is important because an early overrun does not typically go away with the passage of time. We have rarely ever witnessed a front-end overrun mystically disappearing through exemplary (underrunning) performance of the remaining work.

Think about it. Question: In a project baseline, where are the best scope definition, best planning, best budget, and best scheduled dates placed—in the first half or the last half of the baseline? Answer: Likely the best of everything will be incorporated into the first half of the baseline. Thus, if a project incurs an overrun in the first half, what are the chances of making a later recovery of the overrun? Little-to-none. This EAC formula provides a sort of minimum overrun floor that typically does not go away.

Short of a project dropping scope features (i.e., the outright elimination of authorized tasks), an overrun in the early phases of the project is very serious, and likely constitutes a permanent loss of funds for any project. The Mathematical or Overrun-to-Date EAC formula adds utility in that it constitutes the lowest "best case" scenario in the range of possible final costs for any project.

2. The "Cumulative CPI" Estimate at Completion

Likely the most common and most respected of all the earned value statistical forecasting methods is displayed in Figure 11.5, called the *"Cumulative CPI" Estimate at Completion*. Two formulas can be used for this method and both are displayed at the bottom of the chart. A long method is shown on the left and the short formula on the right. This method has had considerable scientific data accumulated and studied to support its reliability as a forecasting method.

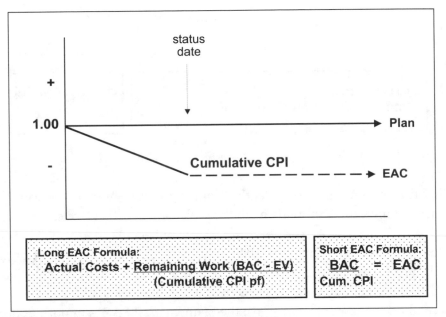

Figure 11.5 *The Low-end "Cumulative CPI" EAC*

Take note of the requirement for use of only <u>cumulative performance data</u>, not periodic or incremental data. While any project team will certainly want to monitor its periodic position to assess recent performance results, periodic data are also subject to anomalies, sometimes caused by placing good data into the wrong time frame. Cumulative performance data tends to smooth out variations, but nevertheless retains its value as a long-term forecasting tool.

The cumulative (not periodic) CPI provides a particularly reliable index to watch because it has been demonstrated to be an accurate and reliable forecasting metric. The cumulative CPI has been shown to stabilize from as early as the 20-percent completion point of the project. One particularly important scientific study described the value of using the cumulative CPI to forecast the final cost results on projects:

"... researchers found that the cumulative CPI does not change by more than ten percent once a contract is twenty percent complete; in most cases, the cumulative

CPI only worsens as a contract proceeds to completion."[2]

Let us pause to reflect on these important empirical findings with all projects employing Earned Value:

1. Project performance results at the 20 percent completion point will stabilize,
2. The remaining performance will not likely change by more than plus or minus 10% at the point of project completion. What a finding! No other project management technique provides such performance insight.

Some people consider the cumulative CPI EAC formula to represent the "most likely" case to predict final costs to complete all work. Others consider it to be simply the "minimum" final estimate of project costs. Either way, the cumulative CPI EAC has been demonstrated to be most accurate in providing a quick statistical forecast of the final required project costs. Such statistical forecasts, when compared against the project manager's "official" estimate, should never be ignored by executive management.

Just how important is this particular method to the Department of Defense (DOD), which has been using earned value data to forecast final cost results for almost four decades? In 1991, when the DOD transferred the requirement for Earned Value Management directly into their DOD acquisition policy, they also added language specifically requiring that the "cumulative CPI" be employed whenever forecasting the final costs:

> Provide the estimate at completion reflecting the best professional judgment of the servicing cost analysis organization. If the contract is at least 15 percent complete and the estimate is lower than that calculated using the cumulative cost performance index, provide an explanation.[3]

There may be valid justification supporting an estimate at completion lower than that calculated using the cumulative CPI. However, since 1991, all DOD project managers must describe how this (unlikely) event will be accomplished. The cumulative CPI EAC forecast is a vital technique for use on all earned value projects.

3. The "Cumulative CPI times SPI" Estimate at Completion

The last statistical formula that has wide professional acceptance in forecasting the final project costs is one that combines both the cost efficiency (CPI) factor and

---

2 Dr. David S. Christensen, "Using Performance Indices to Evaluate the Estimate at Completion," The Journal of Cost Analysis, of the Society of Cost Estimating and Analysis, Spring 1994, page 19.

3 United States Department of Defense, Policy Instruction 5000.2, Part 11, Section B, Attachment 1 (Washington, D.C., February 23, 1991).

the schedule efficiency (SPI) factor. This method is displayed in Figure 11.6 and its formula is shown in the box at the bottom of the chart. Note: there is no short formula to calculate this EAC forecast.

There is a solid rational basis to support the use of a forecasting formula that incorporates both the cost and the schedule efficiency dimensions. The reason: No project team ever likes to be in a position of creating a performance plan, getting management's approval, and then falling behind with their authorized plan. There is a natural human tendency to want to get back on schedule, even if it means consuming more resources to accomplish the same amount of authorized work. The use of paid overtime and additional resources (more people) is often employed, which simply results in permanent, non-recoverable cost damage to the most important efficiency factor, the Cost Performance Index (CPI).

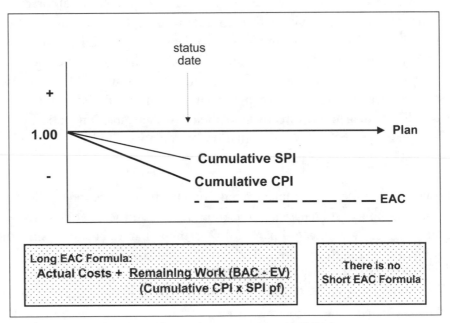

Figure 11.6 *The High-end "Cumulative CPI times SPI" EAC*

Some people consider this formula to be a "worst case" high-end EAC scenario. The authors are in this camp. Others, particularly those within the DOD, consider it to represent the "most likely" forecast. In either case, the CPI times the SPI EAC is one of the more widely used and accepted formulas to statistically forecast the high-end cost requirements for any project. It should be used any time the project is driven by a specific completion date—which includes most projects.

○ ○ ○

Question: What is the utility of providing a statistical range (low/most likely/high) of final cost results for a given project? Answer: Simply put, it is to test the reasonableness of the project manager's "official" cost position against a statistical range of possible earned value forecasts. Earned value forecasts can quickly provide management with an understanding of the cost risks facing any project.

If the project manager predicts a final cost performance of the project outside the statistical range, either above or below it, then the rationale for this position should be explained to all parties with a vested interest in the project. Those parties include the project's owner, senior executive management, corporate shareholders, and so forth.

Under the Sarbanes-Oxley Act of 2002, which is covered in Chapter 14, the Chief Financial Officer (CFO) and the Chief Executive Officer (CEO) will also have an interest in the reasonableness of these final estimated values.

TIME MANAGEMENT: PREDICTING THE PROJECT'S FINAL COMPLETION DATE

How long will it take to complete the project? This is another matter of great interest to any project manager, to executive management, and especially to the owner or paying customer. By definition, a project can only be completed within the outer limits of its critical path, which is defined as such:

The critical path is the longest path through a project, and so determines the earliest completion for the work.[4]

The management of the project's critical path and the near-critical paths are thus vital to the successful completion of any project at the earliest possible date. An important point to understand: The earned value schedule performance data alone will <u>not</u> be sufficient to manage or predict the project's time dimension. Projects need to have a solid scheduling process in place that allows them to manage their critical paths.

As was discussed in the last chapter, earned value schedule variances represent the difference between what was actually physically accomplished (the Earned Value) less what was planned to be accomplished (the Planned Value). The formula is SV = EV − PV.

Negative earned value schedule variances are important because they are often one of the first indications of a problem. Negative schedule variances indicate that the project is falling behind its baseline plan . . . period. Also, earned value schedule variances may be used in conjunction with the critical path method (CPM) as a way

4 Dr. James P. Lewis, *Project Planning Scheduling & Control*, (Chicago: Irwin Professional Publishing, Revised Edition, 1995) page 120.

of reinforcing the forecast date for project completion. However, a word of caution: Don't rely on earned value schedule variances alone to help predict the final completion date for a project.

Figure 11.7 displays a chart that depicts the earned value schedule status. As of the status date, halfway through a two-year project, the baseline plan called for completion of so much work, but the project has only accomplished a portion of that work. The project, therefore, is experiencing a negative earned value schedule position.

If we trace the intersection of the earned value line with the status date, then trace backwards to the planned value line and move downward to the bottom time scale, we can see that the project is running roughly two months behind the planned value or baseline schedule. Does this late condition automatically translate into a two-month slip of the project's completion date? Not necessarily. It all depends on whether the late tasks are on the critical path, or are high-risk activities.

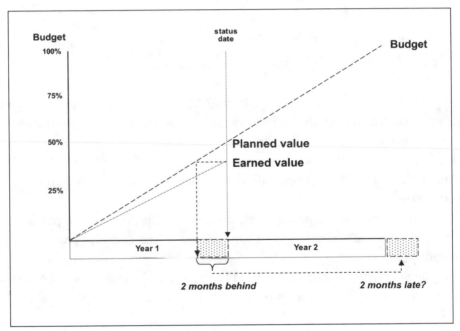

Figure 11.7 *Monitoring the earned value schedule performance*

All that can be concluded from earned value schedule performance data is that the project is currently behind its planned schedule. Nothing more. However, there are some professionals in the field who feel that the earned value schedule position can be used to predict the final completion date for the project. The authors do not endorse this theory. Nor have they ever read any scientific studies that support this position.

The most reliable basis to predict the final completion date of a project is with use of the project's critical path. Earned value schedule data can be useful to reinforce the projections of the critical path. However, in the opinion of the authors, earned value data by itself is not adequate to manage the project's time dimension.

The utility of a project's SV and SPI is that they can be used in conjunction with the CV and CPI to predict the final cost requirements on any project. Also, a negative earned value schedule variance is one of the first indicators a project will receive that it is not performing to its project plan.

IN SUMMARY

The bottom-line questions for any project are, typically: How much will it cost to complete the job? And how much time until the project is over? Two reliable techniques are currently available to any project manager: the use of earned value cost performance data, and the critical path method (CPM).

While many project practitioners today will employ CPM to manage the time dimension for their projects, the use of earned value measurement data has been somewhat limited. It is our belief that the two techniques work well together and are, in fact, complementary. When these two proven techniques are used by people working with a single integrated database, they can provide accurate and reliable forecasts to the age-old questions: How long will my project take to complete? And how much money will it cost?

Use earned value data to predict the project's cost dimension. Use CPM to predict the project's time dimension.

12

MANAGE THE PROJECT PORTFOLIO
USING EARNED VALUE

A PORTFOLIO IS A COLLECTION OF PROJECTS or programs and other work that are grouped together to facilitate effective management of that work to meet strategic business objectives[1].

. . . effective new product development is emerging as the major corporate strategic initiative of the decades ahead.
. . . those companies that fail to excel at developing new products will invariably disappear or be gobbled up by the winners.

A vital question in this new product battleground is: How should corporations most effectively invest their R & D and new product resources? That's what portfolio management is all about: resource allocation to achieve corporate new product objectives[2].

The development and infusion of new products is vital to the continuous success of all companies. But the decisions that executives must make as to which new products to develop is essentially a subjective one dealing with a combination of factors the market and technical issues. Will the new product, once available, satisfy the

---

1 *A Guide to the Project Management Body of Knowledge (PMBOK® Guide)*, Third Edition, (Newtown Square, PA: Project Management Institute) page 16.

2 Robert G. Cooper, Scott J. Edgett, Elko J. Kleinschmidt, *Portfolio Management for New Products*, (Reading, MA: Addison-Wesley, 1998) page 1.

165

perceived wants of the marketplace? And will our particular new product be the one to be embraced by that market?

The employment of Earned Value in the management of a portfolio of projects cannot by itself help executives make the right product choices. That is an intrinsic executive skill. But Earned Value and the metrics it provides can help management make the right choices by providing accurate, reliable, and timely data to support such decisions. What is the real cost and schedule status of our ongoing projects? How much will it actually cost to complete the projects? Do we have enough money to fund all of the desired projects? The solid earned value metrics can also help make those difficult corporate decisions as to which projects to continue to fund, and which to terminate.

Also, a most powerful metric resulting from employing Earned Value hasn't been discussed yet. It is called the "To-Complete Performance Index" (TCPI). We need to understand its meaning and utility because it can be a most valuable aid in the management of a portfolio of projects.

The To-Complete (Remaining Work) Performance Index (TCPI)

One of the most valuable metrics resulting from earned value employment has been kept almost a secret among a few gurus working in the earned value community. How unfortunate. This virtually unknown metric is called the "To-Complete Performance Index" (TCPI), and should be used in conjunction with tracking the cumulative CPI. The TCPI can be one of the most insightful tracking indices . . . if

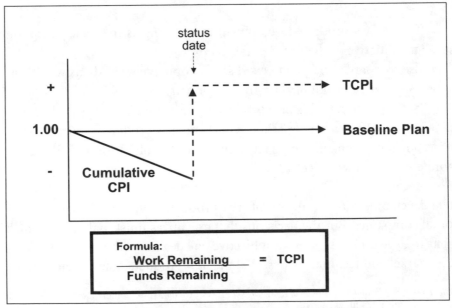

Figure 12.1 *The To-Complete (the work) Performance Index (TCPI)*

TCPI using Management's "Budget at Completion" (BAC):

$$\frac{\text{Work Remaining (BAC - EV)}}{\text{Funds Remaining (BAC - AC)}} \nearrow \; = \; \text{TCPI (BAC)}$$

TCPI using the Project Manager's "Estimate at Completion" (EAC):

$$\frac{\text{Work Remaining (BAC - EV)}}{\text{Funds Remaining (EAC - AC)}} \nearrow \; = \; \text{TCPI (EAC)}$$

Figure 12.2 *Two "To-Complete Performance Index" (TCPI) formulas*

only the project manager and the project team know what it is and how to interpret its data. A typical TCPI display is illustrated in Figure 12.1. The cumulative CPI represents work that has already been completed, and the TCPI constitutes future work.

The TCPI addresses the question: What performance factor (CPI) must the project achieve in order to stay within the tangible future financial goal? It takes the "work remaining" (initially defined as the BAC less EV) and divides it by the "funds remaining."

The funds remaining can be represented by two distinct financial goals, as displayed in Figure 12.2. The first is management's authorized Budget at Completion (BAC) less the funds used (AC). The second is the project manager's latest Estimate at Completion (EAC) less the funds already used (AC).

The first financial goal for any project is to stay within the original budget (BAC) authorized by management. This is a paramount financial objective, until such time as it becomes obvious that this goal is no longer achievable. At that time, the project manager typically provides a new estimate of the funds required to complete the project, called the EAC, and requests management to authorize the increased funds. Once management authorizes the new EAC, all parties track performance to the EAC, using the formula as displayed at the bottom in Figure 12.2.

Both financial goals (the BAC and EAC) are critical to the success of any project, so both must be discussed and understood separately.

THE TCPI USING MANAGEMENT'S BUDGET AT COMPLETION (BAC)

The TCPI metric is important any time a project experiences negative cost performance; that is, when the CPI is running below 1.0 performance. A negative CPI indicates that the project is spending more than it has budgeted for the work completed. It is overrunning its costs. The question then becomes: Will the current overrun cause the project to need more funds than management has authorized in its budget (BAC)? Figure 12.3 displays a project performance chart representing the baseline plan, the cumulative CPI, and the TCPI necessary to stay within management's authorized funds (the BAC).

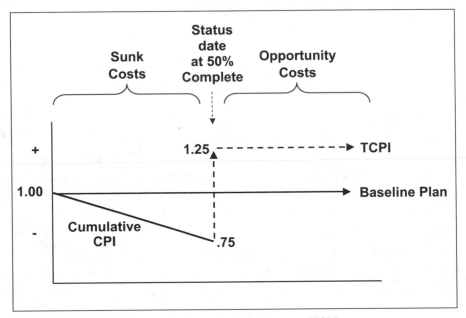

Figure 12.3 *The relationship of Cumulative CPI versus TCPI*

The cumulative CPI can best be thought of as actual "sunk costs." If a project spends more money than it has budgeted for the completed work, those costs are likely gone forever. Early overruns of costs are rarely (if ever) recovered by subsequent performance. The remaining work can thus be considered to be "opportunity costs"; that is, if any cost improvements are to be made, they must come from that remaining work.

When managing a portfolio of projects, executives will want to begin the continuous comparison of earned value performance data as early as possible—10%, 20%, 30%, etc. To illustrate the utility of the TCPI, we will focus on the 50% completion point to describe the concept.

When monitoring the TCPI, the juncture at the 50% completion point is critical to any project. It represents the point at which the sunk costs will precisely equal the opportunity costs. At the point of 50% completion, a cost performance factor (CPI) of .75 can only be offset by completing all future work at the inverse value of 1.25. How likely is this to happen? Probably not very likely, but theoretically possible. However, once the project goes past the 50% completion point, the sunk costs will exceed the opportunity costs, and the required performance factor to meet the financial goal will increase exponentially.

At some point, the project manager and executive management must recognize that "more funds are needed" in order to complete this project. Management then has some hard choices to make.

THE TCPI USING THE PROJECT MANAGER'S ESTIMATE AT COMPLETION (EAC)

Once it becomes obvious that a project can no longer be completed within management's authorized funds (the BAC), the next question then becomes: What is the real number needed to complete the project, the estimate at completion (EAC)? Please note: We are not talking here about the statistically calculated EACs as discussed in the last chapter: the Mathematical, or CPI, or CPI times SPI calculated EACs. Rather, we are referring to the project manager's official position on what it will take to complete the project. This is typically created by taking the actual costs to date, and then preparing a new detailed task-by-task estimate to complete the job.

Project managers, by their very nature, are optimistic individuals. This optimism can sometimes have an influence on what the project manager is willing to accept as a final challenge. One's personal pride often comes into play. Sometimes, the real number of required costs to complete the project is suppressed, at least temporarily. The project manager's official EAC may increase each month . . . a little piece at a time. This condition is unfortunate, but too often real.

However, senior management and the buying customer deserve to know the full truth. They may elect to cancel the project and invest their funds in other endeavors. It is their monies, and they deserve to know the full truth. That is where the TCPI based on available EAC funds becomes a valuable tool. A TCPI based on the EAC funds can be used to validate the reasonableness of the project manager's official EAC.

We suggest that you refer to Figure 12.4 to follow this discussion. In this display, we have portrayed the baseline plan and the cumulative CPI curves. Also shown are the three statistically calculated EAC formulas: the Mathematical EAC, the CPI EAC, and the CPI times SPI EAC. Note that the Mathematical EAC is merely an extension of the baseline plan for all the future work.

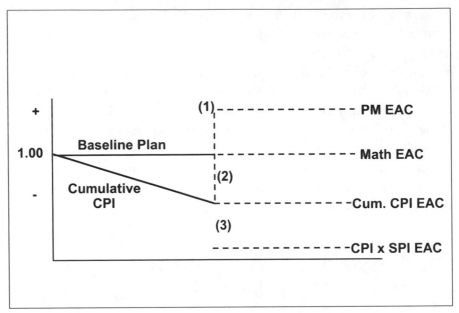

Figure 12.4 *Using the TCPI to validate the Project Manager's EAC*

Assume for a minute that the project manager provides an EAC as displayed at the (1) point for all remaining work. The project manager is suggesting a completion at a value less than that calculated with the Mathematical EAC. Is this likely to happen? No. This EAC assumes a complete absorption of all overrun work to date. Short of a miracle or dropping scope, it will not happen. And yet, project managers will sometimes forecast such estimates to get management "off my back." The number (1) EAC will not happen. But without the TCPI display, the unrealistic EAC may go unchallenged for several months, and the sunk costs will continue to rise.

Now let us assess the second scenario, as displayed with the EAC at the (2) point. This EAC is less than that calculated using the cumulative CPI, but greater than the Mathematical EAC. Because it is forecasting a final value less than that using the cumulative EAC, if it were a DOD-funded project, the military program manager would have to provide an explanation as to why this value was being forecast. Is (2) a reasonable EAC? Possibly, if the project has successfully overcome all or most of the project risks it had initially experienced. If, however, the project still faces substantial challenges, the value at the (2) point may be too optimistic. Management should make an independent assessment. The TCPI display can aid that management assessment.

Lastly, let us examine the project manager's EAC at the (3) point. This EAC assumes a further deterioration of performance at less than the cumulative CPI. Is this a reasonable EAC? Perhaps, if the project is running behind schedule and management wants the project completed by a certain date. In this case, it will likely require additional resources to perform the same planned work. But it is also possible that the project manager may be including some funds as a contingency, in case things go badly. Senior management and the buying customer should inquire as to the basis for the forecast in the range of the (3) level.

o o o

The utility of the TCPI based on either the BAC or EAC is that it allows management at all levels to assess the forecast future of a project based on the past earned value performance. It portrays in graphical form the past performance (sunk costs) versus the future expectations (opportunity costs), so that management at all levels can feel comfortable that their financial goals can, in fact, be achieved. The TCPI can be a valuable aid in this process.

A TEMPLATE FOR PORTFOLIO MANAGEMENT

Any organization that commits to employing the earned value technique on a portfolio of projects gains a wealth of performance data to assess and compare the true health of all its projects. Depending on the desire for oversight, literally dozens of earned value formulas can be applied to each project. That is likely more data than is needed for effective portfolio management. Therefore, some type of selection must occur to monitor the pulse of each project, without encumbering senior management with data of little consequence.

The four critical questions in project portfolio selection using earned value metrics would seem to be: (1) How have we performed to date against the baseline plan?; (2) What are the cost and schedule efficiency factors achieved thus far?; (3) What is the range of statistical EACs as compared to the project manager's latest EAC?; and, finally (4) What completion efficiency factors must each project incur in order to meet the BAC or the project manager's latest EAC?

Figure 12.5 lists a suggested template incorporating earned value performance metrics that the authors contend would allow for a valid comparison of all projects in a portfolio. In addition, it is imperative for management to know the critical-path, total-float position on each project, to assess whether or not the project's expected completion date is still achievable. Earned value portfolio data should be updated each time management sits down to make hard decisions on the portfolio, often referred to as the "Stage-Gate" process.

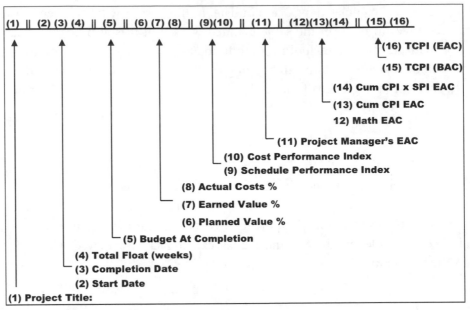

Figure 12.5 *An Earned Value template for portfolio management*

1. Project Title:

   _____

2. Start Date: The date the project was first approved to start by management.
3. Completion Date: The official date management expects the project to be completed.
4. Total Float (weeks): The total float status expressed in weeks, related to #(3) above.

   _____

5. BAC: Management's authorized funding for the total project.

   _____

6. % PV: How much scheduled work was expected as of the cutoff date.
7. % EV: How much scheduled work was completed as of the cutoff date, the % complete.
8. % AC: How much money was spent or committed for the earned value achieved.

   _____

9. SPI: The actual schedule efficiency factor for meeting the baseline schedule.
10. CPI: The actual cost efficiency rate for the work completed.

    _____

11. PM's EAC: If the BAC is in question, the project manager's estimate to complete.

    _____

12. Mathematical EAC: The lowest statistical forecast in a range of estimates at completion.
13. Cumulative CPI EAC: The most likely statistical forecast in a range of estimates at completion.
14. Cumulative CPI x SPI EAC: The highest or worst-case statistical estimate at completion.

15. TCPI (BAC): The performance factor (opposite of #10) needed to stay within the BAC.
16. TCPI (EAC): The performance factor (opposite of #10) needed to meet EAC #11).

With the help of any electronic spreadsheet, the above display of data can be of considerable value to executive managers when they make their critical choices concerning which projects to continue and which to terminate. The use of earned value metrics adds an additional perspective not available with any other project management technique.

13

IMPLEMENT EARNED VALUE
ON ALL PROJECTS

EMPLOYING EARNED VALUE ON A PROJECT can be both easy and challenging. The easy part is that there is nothing inherently difficult about the earned value concept. By simply following fundamental project management practices, anyone can employ the concept on any project.

However, the challenging part is that it takes discipline to consistently employ fundamental project management practices within any organization. And Earned Value, in order to be measured, requires that fundamental project management practices be strictly followed. If corners are cut, certain basic requirements are bypassed; then Earned Value cannot be effectively implemented.

At a minimum, project goals must be set. The project's scope of work must be defined, a measurable baseline plan must be put in place and tightly controlled, and measurement of actual performance must routinely take place. These are fundamental practices often circumvented by organizations not yet ready to move from their "functional fiefdoms" over to "management by projects."

Earned Value Management as a concept is most often defined by professionals as being fully compliant with all of the 32 criteria as described in the Appendix to this book. This is fine . . . for mega-projects. But most of the projects we work are not in the mega-project, multi-billion-dollar class.

The authors have studied the concept and have summarized just ten fundamental steps necessary to implement a "simple" (low-end) form of Earned Value

Management on projects. These are the minimum requirements necessary to employ simple Earned Value. Each of these ten steps, as described below, will also make reference to a specific earned value criterion as described in the Appendix to this book.

Step 1: To the extent possible, you must define the full scope of the project (EVM Criterion #1).

This is perhaps the most important requirement for implementing Earned Value, and perhaps the most difficult to achieve. Certain types of projects, notably software, often give up at this point and refuse to go further. Management often relinquishes.

On any project, you must define the work to be done, if for no better reason than to know where you are and when you are done. To the extent that you can, you must define 100% of the scope of the project. This is true for any project, but it is particularly critical on any project in which you intend to measure Earned Value.

With Earned Value, we constantly focus on the authorized work that has been completed, plus management's official authorized budget for the completed work. We express the status as being "15% complete," "25% complete," "50% complete," and so forth. Question: If we have not defined what constitutes 100% of the project, how can we ever assess our percentage completion point? Answer: We can't.

Realistically, no project will ever define a new job with absolute precision. But one must make educated assumptions about a new project in order to quantify and then decompose the work with sufficient confidence that the effort can then be planned, scheduled and budgeted with some degree of certainty. Anything less, and management will be committing to a new project by providing essentially a "blank check." Vague scope definition begets scope creep.

How does one define a new job when specific details are lacking? There are no absolute answers. But one of the most useful of all tools available to any project manager is the Work Breakdown Structure (WBS). The WBS is to the project manager what the organization chart is to the executive. A WBS allows the project manager to define a new endeavor by laying out all the assumed work within the framework of the WBS, and then decomposing each element into measurable work packages.

Additionally, once the WBS is assumed to constitute a reasonable portrayal of the new project, the WBS can then be used to take the next critical steps in the project planning process, including make-or-buy analysis; risk assessment; scheduling; estimating, and, ultimately, the authorization of budgets to proceed.

Step 2: You must determine who will perform the defined work, including the identification of all major critical procurements (EVM Criterion #2).

It does make a difference to the project determining who will perform the defined work. Experienced workers generally work better and faster than inexperienced people, but they also cost more. Using an experienced work force is usually a good investment. However, sometimes the project's own organization will have no experience in a particular area, perhaps in developing a critical new component, and the project must send the work to another company for performance. These choices are called "make or buy" decisions, and selecting those items that must be procured for the project is an essential extension of the scope definition process.

Why is it important to identify the work that must be procured? Simply because procurements (versus in-house work) are done under non-forgiving legal arrangements. Formal contracts must be executed. It you commit to buy something that is not what you need, or the requirements must be modified, such changes will be accommodated, but at a price. Sellers love to have changes in scope, because each change gives them an opportunity to "get well" from a competitive bid. Projects will find that it takes time to adequately compile a tight procurement package, which can later be enforced, if need be, in a court of law. The earlier the procured work is identified, and responsibilities assigned, the better such packages can be managed.

By contrast, internal budgets can be executed in a more informal way, and the fact that everyone is on the same payroll allows a margin of slack. But there is no slack with the procured work. Procurements must be done properly, at the start, or the project will pay a price.

Lastly, whether the project work is done by the project's own organization, or procured from outside the company, the measurement and reporting of progress must take place. Inside or outside, the project must be able to measure the Earned Value versus the Actual Costs of the work being performed.

Step 3: You must plan and schedule the defined work (EVM Criterion #6).

Perhaps the single most critical tool required to implement Earned Value is to have a formal scheduling process in place. The project's scheduling system will portray the approved work scope, with each task carefully placed into a specific time frame for performance. In earned value vernacular, the scheduled work (plus its authorized budget) will constitute the project's "Planned Value." As performance then takes place on the project, that portion of the Planned Value that is physically completed (plus its budget) constitutes the "Earned Value." Both the Planned Value and the resulting Earned Value emanate from the project's master schedule and must use the same measurement metrics to both plan and then measure the actual performance.

The project's formal scheduling system is thus critical to the employment of Earned Value because it is the vehicle that describes the project scope, the Planned Value, and the resulting Earned Value. The project schedule is vital to Earned Value because it reflects the project manager's baseline "Planned Value" for everyone to follow.

On more complex projects, there should be a method to isolate the constraints between one task and other tasks. Typically, to satisfy this requirement, some form of critical path methodology (CPM) will need to be employed. The critical path (and near critical paths) on projects must be aggressively managed in conjunction with negative earned value schedule variances. A behind schedule variance (less than 1.0 performance) indicates that the project is falling behind its baseline plan. If the late tasks are on the critical path, or they are high-risk tasks, they must be managed to successful completion.

Step 4: You must estimate the required resources and formally authorize budgets (EVM Criterion #9).

Once the work scope has been fully defined and subsequently planned and scheduled, the next requirement to forming an earned value baseline is to estimate the resource requirements for all defined tasks within each level of the specified WBS. Each defined WBS element must have a resource value estimated to complete all the specified work. Management will then assess the requested resources and approve a value in the form of an authorized budget. Individual budgets should never contain contingencies or management reserves. Reserves or contingencies, if they exist, must be isolated and owned by the project manager.

Remember the rule: "Planned Value" represents two things—the scheduled work, plus the authorized budget. "Earned Value" also represents two things—the completed authorized work, plus the same authorized budget. Thus, in order to plan and then measure Earned Value, one needs to schedule all defined tasks along with the authorized budget necessary to complete the tasks.

All authorized budgets must be achievable, in order to have a viable project baseline.

Step 5: You must determine the metrics to convert Planned Value into Earned Value (EVM Criterion #7).

Question: How does one measure the conversion of Planned Value into Earned Value? Answer: One sets up measurable metrics in the baseline project schedules to quantify the authorized work and then the completion of the authorized work. Specific milestones, or tasks with weighted values, are measured as they are physically performed. Remember, Earned Value Project Management is nothing more than managing a project with a resource-loaded schedule.

Over the years, since Earned Value was first introduced, various methods have been devised to measure project performance. However, the most respected methods use some type of discrete measurement. Specific milestones representing points in time are assigned values; when they are fully completed, the assigned budgeted values are earned. Also tasks are assigned values, which can be measured as they are partially completed, at which time some value is assigned to the completed work through the reporting period.

Step 6: You must form a project baseline, determine the points of management control, and formally authorize Control Account Plans (CAPs) (EVM Criterion #8).

Earned Value requires use of an integrated project baseline, meaning that the defined work scope must include both the baseline schedule and the authorized budget. Integration takes place within each of the specified Work Breakdown Structure (WBS) elements.

Project management must next specify the points of management focus, referred to in Earned Value as Control Account Plans (CAPs). CAPS are placed at selected WBS elements and can best be thought of as subprojects, or project teams—subdivisions of the full project. The sum of the CAPS will constitute the total project baseline. The actual earned value performance measurement will take place within each of the specified CAPs. Total project performance is simply the summation of all the detailed CAPs, which can be placed at any level of the WBS.

On commercial contracts, the total project baseline may sometimes include such things as indirect costs, and even profits or fee, to match the total authorized project commitment. The project baseline must, thus, include whatever executive management has authorized the project manager to accomplish.

Internal company projects typically do not contain indirect costs, or profits. Many (perhaps most) internal project baselines will simply represent the sum of the defined CAPs, which are made up exclusively from direct labor hours only. The authorized project baseline constitutes whatever management has decided it should be.

Step 7: You must record all direct project costs consistent with the authorized baseline budgets, in accordance with the organization's general books of accounts (EVM Criterion #16).

A simple requirement: Project managers must be told what they have spent on their projects in order to be held accountable for cost management. Pretty basic stuff. But some organizations find this task extremely difficult, even impossible. How can that be? Simply because many organizations have been "functionally" oriented for so long, they cannot see the projects as distinct components. They can tell how much money was spent by their functions (e.g., engineering, test, maintenance, manufacturing, quality, etc.), but they cannot tell the project managers what they have spent on their projects. They have not made the transition to management by projects.

In order to employ Earned Value on any project, the Actual Costs must be aligned to the authorized project budgets. Remember the rule: Planned Value represents the authorized work plus budget, which is then converted into earned work and the same budget to represent the Earned Value. Earned Value must then be relatable to the Actual Costs in order to determine the cost efficiency factor, called the Cost Performance Index (CPI). The CPI is the single most important metric for any project employing Earned Value. Thus, Actual Costs by total project, and by subproject (CAPs), is an absolute requirement in order to employ Earned Value.

There is a trend in projects that employ Earned Value to measure performance on a weekly basis. We need to understand what this does and does not mean. Weekly earned value measurement means the measurement of internal direct labor hours. On a weekly basis, the company labor reports will produce Planned Value, Earned Value, and Actual Hours for internal direct labor hours only. Direct labor dollars, indirect costs, purchased articles, travel, etc., are generally not available on a weekly basis. Weekly performance measurement takes place on the internal direct labor hours only. However, this factor alone can be significant in effective project control.

The requirement for accuracy in the weekly labor reporting is critical. Any error factor in labor reporting will invalidate its usefulness. Errors in labor can occur for a number of reasons: people charge to the wrong account numbers, insert the wrong numbers, continue to charge to completed projects, charge to projects before authorized, etc.

In order to eliminate errors, some companies have implemented automated direct labor tracking systems in which employees must type in their project codes before starting the reporting cycle. If employees type in an incorrect labor code, the automated system immediately rejects the charge and the employee must correct the error prior to starting work. Accurate labor reporting is critical to measuring weekly Earned Value.

Step 8: You must continuously monitor the earned value performance to determine cost and schedule exceptions to the baseline plan: the schedule variances (Earned Value less the Planned Value) and cost variances (Earned Value less the Actual Costs) (EVM Criterion #22).

Projects employing Earned Value will need to monitor their cost and schedule results against the authorized baseline for the duration of the project. Management will focus its attention on exceptions to the baseline plan, particularly those that are greater than previously defined acceptable tolerances. Earned Value is thus a "management by exception" concept.

A negative earned value schedule variance simply means that the value of the work performed does not match the value of the work scheduled; that is, the project is falling behind its scheduled work plan. Each behind-schedule task should be assessed as to its criticality. If the late tasks are on the critical path, or if the tasks carry a high risk to the project, then efforts must be taken to get the late tasks back on schedule. However, additional project resources should not typically be spent on low-risk tasks or tasks that have positive critical path float.

The single most important aspect of employing Earned Value is the cost efficiency readings that it provides. The difference between the value of work earned, versus the costs incurred to accomplish the work, provides the cost efficiency factor. If the project spends more money than it receives in value, this reflects an overrun condition. Overruns are typically non-recoverable. Overruns expressed as a percentage value have been found to deteriorate . . . unless the project takes aggressive actions to mitigate the condition.

Perhaps of greatest benefit, the earned value cost efficiency rate has been found to be stable from the 20% point of project completion. The cost efficiency factor is thus an important metric for any project manager or enterprise executive to monitor.

Step 9: Using earned value data, you must continuously forecast the final required costs based on actual performance, and keep management apprised so it can take corrective actions if necessary (EVM Criterion #27).

One of the more beneficial aspects of Earned Value is that it provides the capability to quickly and independently forecast the total funds required to complete a project, commonly referred to as the estimate at completion (EAC). Based on Actual Cost and schedule performance against the baseline plan, a project is able to accurately estimate the total funds it will require to finish the job within a finite range of values.

Often, management or customers will have a preconceived notion of what final costs should be or what they would like them to be. If the earned value statistical forecast of estimated final costs is greater than the "official" project manager's estimate to complete the project, someone needs to reconcile these professional differences of opinion.

Actual performance results on any project, good or bad, are, in effect, "sunk costs." Such costs represent what the project has actually achieved in performance. Thus, any improvements in performance must come from the future work, tasks that lie ahead of the project's status date. Earned Value allows the project manager to accurately quantify the cost and schedule performance achieved to date. And if the results achieved to date are less than those desired by management, the project can exert a more aggressive posture to influence future work.

Earned Value, because it allows the project to accurately quantity the value of the work already achieved, also allows the project to quantify the value of the future work in order to stay within the objectives set for the project by management. The single most respected method of forecasting the final cost results is to assume that the project will continue at its established cost efficiency rate—that it will get no better or no worse.

Step 10: You must manage the defined scope baseline by approving or rejecting all changes, and then incorporating the approved changes into the project baseline in a timely manner (EVM Criterion #28).

The project performance measurement baseline which was initially put into place at the start of the project is only as good as the management of all proposed new changes to the baseline for the duration of the project. Performance baselines quickly become invalid simply by failing to incorporate changes into the approved baseline, with the addition or deletion of added work scope.

All new requested changes on the project must be quickly addressed, either by approving such changes, or by rejecting them. Thus, all project managers should have sufficient authority to say "no."

In order for the initial baseline to remain valid, each and every change must be controlled. Maintaining an approved baseline can be as challenging as the definition of the project scope at the start of the project.

IN SUMMARY

Earned Value Project Management is not a difficult concept to understand or to employ. It is certainly not as complicated a process as some have made it to be over the years. The authors have concluded that effective Earned Value can be achieved by simply applying the ten simple steps as listed above. These ten steps can be applied to any project, of any size, in any industry. Earned Value is for the masses.

As you read over these ten suggested steps, we hope you come to the conclusion that employing Earned Value Project Management consists of nothing more than simply following fundamental best project management processes. As was stated nicely by a gentleman from the United Kingdom:

> Whilst you can practice good project management without EVM, you cannot practice EVM effectively without good project management.[1]

We could not have stated it better.

---

[1] Steve Crowther, British Aerospace, *Best of British: Earned Value Management*, appearing in the Magazine of the Association for Project Management, London, June 1999, page 13.

14

FULFILL YOUR FIDUCIARY DUTY AND COMPLY WITH SARBANES-OXLEY

ACCORDING TO BLACK'S LAW DICTIONARY, A FIDUCIARY IS:

A person having a duty, created by his undertaking, to act primarily for another's benefit in matters connected with such undertaking. The term . . . includes such offices or relations as those of an attorney at law, a guardian, executor, or broker, a director of a corporation, and a public officer.

THE SECURITIES ACT OF 1933 STATES:

Any person who – (2) offers or sells a security . . . which includes an untrue statement of a material fact or omits to state a material fact necessary in order to make the statements, in the light of the circumstances under which they were made, not misleading . . . shall be liable to the person purchasing such security from him, who may sue either at law or in equity in any court of competent jurisdiction, to recover the consideration paid for such security with interest thereon . . .

THE SARBANES-OXLEY ACT OF 2002 STATES:

SEC. 906. **Corporate Responsibility for Financial Reports**

Certification of Periodic Financial Reports—Each periodic report containing financial statements filed by an insurer with the Security Exchange Commission . . . shall be accompanied by a written statement by the chief executive officer and chief financial officer . . .

Criminal Penalties—Whoever . . . willfully certifies any statement as set forth . . . knowing that the periodic report accompanying the statement does not comport with all the requirements set forth in this section shall be fined not more than $5,000,000, or imprisoned not more than 20 years, or both.

Well, this section of the Sarbanes-Oxley Act of 2002 will certainly get your attention, particularly if your job title happens to be "chief executive officer." No more excuses like: "I know nothing about accounting" or "I was a bad student" or "I hire accountants to do that stuff." There is now too much at stake: penalties and even jail time!

The second edition of this book was released in the summer of 2000. A lot has happened to Corporate America since that time, particularly affecting publicly traded companies. As the authors stated in their second edition—which, remember, was one year before the Enron (et al.) messes hit the headlines, and two years before the Sarbanes-Oxley Act of 2002 came into effect:

> It has been the contention of the authors that there is often a duty created on the part of selected corporate officers and government officials, based on the offices they hold. That duty would require them to employ all proven management tools in the performance of their jobs, including, and in particular, EVM . . . .
>
> This duty would extend to project managers, the chief financial officers, chief information officers, and certainly chief executive officers of most corporations.
>
> These individuals can in part meet this fiduciary duty by employing a simple but effective form of Earned Value in the management of their projects.[1]

With the revelations coming from Enron, WorldCom, Tyco, and others, it is obvious that certain executives in the corporate world did not take seriously their fiduciary duties to the public. Whether the passage of the Sarbanes-Oxley Act of 2002 will make a difference remains to be seen. We remain convinced that, if performance on projects can have a "material" impact on the profit or loss of any company, at least a simple form of Earned Value Management must be—repeat: must be—employed to accurately predict the final costs of these projects. To do otherwise is to ignore the impressive empirical work done by the Department of Defense over the past four decades.

PUTTING A POSITIVE SPIN ON FINANCIAL REPORTS, OR "COOKING THE BOOKS"

There are numerous ways corporate executives can put a "positive spin" on their financial reporting to the public. Some methods are legal, others are blatantly illegal. The

---

1 Fleming and Koppelman, *Earned Value Project Management* (Newtown Square, PA: Project Management Institute, Second Edition, 2000).

illegal ways are now being addressed by a number of dedicated groups, including the United States Congress, the Securities and Exchange Commission (SEC), Department of Justice, state attorneys general, and others. With the President's signature on the Sarbanes-Oxley Act of 2002 (SOX), the spotlight is now on every CFO <u>and</u> CEO to give an accurate portrayal of their true financial condition. To review this mandate, we need to understand what is required by SOX. To quote directly from the Act:

> . . . The Commission shall, by rule, require, for each company filing periodic reports under section 13(a) or 15(d) of the Securities Exchange Act of 1934 . . . that the principal executive officer or officers and the principal financial officer or officers, or persons performing similar functions, certify in each annual or quarterly report filed or submitted under either section of such act that

> 1. The signing officer has reviewed the report;
> 2. Based on the officer's knowledge, the report does not contain any untrue statements of a material fact or omit to state a material fact necessary in order to make the statements made, in light of the circumstances under which such statements were made, not misleading;
> 3. Based on such officer's knowledge, the financial statements, and other financial information included in the report, fairly present in all material respects the financial condition and results of operations of the issuer as of, and for, the periods presented in the report;
> 4. The signing officers
>   A) are responsible for establishing and maintaining internal controls;
>   B) have designed such internal controls to ensure that material information relating to the issuer and its consolidated subsidiaries is known to such officers by others within those entities, particularly during the period in which the periodic reports are being prepared. . . .[2]

However, there still may be a legal way for corporate executives to effectively cook their books and put a positive spin on questionable long-term project performance. Perhaps it should not be legal because, at best, the practice is highly questionable. This approach is to ignore the early performance indicators on major new projects (capital, software, etc.), which often span several fiscal years. Projects could be directed to wait until all actual funds have been expended in order to predict a final overrun of costs. Not a good course of action to take. By then, it could be too late to recover. Is this a material issue for a public company? The authors are of the belief that it could be.

---

2 Sarbanes-Oxley Act of 2002, Sec. 302 Corporate Responsibility for Financial Reports.

Some obvious examples of major capital investment projects that could impact the firm's bottom line would be: the construction of a new corporate headquarters, an IT outsourcing transition project, a commitment for a new corporate enterprise resource planning (ERP) system, construction of a new factory, the decommissioning of a nuclear reactor, etc. These are just a few examples of multi-year projects that, if performed poorly, could have a "material" effect on the profitability of any organization, and, of course, the resulting annual bonuses of their managing executives.

The prevailing attitude of many firms would seem to be that, whenever they make a long-term commitment to fund a major new project that spans multiple fiscal years, there is no legal obligation to ascertain, and report on, both the current status and final required costs. A recent best-selling book on the Enron affair perhaps typifies this type of corporate attitude:

... the truth is that there is no entirely satisfactory way to account for complex deals that extend over several years.[3]

Respectfully, the authors disagree with this assertion. There is a method, a proven and accurate method, to measure the current status and estimate final required costs on major capital projects that span multiple fiscal years. That technique is called Earned Value Management (EVM). It is a concept originated more than 100 years ago by industrial engineers as they measured cost results in American factories. Furthermore, the U.S. Department of Defense (DOD) has successfully employed this technique for the past 40 years on its major systems acquisitions. Earned Value will not prevent an overrun. But it will tell executive management that an overrun of costs is likely—even highly probable. And it will provide a prediction of final required cost estimates within a range of values. These predictions should not be ignored by management.

Private industry has been slow to adopt this proven technique to manage major projects for a variety of reasons, some valid and some frankly self-serving. Perhaps it is sometimes advantageous not to know the true conditions and final costs of major projects, particularly if such public knowledge would have an adverse impact on year-end corporate revenues, the price of company stock, and resulting executive bonuses. But is there a higher fiduciary duty to report the true conditions, and does the Sarbanes-Oxley Act make it mandatory to report the condition to the public? Perhaps.

Focusing on Value of the Work Accomplished (i.e., the Earned Value)

Today, most corporate financial executives likely measure their cost performance on projects by using only two dimensions: the projected costs versus the actual costs. Thus, if all the allotted budget is spent, they are right on target. If less is spent, then

---

3 Peter C. Fusaro, and Ross M. Miller, *What Went Wrong at Enron* (Hoboken, NJ: John Wiley & Sons, Inc. 2002), page 34.

there is an underrun of costs. If more is spent, then an overrun exists. To the authors, this is not *cost* performance, but rather *funding* performance. What is missing is the measurement of the "value of the work" performed for the monies spent. We call this Earned Value Management (EVM).

Let us discuss an example of a project with assumed numbers. If a given project's budget was set at $100 million and only $90 million was spent, but it had only accomplished $80 million in work value, what should you call this condition? Respectfully, we feel that it should be called what it is: a $10 million overrun of costs. The missing third dimension on most corporate scorecards today is a measure of the value of the physical work accomplished for the monies being spent.

The Sarbanes-Oxley Act raises a question: In this scenario, would a $10-million-dollar overrun of total project costs be considered a "material" financial issue to a company? Perhaps. It all depends on the impact that a $100-million-dollar project might have on a given firm's financial status. This will vary from company to company.

A century ago, the industrial engineers led by the father of scientific management, Frederick W. Taylor, were correct in their assessment of what represented "true" cost performance in their factories. Cost performance represented the difference between the accomplished work (represented by earned standards) versus the actual costs incurred. It was not the difference between the planned costs and actual costs. Today, many corporate executives still do not grasp this simple concept, and are content to focus on projected costs versus actual costs, calling this their "cost performance."

The early industrial engineers created what they called their "planned standards" representing two components: the authorized physical work and the authorized budget for the authorized work. Planned standards simply represented their baseline plan. It was only when such work was completed that they could determine their true cost performance.

Thus, a century ago, Taylor et al. focused on the "earned standards" that represented physically accomplished work, plus its original authorized budget. They then compared the earned standards against the actual hours expended to determine their true "cost performance." It worked then. It can work now.

Earned Value Management (EVM)

The Department of Defense (DOD) was the first group in modern times to adopt this early industrial engineering factory concept for use in the management of projects.

In 1962, the DOD had a major capital project called the "Minuteman Missile." This project employed hundreds of people, cost millions of taxpayer dollars, and spanned several fiscal years. The U.S. Air Force project staff recognized their duty to the taxpayers to report the accurate financial status of this major project. They adopted this simple industrial engineering concept to their one-time-only major project, and, to their surprise, earned value measurement worked for them.

They broke the project into discrete pieces and separate tasks. They then added an authorized budget to each task. When each task was completed, they credited its completion and "earned" its original authorized budget. They compared this completed work, which they called the "Earned Value," against the costs spent to accomplish this work. The result gave them an accurate reflection of their true cost performance, available with no other project management technique.

Since 1977, the DOD's Pentagon has kept track of the performance of hundreds of projects, reflecting actual performance—the good, the bad, and the downright ugly. In total, they have now analyzed more than 800 separate projects. Individual company names have been kept private. The results have been spectacular: they have been able to demonstrate the predictability of final project cost requirements based on earned value data. These studies have also supported the belief that early cost overruns are rarely (if ever) offset by subsequent performance. Thus, overseeing early cost performance is vital to successful project cost management.

With EVM, the single most important tracking metric is called the "CPI" or the "cost performance index." The CPI represents that delicate relationship between the Earned Value accomplished, divided by the Actual Costs spent to accomplish the work. The cumulative CPI has been demonstrated to be a stable predictor of final costs at completion, even as early as the 20-percent completion point of any project.

The CPI can thus be used to accurately predict the final cost position of any project, even one spanning multiple years in performance. If the cumulative CPI registers a .80 performance value, it means that for every dollar that was spent, only 80 cents of value was earned. This can also be called an overrun. Early overruns are very serious indicators, as subsequent performance rarely ever recovers early overruns.

Most importantly, the cumulative CPI can be used (starting at the 20-percent completion point) to accurately forecast the final project cost results with amazing precision. For example, if a five-year $100-million-dollar project has experienced a cumulative CPI of only .80 at the 20-percent completion point, one can forecast the final cost results within a finite range.

Simply take the $100 million project budget and divide it by the CPI of .80. Immediately, the forecast costs of the final project would be about $125 million, or a cost overrun of approximately $25 million. How accurate is this forecast? Empirical studies support the position that it will be accurate within plus or minus 10 percent from the $125 million final costs.

Important point: The $100 million authorized budget would not be adequate to finish this project. This raises a Sarbanes-Oxley question: Would a $25 million projected overrun of final costs constitute a "material" financial issue? Perhaps.

Analytical scientific research by the DOD supports the use of this doctrine.

Financial Reporting Today

There is no valid reason today why all companies cannot accurately measure and report on the true cost position of all their capital projects by employing a simple form of Earned Value Management. This technique should also be applied to perhaps the most challenging jobs we face today, the management of software projects. Using Earned Value to manage long-term capital projects is essential to meeting the corporate executives' fiduciary duty to their shareholders.

The Sarbanes-Oxley Act was signed into law on July 30, 2002. It would seem to reinforce the contention that there is a fiduciary duty placed on corporate executives to tell the whole truth when reporting the financial condition of their companies. This duty would include an accurate assessment of the true current status, and the final required costs to finish all multi-year projects.

Employing a simple form of Earned Value Management can help corporate executives meet this fiduciary duty, and, in particular, their legal obligations under the Sarbanes-Oxley Act.

THE EARNED VALUE MANAGEMENT (EVM) SYSTEM CRITERIA

FOUR DECADES AGO, IN 1965, the United States Air Force defined what it required from private industry in order to employ Earned Value in the performance of government-funded projects. The result was a document entitled the Cost Schedule Planning and Control Specification (C/SPCS). It contained 35 specific criteria to be employed on all major projects. Two years later, the Department of Defense (DOD) formally accepted these same criteria with a slightly changed title—the Cost/Schedule Control Systems Criteria (C/SCSC). Any firm wanting to perform on new projects for the DOD had to comply with these 35 standards as a precondition to winning a new contract. C/SCSC was to be consistently applied to DOD projects.

Several years later, in 1995, at a formal meeting of the Management Systems Subcommittee of the National Defense Industrial Association (NDIA), the NDIA subcommittee accepted the task of examining and rewriting the DOD's criteria for Earned Value Management. Their objective was to make the criteria more user-friendly, more compatible with the needs of private industry.

Over the next eighteen months, the NDIA subcommittee met, discussed and established their own reworded version of the DOD's Cost/Schedule Control Systems Criteria. When released, the new industry document was titled the Earned Value Management (EVM) System Criteria and contained just 32 criteria, three less than the original C/SCSC. On December 14, 1996, to the surprise of many, the Under Secretary of Defense for Acquisition & Technology accepted the NDIA industry rewrite of the earned value management criteria verbatim.

The significance of this change was not in the revised wording of the criteria, or in the minimal reduction in their number from 35 to 32. Rather, the critical difference was in the "attitude" towards the earned value management process. In 1997, there was a shifting of the earned value management (EVM) system ownership from that of a United States Government requirement, to that of ownership by private

191

industry. Private industry would now embrace the earned value management technique not because it was a government mandate, but because it represented a set of "best practice" processes available to project managers in the private sector.

One additional event deserves mention. The NDIA subcommittee continued its effort of converting Earned Value Management into a broad-based international best practice. The NDIA subcommittee requested that the revised earned value management criteria be formally issued as an American National Standards Institute-Electronic Industries Association standard. In July 1998, the NSIA/EIA Standard 748 was formally published. Then, on August 17, 1999, the DOD accepted the ANSI/EIA 748 standard for applications to all DOD projects, formally replacing the C/SCSC.

What follows is a verbatim quote of the 32 industry Earned Value Management (EVM) System criteria, followed by the author's "unofficial" interpretation of each criterion. Please understand that the narrative interpretation that follows each criterion represents the authors' views, and only their views. It is provided for your general guidance only.

The thirty-two EVM criteria are divided into five logical major groups.

○   ○   ○

GROUP 1—ORGANIZATION CRITERIA (FIVE)

Purpose of the Organization Criteria:
- To require that the entire project scope be defined, including make-versus-buy choices.
- To require an integrated project baseline (scope + schedule + costs) with use of a WBS.
- To establish management control responsibilities with use of Control Account Plans (CAPs).
- To assign performance responsibilities for all CAPS to the functional organizations.

Problems with the Organization Criteria:
- Functional organizations starting work with an inadequate project scope definition.
- Rejection of the project's WBS by functional "fiefdoms."

The first group of criteria deals with the requirement for any new project to be completely defined and planned, prior to starting performance of the work. Today, we would typically call this effort defining the scope of the project. Think about it: Earned value measurement cannot take place without some definition of what constitutes 100% of the project.

This effort starts with a requirement to specify all of the assumed project deliverables to be accomplished. Such definitions are best accomplished with use of a Work Breakdown Structure (WBS) in order to completely capture all of the proposed work. The WBS provides for the integration of all project tasks, together with their estimated resources, with each task planned within a specific time frame for performance. Once defined, one individual or specific organization must be held accountable for the performance of each of the defined project tasks.

Any comprehensive definition of project scope must also include the make-versus-buy choices for all segments of work, isolating in particular that effort that must be procured from other (outside) organizations. Managers responsible for the authorization and control of indirect costs must also be identified.

The major problems in meeting these initial criteria have been an inadequate definition of the total project scope, a poor definition of make-versus-buy, and the rejection of the project manager's WBS by selected functional organizations.

EVM Criterion # 1:
Define the authorized work elements for the program. A Work Breakdown Structure (WBS), tailored for effective internal management control, is commonly used in this process.

The first criterion requires that any new project be defined, to the extent possible, before starting the work. A Work Breakdown Structure (WBS) is typically recommended (required) for use in this process. The WBS is a product-oriented hierarchical family tree that describes the major segments of the project and is used to specify all deliverables: hardware, software, services, and data. The WBS is used to specify all of the assumed work, and is perhaps the single most important requirement to the successful employment of Earned Value. Each level of the WBS provides a progressively more detailed description of the work to be accomplished.

All major line items and project deliverables must be identified somewhere within the WBS. All functional organizations must then work within the scope defined by the project's WBS. Any effort requested of the project that cannot be identified within the WBS is potentially out of scope effort, and authorization is needed in order to accommodate such work.

The project WBS allows management to concentrate on logical groupings of project work, the sub-projects, for measurement of performance. At the lowest selected levels of specified WBS elements will be placed Control Account Plans (CAPs), which are the points at which earned value performance and management control will take place for the project. A CAP can best be thought of as a sub-project, a project team, an integrated product development team, or perhaps simply as a point of project management responsibility and control.

All project management CAPs must contain four elements in order to be viable:

the authorized scope of work for the CAP; a specified time frame for performance; an authorized budget; and a specific individual or organization to be held accountable for performance of each CAP. The summation of all specified CAPs, plus management reserves if any, will constitute the total project.

EVM Criterion # 2:
Identify the program organizational structure including the major subcontractors responsible for accomplishing the authorized work, and define the organizational elements in which work will be planned and controlled.

This criterion requires that all tasks defined within the project's WBS be identified and assigned to a specific (internal) functional organization for performance, or designated as an external buy item as a part of the project's make-versus-buy process. The project's WBS is related against the company organizational breakdown structure (OBS) to allow for the assignment of each of the project's tasks to a specific organization for performance. This process will produce what is typically called a project responsibility assignment matrix (RAM).

All tasks identified in the project WBS must be assigned to a specific organization for performance, including that work that will be procured from outside of the company; that is, contracted or subcontracted to another company for performance. This criterion requires that the project make specific organization assignments of all identified work.

EVM Criterion # 3:
Provide for the integration of the company's planning, scheduling, budgeting, work authorization and cost accumulation processes with each other, and as appropriate, the program work breakdown structure and the program organizational structure.

The intent of this criterion is to require the integration the project's management process with both the way the work is defined with use of the WBS, and the functional organizations that will be performing the effort. This requirement specifies that projects employ a single management control system with a common information database flowing though the contractor's functional disciplines. The Control Account Plans (CAPs), which will have tasks allocated to specific functions, provide the basis for organizations to perform with a common database.

Companies, particularly those with large and well-established functional organizations, often have had difficulty satisfying this criterion. Typically, each of the various functional organizations has its own performance agendas, and each wants to manage its own affairs in its own particular manner. Sometimes functional goals can be at odds with project goals. Master scheduling, cost estimating, work authorizations, budgeting, cost accumulation, and each of the various functions must work within a single database as specified by the project WBS.

The Control Account Plan (CAP) provides the fundamental building block for earned value performance management, and makes it possible for the various functional units to work from a common database. The defined CAPs (subprojects) allow projects to monitor performance from two perspectives: by WBS, to determine the project results, or by OBS, to focus on functional results.

EVM Criterion # 4:

Identify the company organization or function responsible for controlling overhead (indirect costs).

The United States Government acquisition personnel are acutely aware that costs associated with any given project contain both direct and indirect costs. While there is generally minimal controversy over the application of direct project costs, there is much concern over both the content and the proportionate application of indirect costs applied to a given project. Thus, four (#s 4, 13, 19, 24) of the 32 criteria deal specifically with the management of contractor indirect costs . . . even though any given project manager will have minimal (likely zero) influence over such costs. That is why they are called indirect costs; because they are non-specific to any given project. Only the very senior corporate executive managers, as opposed to any give project manager, can influence indirect costs.

This criterion requires that all indirect costs be clearly defined as a category, and responsibilities formally documented. Those individual managers who are responsible for authorizing and controlling overheads must be identified, generally with some type of delegation of authority that stipulates the limits of such authority. Such activities may be centralized or decentralized, as long as there is consistency in application, and a clear assignment of responsibility.

The allocation of indirect costs to specific projects must be consistent for all projects in the organization, and defined somewhere in procedural documentation. Such costs may not be arbitrarily applied to a given project, inconsistent with such procedures. The government is particularly sensitive to the consistency of application of such costs as they are allotted to different types of contracts within a firm's cost-reimbursable versus fixed-price contract base. Their concern is that contractors could be tempted to try and maximize profits on their fixed price work, at the expense of cost (open-ended) reimbursable contracts.

EVM Criterion # 5:

Provide for integration of the program work breakdown structure and the program organizational structure in a manner that permits cost and schedule performance measurement by elements of either or both structures as needed.

Four (# 5, 17, 18, 25) of the 32 criteria deal with the same issue of forming a project baseline that can be measured from two perspectives: by the project's WBS, and by the functional organization's OBS. This is the first of the four criteria dealing with this single issue.

This requirement is met by forming Control Account Plans (CAPs), which can be summarized by either the project WBS or by the functional OBS. With the use of multi-functional project team CAPs, the individual Work Package tasks within each CAP must be identified to a specific function in order to be able to satisfy the requirement for an OBS roll-up.

○ ○ ○

GROUP 2—PLANNING, SCHEDULING, AND BUDGETING CRITERIA (TEN)

Purpose of the Planning, Scheduling, and Budgeting Criteria:
- To require the employment of a formal planning, scheduling and budgeting system.
- To require the formation of a project baseline which allows performance to be measured.

Problems with the Planning, Scheduling, and Budgeting Criteria:
- Lack of discipline in the functional organizations.
- Project baselines that are either "front-loaded" or "rubber."

In the second major grouping of the criteria, there are ten requirements, the single largest group, which must be satisfied. Here it must be demonstrated that the project employs a single, integrated management control system within which it can implement a formal project performance baseline for all of the defined project scope. Each project must be authorized by management, planned, scheduled, the resources estimated, then formally budgeted, and all work performed within the project's formal baseline.

Should the project have set aside any management (or contingency) reserves, such values must be strictly controlled by the project manager (or other senior management) and isolated outside the project's performance baseline. All such reserves subsequently released by the project must be formally transferred into the project's performance baseline. This group requires that a formal management control system be in place for the full life cycle of the project.

There have been several problems experienced with this group of criteria. One of the most common has resulted from a general lack of discipline by the functional organizations supporting the authorized project. It is not possible to measure project performance when the functional departments doing the work are casual about keeping records of their own performance.

Other problems have been experienced with the control of authorized budget for authorized work in the performance baseline. The inadvertent (sometimes intentional) front-end placement of budget without a corresponding level of work scope, called baseline "front-loading," and/or the inadvertent (sometimes intentional) shifting of authorized budget into earlier periods, without a corresponding shift of authorized work, called "rubber base-lining," have created opportunities for any company wanting to "game" the earned value management process.

Earned Value Management requires formality and organizational discipline from those performing the work on a project, or the measurement of actual performance will be questionable.

EVM Criterion # 6:
Schedule the authorized work in a manner that describes the sequence of work and identifies the significant task interdependencies required to meet the requirements of the program.

This criterion requires that contractors have in place a formal scheduling system to support their projects. In particular, the organizations must issue a comprehensive project master schedule (PMS) for each project that sets forth all critical milestones and key tasks representing the project. The project's Planned Value will be determined by compliance with this criterion.

On the larger and more complex projects, and in organizations where there are numerous projects being performed simultaneously, the project master schedules (PMS) may be reinforced by subordinate schedules as appropriate, often in the form of detailed functional schedules. However, all schedules within the enterprise must be in concert with the requirements contained in each project's PMS.

The key issue is the traceability and consistency of the key program milestones specified in each PMS. Functions must schedule their work in accordance with the requirements defined in project master schedules. The schedules must portray the logical sequence of all work to be accomplished, and each Control Account Plan (CAP) must contain the baseline start and stop dates, from which project completion dates can be forecast.

Nowhere in any of the criteria do they specify that a particular scheduling technique must be used. However, the criteria do require that contractor scheduling systems reflect interdependencies and constraints. Because only critical path method (CPM) schedules show such relationships, a strict interpretation of this criterion might suggest that Earned Value Management requires the use of some type of a CPM network schedules.

EVM Criterion # 7:
Identify physical products, milestones, technical performance goals, or other indicators that will be used to measure progress.

This criterion is related to the one above, and requires that projects have the ability to measure their physical performance, as defined within the tasks displayed in project schedules. Just what constitutes the physical completion of the work is the central issue.

Projects must specify what physical products, outputs, metrics, milestones, and technical performance indicators will be used to measure actual work accomplished against the schedule plan. How the Earned Value will actually be measured is the requirement of this criterion.

There are numerous methods with which to measure physical work accomplishment, and the projects must specify which of these methods they will employ.

EVM Criterion # 8:

Establish and maintain a time-phased budget baseline, at the control account level, against which program performance can be measured. Initial budgets established for performance measurement will be based on either internal management goals or the external customer negotiated target cost including estimates for authorized but undefinitized work. Budget for long-term efforts may be held in higher-level accounts until an appropriate time for allocation at the control account level. On government contracts, if an overtarget baseline is used for performance measurement reporting purposes, prior notification must be provided to the customer.

When this criterion specifies "a time-phased budget baseline," it is imposing a precise term in Earned Value Management called the "Performance Measurement Baseline (PMB)." It is important that this term be fully understood. We are discussing the project baseline against which performance will be measured.

The PMB is defined aptly in the industry ANSI/EIA 748 standard for Earned Value Management Systems as:

> PERFORMANCE MEASUREMENT BASELINE - The total time-phased budget plan against which program performance is measured. It is the schedule for expenditure of the resources allocated to accomplish program scope and schedule objectives, and is formed by the budgets assigned to control accounts and applicable indirect budgets. The Performance Measurement Baseline also includes budget for future effort assigned to higher Work Breakdown Structure levels (summary level planning packages) plus any undistributed budget. Management Reserve is not included in the baseline as it is not yet designated for specific work scope.

The project's performance measurement baseline is made up of the sum of the project's subprojects or Control Account Plans (CAPs). Management reserve (MR) is considered to be outside of the PMB, until specifically authorized and allocated for specific work within the PMB.

The PMB must include all authorized project work. Authorized, but not yet definitized project work may exist in various soft forms: authorized, but not yet estimated; authorized, but not yet proposed; authorized, but not yet negotiated; negotiated, but not yet covered by a change order; etc. However, in order to accurately measure performance, all work being done by the project must be included in the PMB.

On projects that run for a long duration, it may be inadvisable or even impossible to budget the long-term effort down to the specific CAP level. In such cases, long-term budgets may be allocated and kept at the higher level WBS elements, in what are called "planning packages." This is simply the "rolling-wave" budgeting technique. It is critical to the integrity of EVM systems that the long-term budgets be tightly controlled to prevent the commingling with the short-term fully budgeted CAPs.

Generally, Control Account Plans (CAPs) should be opened consistent with, not before, their scheduled start date. If a situation calls for starting work on a CAP prior to the planned start date, such work must be authorized by the project manager on an exception basis. The across-the-board initiation of work earlier than planned could adversely impact the authorized funding and distort the performance measurement. The concern is that overruns might be disguised if budgets were allowed to be shifted back and forth casually between time periods.

This criterion also requires that indirect project costs be allocated into the PMB, but not necessarily within the individual CAP budgets. There is no requirement that indirect costs be included within each CAP. However, if left outside of individual CAP budgets, indirect costs must be allocated in some way so that the full value of the PMB includes both the direct and indirect costs. Some projects accomplish this by creating a separate CAP covering indirect costs.

The term "over target baseline" (or OTB) as used in the criterion is a kind, gentle and ambiguous term for describing an "overrun." For some reason, EVM practitioners, or more likely their managers, have always been shy about calling an overrun what it is. The final sentence of this criterion merely suggests that if the project sets its budgets to an OTB or overrun, they should only do so with the blessing and concurrence of the customer and/or management. We would certainly hope so.

All projects require a well-defined and formally controlled PMB in order to measure earned value performance for the life of the project.

EVM Criterion # 9:
Establish budgets for authorized work with identification of significant cost elements (labor, material, etc.) as needed for internal management and for control of subcontractors.

The total project must be budgeted, and such budgets must reflect the type of costs associated with the budgets. Costs that must be identified include direct labor;

indirect burdens; various types of procured items, including materials, contracts, or subcontracts; and all other direct costs, such as travel, computer, etc. Such budgeted items must be formally controlled according to internal company procedures. The functional organizations receiving the budgets must be identified.

Budgeted values must represent the project costs that have been negotiated. If there have been authorized changes that have not yet been negotiated, the budgets must include an estimated value for all such authorized work. Project budgets must be issued in a formal, documented and controlled manner down to the various Control Account Plan (CAP) levels.

EVM Criterion # 10:
To the extent that it is practical to identify the authorized work in discrete work packages, establish budgets for this work in terms of dollars, hours, or other measurable units. Where the entire control account is not subdivided into work packages, identify the long-term effort in larger planning packages for budgeting and scheduling purposes.

Many of the 32 criteria are related to other criteria, and often will expand on the requirements imposed in other criteria. This one further expands the requirements for a definitive Performance Measurement Baseline (PMB). Here, discrete work packages must be created for short-term tasks to the greatest extent possible, followed by larger planning packages in the long-term. All budgets must be time-phased over the full life of the project.

Under this criterion, the project must demonstrate that it has established discrete budgets to the greatest extent possible in a way that represents the manner in which the work will be performed. All effort shown in long-term, time-phased planning packages will subsequently become definitive work packages as they approach the short-term periods for performance. This criterion had previously specified that discrete work packages must be of relatively short duration, but that wording was dropped in the industry revision of the criteria.

All work packages must contain measurable metrics to allow for the objective measurement of work accomplishment. The project must be able to differentiate between short-term work packages and long-term planning packages so that specified work and budget cannot be indiscriminately commingled.

All direct budgets must be expressed in measurable units—for example, hours, dollars, standards, or other types of measurable costs. All work package tasks must be assigned to a specific function for performance.

EVM Criterion # 11:
Provide that the sum of all work package budgets, plus planning package budgets within a control account, equals the control account budget.

This criterion simply requires that the sum of all work package budgets and planning package budgets within any Control Account Plan (CAP) must equal the authorized budget for the CAP. All authorized budgets must relate to a specific statement of work to be performed, except for management reserve budgets, which are held outside of the performance baseline.

EVM Criterion # 12:

Identify and control level of effort activity by time-phased budgets established for this purpose. Only that effort which is unmeasurable or for which measurement is impractical may be classified as level of effort.

This criterion allows for earned value measurement by use of level of effort, but only for that work that cannot be measured with either discrete or apportioned means. Of the three types of work tasks to be measured with Earned Value (discrete, apportioned, or level of effort), level of effort (LOE) measurement is, without question, the least desirable.

LOE tasks must be identified, time-phased, and kept to a minimum. With LOE tasks, the Earned Value accomplished always equals the Planned Value, irrespective of whether any work was done. In effect, LOE measures nothing but the passage of time, not physical work accomplishment.

This criterion requires that LOE budgets, when used, be formally budgeted and controlled as with any other effort. Neither budget nor Earned Value for the LOE tasks may be shifted independently to the left or right, for this would distort the reported status of a project.

Examples of typical LOE effort are the project manager and staff, a field support engineer, guard services, scheduling, help information desks, etc., each of which performs activities more related to time passage than to physical output. Certain tasks may be justifiable as LOE, but they must be kept to a minimum to prevent the distortion of measured performance.

EVM Criterion # 13:

Establish overhead budgets for each significant organizational component of the company for expenses that will become indirect costs. Reflect in the program budgets, at the appropriate level, the amounts in overhead pools that are planned to be allocated to the program as indirect costs.

Most firms will have some type of indirect expenses allocated over the direct costs. Larger firms may have several categories or pools of indirect costs. Typical categories of such pools might be: engineering burden, manufacturing burden, material burden, general and administrative expenses, and sometimes even a special study or partial field burdens.

Each company must specify the number of indirect pools that it will have, the types of costs and methods for controlling each of their independent burden centers. Such costs must be tightly managed with each of the respective pools to preclude the possibility of the manipulation of such costs by a contractor. Any changes to either the direct bases or burden pools must be accommodated according to formal internal procedures.

Lastly, in the event that burdens are not applied to individual control accounts, and the criteria do not require application of burdens to Control Account Plan budgets, the contractor must indicate at what point in the WBS and organizational summaries such burden costs will be added.

EVM Criterion # 14:
Identify management reserves and undistributed budget.

This criterion deals with two categories of project costs: Management Reserve (MR) and Undistributed Budget (UB).

Management Reserve (MR), sometimes called contingency funds, represents an amount of the total budget baseline that is withheld by the project manager to cover the unknowns, the bad things that are sure to happen but that cannot be specified with certainty. MR funds are held outside of the project's Performance Measurement Baseline (PMB).

All MR must be tightly controlled and every transaction that either adds to or takes from the MR must be documented and approved by the project manager. MR is, by definition, outside the PMB. Therefore, no management reserve may be included in either control account budgets or organizational budgets. MR is typically expected to be consumed during performance of the project. If unconsumed at the conclusion of the project, MR becomes underrun.

Undistributed Budget (UB) represents funds applicable to project work that has not yet been placed into authorized budgets. Undistributed Budget is, by definition, a part of the project's PMB, as contrasted with Management Reserve, which is outside the PMB until a management decision is made to transfer some portion of it into the PMB.

Undistributed budget must be allotted against a specific statement of work, and must be time-phased and tightly controlled so as to not be used for other work that could mask an overrun. Typically, there are three situations in which undistributed budget may be used:

1. For authorized project changes not yet negotiated, where interim budgets are kept at a higher WBS level until negotiations are concluded;
2. For negotiated changes not yet budgeted into Control Account Plans;
3. For long-term tasks for which it might be pointless to define budgets down to the detailed control account level at the present time (using the rolling-wave budgeting concept).

EVM Criterion # 15:

Provide that the program target cost goal is reconciled with the sum of all internal program budgets and management reserves.

This criterion has its focus on the ability to account for all project funds. Likely it is a carryover from the time when large cost reimbursable-type contracts were commonplace and certain unscrupulous contractors would actually overbudget the total funds on a contract, thus assuring a cost overrun of the project. Today, with the electronic spreadsheets available to us, the utility of this criterion is perhaps debatable.

Contractors must demonstrate that they have not exceeded the total project costs with their approved budgets, and must have such control processes documented with internal company procedures.

o o o

GROUP 3—ACCOUNTING CRITERIA (SIX)

Purpose of the Accounting Criteria:
- Require that all projects be given accurate and timely cost reports.
- Require that project costs be recorded as consumed or incurred.
- Require accounting systems that can measure: Planned Value, Earned Value, and Actual Costs.

Problems with the Accounting Criteria:
- Difficulty of measuring earned value performance on the procured items.
- Difficulty of determining actual "price" and "usage" variances for work accomplished.

In this third grouping of criteria, the emphasis is on the recording of costs for the projects. It requires the segregation of all legitimate direct costs for a given project, together with the appropriate application of the indirect costs allocated to the project.

All firms doing business in the public sector will have some type of formal accounting system in place that will utilize generally acceptable standards of accounting. Such records must be available for a subsequent audit, if necessary.

However, earned value performance measurement also demands a unique accounting requirement. EVM projects must be able to record their direct costs at the point at which performance measurement takes place, typically within the Control Account Plans (CAPs). Such direct costs must be able to be summarized both through the project's Work Breakdown Structure and the company's functional organizations.

Earned Value also requires that a "performance measurement baseline" be created that permits the project to be able to measure the three dimensions of Earned

Value: the Planned Value versus the Earned Value to measure its schedule performance, and its Earned Value versus the Actual Costs to measure its cost performance.

The major difficulty in meeting this group of criteria has been with the synchronization of the Planned Value, Earned Value, and the actual or accrued costs for the work performed. Also, accounting for purchased materials and contracted or subcontracted work to other companies has always been a challenge, particularly when progress payments are given. Measuring the Planned Value against the Earned Value and Actual Costs for purchased items has represented the ultimate challenge for many projects.

EVM Criterion # 16:
Record direct costs in a manner consistent with the budgets in a formal system controlled by the general books of account.

This criterion requires that project managers be told what they have spent (in direct costs) on their project. Not an unreasonable requirement. However, because some organizations have been functionally dominated for so long a time, they sometimes have difficulty isolating their direct costs against specific projects. They may know how much "design time" has been spent in total for the entire organization, but cannot tell you how much by individual project.

To satisfy this criterion, companies must use generally acceptable methods of accounting for all direct project costs. Any conventional method of accounting may be used, but the preferred technique is the "applied direct cost" method, which simply means that direct resources are accounted for as they are used, or as consumed.

It is fairly easy to allocate direct labor costs with their corresponding labor burdens, and other direct costs to a specific project. However, costs for the procured items, because they are often consumed in different time periods, sometimes purchased for inventory, or may be transferred into or out of an inventory to another project, often provide the ultimate challenge to measure direct costs consumption on any given project.

The next two criteria are related and will be discussed together.

EVM Criterion # 17:
When a Work Breakdown Structure is used, summarize direct costs from control accounts into the work breakdown structure without allocation of a single control account to two or more work breakdown structure elements.

EVM Criterion # 18:
Summarize direct costs from the control accounts into the contractor's organizational elements without allocation of a single control account to two or more organizational elements.

Criteria 17 and 18 are related, the only difference between them being the direction of the summation of the detailed control account data. Number 17 requires the ability to sum control accounts upward into a WBS segregation to reach the total project costs. Criterion number 18 requires the summation of the same control accounts by the functional organization, to higher organizational levels—for example, engineering, manufacturing, quality, purchasing, testing, etc.—to also match the total project costs. Both summations will have the same grand total costs.

Both criteria prohibit the allocation of a single control account to more than one WBS element, or more than one functional organizational unit. Question: With the increased use of multi-functional project team control accounts, how do you satisfy these criteria without an allocation of costs within a single CAP? Answer: You identify specific work packages within the CAPs to specific organizations; thus the allocation of each work package is directly linked to specific organizational units.

EVM Criterion # 19:
Record all indirect costs that will be allocated to the contract.

Here is another criterion which addresses the issue of organizational control of indirect costs. This one requires that the contractor be in a position to apply indirect costs uniformly from the point at which they are incurred, perhaps allocated into specified pools if multiple pools are used, and ultimately charged against a contract or project. To satisfy this criterion, there must be a formal documented relationship between those persons who have responsibility for the control of indirect budgets, and those persons who are able to incur such costs against budgets.

Here the contractor must demonstrate that no manipulation of costs can take place with the allocation of indirect costs between projects, or contracts, and that both the commercial work and government contracts are treated consistently with the allotment of burden costs.

Lastly, the contractors must be in a position to show that the methods they use to allocate indirect costs to the final source are reasonable. Whether the indirect application method chosen calls for an annual financial plan with monthly adjustment of indirect actuals, or a constant rate applied monthly with adjustments at year's end for actuals incurred, the procedures governing such activity must be formally documented, followed, and fully auditable.

EVM Criterion # 20:
Identify unit costs, equivalent unit costs, or lot costs when needed.

The full life cycle of any new product generally consists of two distinct phases: one phase for the product development, and another to manufacture the item over and over again. The developmental phase is considered to be "non-recurring," the production effort "recurring."

However, even in the development of a new product, there will often be initial recurring costs involved, and it is a good practice to isolate the non-recurring from the recurring costs in order to be in a position to later estimate the repetitive costs for producing the new product. Under this criterion, the project must be able to distinguish between non-recurring (developmental) effort and recurring (production) effort.

This criterion also requires that the project be able to establish unit, equivalent unit, or lot costs for articles to be subsequently produced in the recurring phase. Unit costs may be developed by direct labor hours, direct labor dollars, material dollars, or the total unit price.

Unit costs may be established by isolating the individual costs for producing one unit, or by equivalents of several units, or by lot costs. Under lot costs, a block of selected units will be produced in a single batch at one time. The contractor must isolate the actual average costs of one unit in a given block to satisfy this criterion. The average cost of units in block 1 are then equated to the average unit costs in subsequent blocks 10, 100, 1,000, etc., to determine whether the costs per unit are being reduced, with the efficiency increasing, as the number of articles being manufactured increases.

EVM Criterion # 21:

For EVMS, the material accounting system will provide for:

1. *Accurate cost accumulation and assignment of costs to control accounts in a manner consistent with the budgets using recognized, acceptable, costing techniques.*
2. *Cost performance measurement at the point in time most suitable for the category of material involved, but no earlier than the time of progress payments or actual receipt of material.*
3. *Full accountability of all material purchased for the program, including the residual inventory.*

Without question, this criterion has been the most difficult for most contractors to satisfy. Certain contractors have actually lost the government's "approval" of their management control systems because they failed to satisfy the demands of this criterion.

The requirement is that all purchased materials be measured in the same accounting period, reflecting the Planned Value versus the Earned Value (to determine any schedule variance), and the Earned Value versus the Actual Costs (to reflect any cost variance). The problem with procurements is that these actions do not normally happen at the same point in time.

In order to buy something from another company, that something must be defined; that is, a technical procurement specification must be prepared. But a strict interpretation of item (2) in this criterion precludes giving credit for work in the preparation of a procurement specification, and yet, procurements cannot happen without specifications.

Another problem is that, when giving progress payments to suppliers, it is a common practice to have "withholds" or "retention" values withheld from the supplier until the entire job has been completed. Thus, there will sometimes be a discrepancy between the Earned Value credited as compared to the Actual Costs recorded, unless an accounting accrual is made for the withheld cost values—which results in an added task on the CAP manager.

Lastly, it is common practice for one project (the largest project) to buy materials for other projects and place such items into an inventory until used. Item (3) requires a full accountability for all residual inventory; not unreasonable, but a difficult task to satisfy.

One recommendation to all projects is to keep the purchased items versus in-house labor costs in separate Control Account Plans, or separate work packages. The two (make work versus buy work) do not mix well. Materials must be monitored and sometimes the Actual Costs adjusted by the CAP manager in order to reflect an accurate portrayal of the performance of materials.

o   o   o

GROUP 4—ANALYSIS CRITERIA (SIX)

Purpose of the Analysis Criteria:
- Require the "measurement" of actual performance against the authorized baseline.
- Require the "analysis" of actual performance against the authorized baseline.
- Require the "forecasting" of final results based on actual project performance.

Problems with the Analysis Criteria:
- Subjective (soft) measurement of physical performance.
- Excessive use of Level of Effort measurement in the performance baseline.
- Senior management's influence over the final forecast numbers.

This fourth grouping of the criteria imposes two distinct requirements on projects employing Earned Value. Both are critical to the proper employment of Earned Value Management.

First, the actual performance against the project baseline plan must be monitored, objectively measured, and accurately reported for the project. All significant variances from the project baseline plan must be analyzed, understood and corrective actions taken by management.

Second, based on the actual performance of the project against its own plan, the final required costs and time estimates to complete the project must be routinely forecast. Such forecasts must be timely in order for the project manager to be able to take corrective measures, and, thus, alter adverse projections.

The difficulties typically experienced with this criteria group often include too much "subjective" measurement of actual performance, thus allowing individuals to put a "positive spin" on adverse results, to artificially improve the progress being reported to senior management.

Also, projects that have an excessive use of "level of effort" tasks incorporated into their baseline will often experience distorted measurements when actual implementation levels fall short of their baseline plans. LOE results will often mask real problems being experienced, problems which need management attention.

Lastly, senior executive managers have been known to exert an unduly optimistic influence on both the reported actual project performance, and on the forecasts of final costs needed to complete given projects. It isn't necessarily that senior managers intend to deceive anyone. Rather, they simply often decree: "Make this overrun go away!" Sometimes it works. Often it does not.

EVM Criterion # 22:
At least on a monthly basis, generate the following information at the control account and other levels as necessary for management control using actual cost data from, or reconcilable with, the accounting system:

1. *Comparison of the amount of planned budget and the amount of budget earned for work accomplished. This comparison provides the schedule variance.*
2. *Comparison of the amount of the budget earned and the actual (applied where appropriate) direct costs for the same work. This comparison provides the cost variance.*

This criterion is one that clearly separates Earned Value Management from the traditional approach of measuring cost performance by simply relating the planned costs to the actual costs. Here the requirement is for a monthly (minimum) comparison of project performance at the control account level with a focus on earned value results:

1. Measure the Earned Value achieved less the Planned Value to determine any schedule variance, and . . .
2. Measure the Earned Value achieved less the Actual Costs to determine any cost variance.

While this criterion only specifies a monthly analysis of results, recent experience in industry would suggest a trend towards the weekly measurement of direct labor hour performance. The comparison should be sufficiently detailed to allow for performance measurement by category of direct costs, by external supplier performance, and by organization.

Internal procedures must be in place to require such measurements. If other than Actual Costs from the general ledger are used to report cost performance, there must be a reconciliation with the estimated costs methodology. Potential overruns or underruns of costs should be predictable with compliance of this criterion.

EVM Criterion # 23:

Identify, at least monthly, the significant differences between both planned and actual schedule performance and planned and actual cost performance, and provide the reasons for the variances in the detail needed by program management.

Previously, this criterion only addressed schedule variances, but with the industry rewording of the criteria, variances in cost performance were also added.

Whenever a project exceeds either a schedule variance or a cost variance from a previously set baseline parameter, typically called a variance threshold, the project must automatically perform an analysis to determine why the acceptable tolerances were exceeded. The analysis should assess the types of costs involved—for example, labor, material, and other direct costs—and discuss the reasons for such variances. Typically, a plan for recovery should be developed and the future impact on both the final project's cost and schedule determined.

When the project has major segments of the effort performed by another outside company, contracted or subcontracted, and when the supplier's performance exceeds acceptable parameters, the same analysis of results must be performed on the procured work.

EVM Criterion # 24:

Identify budgeted and applied (or actual) indirect costs at the level and frequency needed by management for effective control, along with the reasons for any significant variances.

This criterion requires that a contractor perform an analysis of any variances of indirect expenses against the original budget. The analysis must cover the types of costs involved, and the indirect pool or pools involved, as may be appropriate.

Indirect expenses are applied as a percentage value against a direct cost base. Actual indirect rates experienced may vary from what was originally planned for two principal reasons:

1. Because actual indirect expenses change upward or downward from the original budgeted amounts, or . . .
2. Because the direct business base over which the indirect costs are allocated change upward or downward, resulting in a higher or lower allocation to a given project.

The changes of primary concern to project management are <u>increased</u> indirect expenses over those originally planned, or a <u>smaller</u> direct base over which to absorb such costs. In either case, the result will be increased indirect costs applied against a given project. This criterion also requires that some management action be taken in response to adverse changes in the indirect rates.

EVM Criterion # 25:

Summarize the data elements and associated variances through the program organization and/or work breakdown structure to support management needs and any customer reporting specified in the contract.

Projects are typically required to analyze all significant variances at the control account level. However, projects may not be required to formally report all variances to the customer. Rather, formal customer reporting usually takes place at higher level of the WBS and at a higher organizational unit.

This approach gives the project some flexibility in managing effort. Many variances that occur at the control account level are never actually reported to the customer or senior management, simply because there are offsetting variances at the same levels of the WBS or OBS. Through corrective actions, projects are often able to bring variances back to acceptable levels without the involvement by the customer or senior management. There is nothing inherently wrong with this concept, and it does give project managers the opportunity to manage their work without undue external involvement.

This criterion requires that a project have the capability of summarizing variances upward through the WBS, or horizontally by organization unit. Also, there must be consistency in what is being reported to the customer, versus that which is reported internally to senior management: only one set of books on any project.

EVM Criterion # 26:

Implement managerial actions taken as the result of earned value information.

This criterion addresses the issue of whether earned value performance data is being used by management throughout the organization. It requires that there be a procedure in effect that initiates corrective actions whenever established cost or schedule performance parameters have been penetrated.

Variance thresholds may be set at a number of monitoring points, reflecting either positive or negative values. Some projects will set a combination of variance points that trigger management action. Variances either over or under a given threshold can indicate either a performance problem, or sometimes simply a problem with the authorized baseline plan. Positive variances are often set at a greater value than negative variances, sometimes twice the value, simply because they often represent questionable planning, rather than poor performance.

EVM Criterion # 27:

Develop revised estimates of cost at completion based on performance to date, commitment values for material, and estimates of future conditions. Compare this information with the performance measurement baseline to identify variances at completion that are important to company management, and any applicable customer reporting requirements, including statements of funding requirements.

A key issue for all projects is how much it will cost to complete the total project, typically referred to as the estimate at completion or EAC. Likely, this is precisely why many projects elect to employ Earned Value Management, to require a timely and accurate forecast of the total funds needed to complete the project. If it is going to cost more than management has authorized to complete a given job, management deserves to know this fact as early as possible. Management may elect to not complete a given project and use the remaining funds elsewhere.

Some project managers have been known to put a positive spin on their actual performance results, and perhaps mislead management into unrealistic expectations of the final bill. At other times, it may be senior managers who will insist on ignoring the actual performance results, and direct the project manager to make overruns "go away." Call it being optimistic, unrealistic, misrepresenting the facts, whatever, some firms have established a reputation for themselves of consistently making poor projections of the total funding requirements. This is often the case when they are working under cost-reimbursable contracts. Therefore, an essential ingredient in any management control system must be the capability of making accurate and timely forecasts of the final costs on jobs.

This criterion requires that EACs be performed routinely based on actual performance to date and a reasonable assessment of the work to complete all unfinished work. Such estimates to complete must relate to the current authorized statement of work, and are best supported by bottom-up estimates of the remaining tasks.

Because of their magnitude on the total costs, overhead or indirect costs are also an essential part of any accurate EAC, even though indirect costs will be beyond the control of any given project manager. Historical performance of indirect pools should be considered while forecasting the EAC. Many of the overhead cost items are essentially amortized fixed assets—for example an administration building—and such costs will not change even though there may be a major drop of direct bases.

A number of issues will pertain to the EAC preparations that can be best handled through documented internal procedures. For example, the frequency with which EACs must be prepared is an important issue best determined with documented procedures.

○ ○ ○

GROUP 5—REVISIONS CRITERIA (FIVE)

Purpose of the Revisions Criteria:
- Require the management of all changes to the approved project baseline.
- Require the timely approval or rejection, and the incorporation of approved changes.

Problems with the Revisions Criteria:
- Work done by the functions without approval of the project manager.
- Slow incorporation of changes into the baseline.
- Poor or no estimates for scope changes.

This last of the five groups of criteria deals with the control of revisions to the approved project baseline. All changes to the approved baseline must be aggressively managed and either approved or rejected in a timely fashion. The quickest way to lose the capability of measuring project performance is to ignore changes and work to an obsolete baseline. All such changes to the original baseline must be documented and be traceable back to the original approved baseline.

Changes to a baseline often result from two primary sources: external customer direction, or internal management ideas. No project of any magnitude ever runs its full course without encountering some change, and it is incumbent upon a project manager to dispose of all changes in an orderly and documented manner.

Difficulties often arise in the management and incorporation of project changes. Often new out-of-scope work is performed without proper authorization, and subsequent approval for the changes never comes. Actual costs are sometimes incurred without commensurate budget. Often the change approval process is:

EVM Criterion # 28:
Incorporate authorized changes in a timely manner, recording the effects of such changes in budgets and schedules. In the directed effort prior to negotiation of a change, base such revisions on the amount estimated and budgeted to the program organizations.

All projects encounter changes both from external and internal sources. In order to maintain a relationship between the work authorized and the actual physical work being performed, a project must incorporate approved changes into budgets in a timely manner.

Just what constitutes "timely" is a debatable question. In some cases, "timely" could represent minutes, as when stopping work for a safety issue. In other situations, "timely" might allow for days or weeks to pass before incorporation. The outer limit of "timely" would likely be dictated by the project's reporting cycle to management.

There must be consistency on what is being reported, and what is being actually worked.

Changes to the working budgets and schedules must be accommodated in an expeditious manner and reflected in the project's baseline. Work that has been authorized but not negotiated with the customer must be folded into the project baseline based on an estimated value of the new work, and, once negotiated, adjusted to reflect the final settlement with the customer. Newly authorized but unpriced work must be planned and controlled as with all definitized work.

EVM Criterion # 29:

Reconcile current budgets to prior budgets in terms of changes to the authorized work and internal replanning in the detail needed by management for effective control.

This criterion requires the traceability of all changes currently being worked back to the original project baseline. Because earned value baselines are constructed from bottoms-up detail, this requirement is satisfied by providing traceability down to the lowest level of the project WBS.

EVM Criterion # 30:

Control retroactive changes to records pertaining to work performed that would change previously reported amounts for Actual Costs, Earned Value, or budgets. Adjustments should be made only for correction of errors, routine accounting adjustments, effects of customer or management directed changes, or to improve the baseline integrity and accuracy of performance measurement data.

Earned Value Management requires discipline from the performing organization. Measurement of project performance must be objective to the greatest extent possible. If "after the fact" changes to the Planned Value, Earned Value, or Actual Costs can be made, the temptation to manipulate the report card will exist. This criterion prevents the indiscriminate altering of past period data, without a documented justification, and includes both direct and indirect costs.

An exception to this rule may be to allow the correction of errors in calculations, and correction of legitimate routine accounting adjustments. In each case, such adjustments should be documented by the person making those changes.

EVM Criterion # 31:

Prevent revisions to the program budget except for authorized changes.

A project's total baseline will be comprised of that effort which has been authorized in formal budgets, plus any management reserve held by the project manager. Management reserve is typically expected to be consumed during the course of project performance.

Sometimes a project will experience difficulties in staying within the total limits of its authorized funds and, after careful analysis of the work remaining, may determine that it would make no sense to continue to measure progress against unattainable cost goals. When such conditions occur, this criterion permits the contractor to budget the remaining work greater than the project baseline, but only with strict approval of senior management or the customer on cost-reimbursable contracts.

The project must have procedures that prevent proceeding with any altered baseline until approval is received from senior management.

EVM Criterion # 32:
Document changes to the performance measurement baseline.

Maintenance of the approved project baseline is fundamental to Earned Value Management. This criterion requires that the project have in place the necessary procedures to preclude unauthorized changes to the project baseline, and that all such changes be traceable back to the original baseline.

GLOSSARY OF EARNED VALUE
PROJECT MANAGEMENT TERMS

A Guide to the Project Management Body of Knowledge (PMBOK® Guide): An official publication of the Project Management Institute (PMI), a basic reference and the world's de facto standard for the project management profession.

Activity: Effort that occurs over time and generally consumes resources, sometimes also called a "task."

Actual Cost: As used in a typical business setting, the actual costs recorded on the books, expended and sometimes incurred, against a given project.

 As used with Earned Value Management, the costs actually expended and or incurred that relate to the project's budgeted costs. Since these costs must relate to the budgeted costs, they must be in the same format as the budget, which will sometimes cover direct labor hours only, direct labor costs, all direct costs, sometimes burdens, and sometimes profits. Actual Costs employing Earned Value must relate by category to the budgeted costs.

Actual Cost of Work Performed (ACWP): The total costs incurred in accomplishing the work performed. *See "Actual Cost."*

Actual Direct Costs: Those costs specifically identified with a specific contract or a project, based upon the contractor's cost identification and accumulation system. *See "Direct Costs."*

ACWP: See "Actual Costs of Work Performed."

Advanced Material Release (AMR): A document sometimes used by organizations to initiate the purchase of long-lead-time or time-critical materials prior to the final release of a design.

American National Standards Institute/Electronic Industries Association 748 (ANSI-EIE 748): The document representing the industry rewrite of the original thirty-five (35) Cost/Schedule Control Systems Criteria. ANSI/EIA 748 Standard was issued in July 1998 and consists of 32 criteria.

Applied Direct Costs: The actual direct costs recognized in the time period associated with the consumption of labor, material, and other direct resources, without regard to the date of commitment or the date of payment.

Apportioned Effort: Apportioned is one of the three approved methods to measure earned value performance (discrete, apportioned, level of effort). Apportioned work measures the performance of another specifically related task, called a base task, and assumes that the performance of the base task represents the same performance results as the apportioned task.

215

Authorized Unpriced Work (AUW): Any scope change for which authorization to proceed has been given, but the estimated value of the change has not yet determined or negotiated.

Authorized Work: All effort that has been authorized and negotiated, plus any work for which authorization has been given but a negotiated value has not yet been agreed upon.

BAC: See "Budget at Completion."

Bar Chart: *See "Gantt Chart."*

Baseline: The approved time phased project plan. *See also: "Performance Measurement Baseline" and "Contract Budget Base."*

Baseline Review (BR): A customer review conducted to determine with a limited sampling that a contractor is continuing to use the previously approved performance management system and is properly implementing a baseline on the contract or option under review.

Basis of Estimate (BOE): The justification or rationale supporting an estimate of required costs, or request for time in a schedule.

BCWP: See "Budgeted Costs for Work Performed."

BCWS: See "Budgeted Costs for Work Schedules."

Bill of Material (BOM): A complete listing of all parts, raw materials and purchased items that will go into an article showing the quantity required of each item to make the deliverable units.

Booking Rates: The rates used to record estimated actual indirect costs to a project. The overhead booking rates are typically applied to direct labor, materials and other direct costs.

Bottom-Up Cost Estimate: *See "Engineering Cost Estimate."*

BR: See "Baseline Review."

Budget: A fiscal plan of operations for a given period.

Budget at Completion (BAC): The sum of all authorized budgets allocated to a project. It is synonymous with the earned value term, "Performance Measurement Baseline (PMB)." The term BAC can have different meanings from organization to organization depending on what management has authorized for the project: sometimes direct labor hours only, direct labor dollars, other direct costs, burdens, profit, etc. The precise authorized BAC depends on management's expectations.

Budgeted Cost for Work Performed (BCWP): The sum of the authorized work that has been completed, and partially completed, plus management's budget for the completed work. BCWP has been replaced with the term, "Earned Value."

Budgeted Cost for Work Scheduled (BCWS): The sum of the work that has been authorized, plus management's budget for the authorized work. The total of the authorized work equals the Budget at Completion (BAC) The term BCWS has been replaced with the term, "Planned Value."

Budgeting: Time-phased financial requirements.

Burden: Overhead expenses distributed over appropriate direct labor and/or sometimes the material base. *See also "Indirect Cost."*

CA: See "Control Account."

CAM: See "Control Account Manager."

CAP: See "Control Account Plan."

CBB: See "Contract Budget Base."

CFSR: See "Contract Funds Status Report."

Chart of Accounts: Sometimes called "code of accounts." Any numbering system used to place costs into logical categories—for example, labor, materials, travel, indirect, etc. A project's chart of accounts is typically based on the corporate chart of accounts.

Code of Accounts: A numbering system often used to identify unique elements of the project's work breakdown structure (WBS).

Commitment: A binding financial obligation, often taking the form of a purchase order.

Compliance Evaluation Review (CER): A new term that has replaced the earlier term, "Demonstration Review (DR)." The CER is the initial formal review of a contractor's management control system and the process to determine whether or not it satisfies the requirements of the Earned Value Management system criteria.

Concurrent Engineering: An approach to the development of new products with the use of multi-functional teams, working in unison from the initial concept until completion of the product. This process is sometimes called "multi-functional teams" or "integrated product development teams."

Contingency Funds: *See "Management Reserve."*

Contract Budget Base (CBB): The negotiated contract cost value, plus the estimated value of authorized but unpriced work.

Contract Funds Status Report (CFSR): A U.S. Government financial report that provides forecast contract-funding requirements.

Contract (formerly Cost) Performance Report (CPR): A monthly formal contract cost report generated by the performing contractor to reflect earned value cost and schedule status information for management.

Contract Target Cost (CTC): The negotiated target costs without fee for the original definitized contract and all contractual changes that have been definitized, but excluding the estimated cost of any authorized but unpriced changes.

Contract Target Price (CTP): The negotiated estimated contract costs, including profit or fee.

Contract Work Breakdown Structure (CWBS): A customer-prepared breakout or subdivision of a project, typically down to WBS level 3 which: (1) subdivides the project into all its major hardware, software, and service elements; (2) integrates the customer and contractor effort; and (3) provides a framework for the planning, control and reporting of the project.

Contractor Cost Data Report (CCDR): A DOD report developed to provide actual contract cost and related data in a standardized format.

Control Account (CA): A management control point or subproject where earned value measurement will take place. It is synonymous with the earlier term, "cost account."

    A point representing the intersection of the Work Breakdown Structure (WBS) and Organizational Breakdown Structure (OBS) at which functional responsibility for work is assigned. Control accounts are the point for the integration of scope, cost, and schedule.

Control Account Manager (CAM): A member of a project, often assigned to the project by a functional organization, who is responsible for performance of a control account, and for the management of resources necessary to accomplish such work.

Control Account Plan (CAP): A management control unit or subproject in which earned value performance measurement will take place. Was formerly called a "Cost Account Plan."

Cost Control: Any process of keeping costs within the bounds of budgets or standards based upon work actually performed.

Cost Element: A unit of costs typically in the form of direct labor, direct materials, other direct costs, and indirect or burden costs.

Cost Estimate: The expected costs to perform a task internally or to acquire an item from an outside source. Cost estimates may be expressed as a single value, or represent a range of values.

Cost Incurred: Costs identified through the use of the accrued method of accounting, or costs actually paid. Such costs will typically include direct labor, direct materials, and all allowable indirect costs.

Cost Overrun: The amount by which a project exceeds, or expects to exceed, the authorized costs.

Cost Performance Index (CPI): The cost efficiency factor representing the relationship between the physical work performed plus management's budget for the completed work (the Earned Value), divided by the Actual Costs expended and/or incurred to complete such work. The CPI is likely the most critical metric provided by Earned Value Management. Formula: Earned Value divided by Actual Costs.

Cost Reimbursement Type Contracts: A category of contracts based on payments to a contractor for all allowable costs, normally requiring only a "best efforts" performance standard from the contractor. Risks for all cost growth over the estimated value rests with the project owner.

Cost/Schedule Control Systems Criteria (C/SCSC): Thirty-five defined performance standards that had to be met by private contractors in order to insure the government that cost-reimbursable and incentive-type contracts were being properly managed. The (35) C/SCSC were issued in 1967, but were superseded in 1996 by the (32) Earned Value Management System Criteria, and later the ANSI/EIA Standard 748 in 1998.

Cost/Schedule Planning and Control Specification (C/SPCS): The United States Air Force initiative in the mid-1960s that later became the C/SCSC.

Cost/Schedule Status Report (C/SSR): The low-end cost and schedule earned value report generally imposed on smaller contracts, those not warranting full C/SCSC compliance.

Cost to Complete Forecast: A time-phased forecast for the completion of all project work. It is typically synonymous with "Estimate to Complete."

Cost Variance (CV): The numerical difference between the Earned Value less the Actual Costs.

CPI: See "Cost Performance Index."

Critical Path: A connected series of tasks in a network schedule representing the longest duration for a project. Any slippage of tasks along the critical path increases the duration of a project.

Critical Path Method (CPM): A project scheduling technique that uses a logic network to predict final project duration by managing those sequences of activities that have the longest duration to accomplish, thus representing the shortest completion date for the project.

Critical Subcontractor: A contractor or supplier performing a decisive portion of a project generally requiring close oversight, control, and reporting. Critical subcontractors are sometimes designated as a result of customer or management direction.

CTC: See "Contract Target Cost."

CTP: See "Contract Target Price."

CV: See "Cost Variance."

CWBS: See "Contractor Work Breakdown Structure."

Deliverable: Any measurable, tangible, verifiable effort produced on a project. Project deliverables are often given a weighted value and are used to measure discrete earned value performance.

Demonstration Review (DR): A former term that has been replaced by a new term, "Compliance Evaluation Review (CER)." The DR was the initial formal review of a contractor's management control system and processes to determine whether or not they satisfied the requirements of the earned value management system criteria.

Direct Costs: Those costs, labor, material, and other direct costs (e.g., travel) that can be consistently related to work performed on a particular project. Direct costs are best contrasted with indirect costs that cannot be identified to a specific project.

Discrete Effort: Discrete is one of the three approved methods to measure earned value performance (discrete, apportioned, level of effort). Discrete tasks will have a specific measurable end product or end result. Discrete tasks are ideal for earned value measurement, and are the preferred method.

Discrete Milestone: A milestone that has a definite scheduled occurrence in time, signaling the start and finish of an activity. Synonymous with the term "Objective Indicator."

EAC: See "Estimate at Completion."

Earned Hours: The time in standard hours credited to work as a result of the completion of a given task or a group of tasks.

Earned Value (EV): The authorized work physically accomplished, plus management's budget for the completed work. Earned Value and percent complete are synonymous terms.

Earned Value Management (EVM) System: See "Earned Value Project Management."

Earned Value Project Management (EVPM): A project management technique that focuses on the completion of authorized work and its authorized budget, called the "Earned Value," for the purpose of monitoring performance and predicting the final required costs and time necessary to finish the project.

Engineering Cost Estimate: A detailed cost estimate of the work and related burdens, usually made by the industrial engineering or the price/cost estimating groups.

Estimate at Completion (EAC): A forecast value expressed in either dollars and/or hours, to represent the projected final costs of a project when all work is completed. The EAC equals the Actual Costs incurred, as well as liabilities, plus the estimated costs for completing all the remaining project work.

Estimate to Complete (ETC): Forecasts that are expressed in either dollars or hours, developed to represent the value of the work remaining to complete a task or a project.

ETC: See "Estimate to Complete."

Event: Something that happens at a point or a moment in time. A significant event is often called a "milestone."

Expenditure: A charge against available funds, evidenced by a voucher, claim, or other documents. Expenditures represent the actual payment of funds.

Fast Tracking: An attempt to shorten a project's duration by overlapping separate activities normally done sequentially; for example, design and then manufacturing. Fast tracking typically adds risks to a project, and is not considered to be a "project teams" or "concurrent engineering" approach.

Fixed-Price Contracts: A category of contracts based on the establishment of firm legal commitments to complete the required work. A performing contractor is legally obligated to finish the job, no matter how much it costs to complete. Risks of all cost growth thus rest on the performing sellers.

Formal Reprogramming: *See "Reprogramming."*

Front Loading: An attempt by a performing contractor to provide adequate budgets for the short-term work, but at the expense of the later-periods' efforts, which are left underfunded. It is an attempt to delay the acknowledgment of a potential cost overrun, in the hope that the contractor may "get well" through changes in the contract statement of work. Front loading often results from severe competition with inadequate or unrealistic negotiated contract target costs.

Funding Profile: A time-phased estimate of funding requirements.

Gantt Chart: A schedule display named after Henry Lawrence Gantt. Likely the most common scheduling display, graphically portraying tasks over a time scale, frequently also called a "bar chart."

General and Administrative (G&A) Expenses: A category of indirect expenses incurred for the administration of a company, typically covering senior executive expenses and corporate headquarters. Such expenses are typically spread over the total direct and burden costs for the organization.

IBR: See "Integrated Baseline Review."

Independent Cost Analysis: An analysis of project cost estimates conducted by an impartial body, not directly associated with the project.

Independent Cost Estimates: An independent estimate of required project costs developed outside the normal channels, to give senior management assurances that they are authorizing reasonable costs for a given project.

Indirect Cost: Resources expended that are not directly identifiable to any specific project or contract. These costs are, thus, allocated over projects based on a formula, typically applied to direct labor costs.

Indirect Cost Pools: A categorical grouping of indirect costs; for example, engineering, manufacturing, test, etc.

Integrated Baseline Review (IBR): A form of earned value process verification in which the technical project management staff leads the effort to verify that the entire project baseline has been budgeted with realistic values to accomplish all the planned work. The IBR is intended to expose the front-loading of baselines.

Integrated Product Development Team (IPDT): The development of new products with use of multi-functional teams, who work in unison from the conceptual start until completion of the product. IPDTs are sometimes also called "concurrent engineering," and are best contrasted with the traditional form of sequential functional development.

Internal Replanning: Replanning actions performed by the project for any remaining effort within approved project scope.

IPDT: See "Integrated Product Development Team."

Labor Rate Variances: Difference between planned labor rates and actual labor rates.

Latest Revised Estimate (LRE): *See "Estimate at Completion."*

Level of Effort (LOE): LOE is one of the three approved methods to measure earned value performance (discrete, apportioned, level of effort). LOE represents work that does not result in a final product. Examples are field engineering, liaison, coordination, follow-up, or other support activities that are not associated with a definable end product. LOE simply measures the passage of time. LOE is the least desirable method of measuring Earned Value.

LOE: See "Level of Effort."

LRE: Latest Revised Estimate, *see "Estimate at Completion."*

Make or Buy: The classification of project scope as to whether it will be performed by the project's organization (make work) or procured from an outside company (buy work).

Management by Exception: A management technique that focuses on performance that falls outside of a predetermined baseline.

Management Reserve (MR): A portion of the total project budget that is set aside and typically controlled by the project manager to cover the unplanned problems likely to occur, but that cannot be defined in advance. Sometimes also called "contingency funds," MR budget is in addition to the project's Performance Measurement Baseline.

Management Reserve Budget: *See "Management Reserve."*

Master Project Schedule (MPS): Typically, the highest summary-level schedule for a project, depicting the overall phasing and all major interfaces, critical milestones, and key elements.

Material: Property which may be incorporated into or attached to an end item to be delivered on a project or which may be consumed or expended in the performance of the effort. It includes, but is not limited to, raw and processed materials, parts, components, assemblies, fuels and lubricants, small tools and supplies which may be consumed in normal use in the performance of a project.

Material Requirements Planning (MRP): An automated procurement system that uses the bill of material to define requirements, less actual inventory records, and the master project schedule to calculate purchasing requirements for materials.

Milestone: An event of particular importance (i.e., a "big event").

MPS: See "Master Project Schedule."

MR: See "Management Reserve."

Multi-Functional Project Team: *See either "Concurrent Engineering" or "Integrated Product Development Team."*

Negotiated Contract Cost: The estimated costs negotiated in a cost-reimbursable-type contract, or the negotiated contract target costs in either a fixed-price incentive contract or a cost-plus incentive fee contract. *See also "Contract Target Cost."*

Network Schedule: A logic flow diagram consisting of the activities and events that must be accomplished in order to reach project objectives, which show their planned sequence, interrelationships, and constraints.

Non-Recurring Costs: Resources that are expended against tasks expected to occur only once on a given project cycle, as contrasted with costs that will occur over and over as the product is subsequently manufactured. Examples are such items as design, qualification testing, and initial tooling.

Objective Indicator: Earned value performance measurement by monitoring tangible deliverables, considered to be the most desirable form of measurement. *See also "Discrete Milestone."*

OBS: See "Organizational Breakdown Structure."

ODC: See "Other Direct Costs."

Organizational Breakdown Structure (OBS): A functionally-oriented organizational hierarchy used as the framework for the assignment of project task performance responsibilities.

Original Budget: The initial budget established at or near the time a project is authorized, based on management's authorization or the negotiated contract costs.

OTB: See "Over Target Baseline."

Other Direct Costs (ODC): A category of accounting elements that can be isolated to specific tasks, other than labor and material items. Typically included in ODC are such items as travel, computer time, and direct supporting services.

Over Target Baseline (OTB): A project baseline that results from the acknowledgement of an overrun, and actually incorporates the forecast overrun into the performance baseline for the remainder of the work. OTBs should be used only with the approval of senior management and the customer.

Overhead: Costs incurred in the operation of a business that cannot be directly related to the individual products, projects or services being produced. *See also "Indirect Cost."*

Overrun: Costs incurred in excess of the project target costs on a cost- or incentive-type contract, or the estimated costs value on a fixed price contract. An overrun is that value of costs needed to complete a project, over the value originally authorized by management.

PAR: See "Problem Analysis Report."

Percent Complete: A measured estimate, typically expressed as a percentage, of the amount of work completed on a total project, or on specific tasks within the project. Percent complete estimates are often used to measure discrete earned value performance, but in a subjective manner.

Performance Measurement Baseline (PMB): On earned value projects, the PMB is a time-phased budget plan against which project performance will be measured. It is formed by the summation of the budgets assigned to Control Account Plans (CAPs), plus their applicable indirect budgets. For future effort, not planned to the control account level, the Performance Measurement Baseline also includes budgets assigned to higher-level WBS elements. The PMB should not include any management or contingency reserves, which are controlled budgets above the PMB.

Performing Organization: The organizational unit responsible for the performance and the management of resources to accomplish a task.

Period of Performance: The time interval of project performance that includes the effort required to achieve all significant project deliverables and schedule milestones.

Planned Value (PV): The baseline measurement plan for an earned value project. The sum of the budgets for all authorized work, scheduled to be accomplished within a given time period. The Planned Value consists of the authorized work and authorized budget for the work. Previously called the "Budgeted Costs for Work Scheduled." The sum of all PV equals the Budget at Completion (BAC).

Planned Value for Work Accomplished (PVWA): An early term used to represent "BCWP" and now "Earned Value."

Planned Value for Work Scheduled (PVWS): An early term used to represent "BCWS" and now "Planned Value."

Planning Package: A logical aggregation of long-term work within a Control Account Plan that can be identified and budgeted, but is not yet defined into specific work packages. Planning packages are usually identified during the initial baseline planning to establish the time-phasing of the major activities within a control account and the quantity of resources required for their performance. Planning packages will be subsequently placed into detailed work packages consistent with the rolling wave concept prior to the start of performance of the authorized work.

PMB: See "Performance Measurement Baseline."

PMBOK® Guide: *See "A Guide to the Project Management Body of Knowledge."*

Portfolio: Typically, a logical grouping of related projects, sometimes called a "program," to facilitate the management of a business unit. The term "portfolio" often has different meanings in various organizations.

Price Variance (PV): The numerical difference between the costs budgeted for a purchased item and the costs actually paid or committed for the item.

Problem Analysis Report (PAR): A narrative report made by the responsible control account manager (CAM) to explain a significant cost or schedule variance, its probable impact on the project, and the corrective actions to be taken to resolve the problem(s).

Program: Typically, an organizational unit made up of the grouping of related projects, often a business unit, sometimes also called a "portfolio." Whereas projects are one-time-only, programs continue over time until the business objectives are met.

Progress Payments: Payments made to a seller during the life of a fixed-price-type contract on the basis of some agreed-to formula. Such formulas can be: percentage of work completed, as typically used in construction; or simply on costs incurred, as with most government contracting. Performance-based payments are a form of progress payments.

Project: A one-time-only endeavor, to satisfy a specific statement of work, meeting all deliverables, within a specific start-to-stop time frame, typically with finite resources.

Project Charter: A formal document prepared by a project, and authorized by senior functional management, that describes the approach to be employed in the management of a particular project. The charter often is used to give organizational authority to a project manager.

Project Cost Base: *See "Contract Budget Base."*

Project Cost Management: A subset of project management that covers the processes required to improve the chances of performing a project within the authorized budget of management. It consists of planning, resource estimating, formal budgeting, and cost control. Earned value performance measurement and forecasting the final costs based on such performance should also be a part of cost management.

Project Management Institute (PMI): The Project Management Institute, with over 190,000 members worldwide, is the leading professional association dealing in the discipline of the management of projects.

Project Manager: An individual who has been assigned responsibility (and, hopefully, commensurate authority) for accomplishing a specific unit of work. The project manager is typically responsible for the planning, implementing, controlling, and reporting of status on a particular project.

Project Risk Analysis: An analysis of identified project risks as to their potential impact on cost, schedule, and technical performance.

Project Teams: *See either "Concurrent Engineering" or "Integrated Product Development Teams."*

PV: See "Price Variance."

PVWA: See "Planned Value for Work Accomplished."

PVWS: See "Planned Value for Work Scheduled."

Recurring Costs: Expenditures against specific tasks that would occur on a repetitive basis in a production run. Examples of these costs would be production labor, materials and equipment, and tool maintenance.

Replanning: A change in the original project plan for accomplishing authorized requirements. There are two types of replanning efforts: "internal" replanning, which is any change in the original plan that remains within the scope of the authorized contract, typically caused by a need to adjust for cost, schedule, or technical problems that have made the original plan unrealistic; or "external" replanning, which are customer-directed changes to a contract in the form of a change order that calls for a modification of the original plan to accommodate the change order.

Reprogramming: A comprehensive replanning of the effort remaining in a project, resulting in a revised total allocated budget, which sometimes exceeds the current contract budget base. Reprogramming is another term for describing an "overrun" condition.

Responsibility Assignment Matrix (RAM): A one-page summary display used to show the relationship of a project's Work Breakdown Structure (WBS) with the specific functional organizations assigned responsibility for performing the project work, typically with use of an Organizational Breakdown Structure (OBS). Usually, the WBS will be displayed along the horizontal axis, and the OBS on the vertical axis.

Responsible Organization: A defined unit within a contractor's organization that is assigned responsibility for accomplishing specific tasks or Control Account Plans.

Rolling Wave Concept: A method to provide a viable long-term project measurement baseline by dividing it into two parts: detail (work package) planning in the near-term, and gross (WBS element) planning in the long-term. As the project performs the short-term work, the long-term gross packages are then planned in specific detail as their period of performance nears. What constitutes short-term versus long-term must be decided by the project manager.

Rubber Baseline: An attempt by a performing organization to take the long-term tasks and move portions of their budgets to the left, into short-term periods, to disguise cost overrun problems. This approach will move budget only, without corresponding work, to mask short-term cost difficulties. It is an indicator of a likely cost overrun condition.

"S"-Shaped Curve: A graphic display of cumulative costs, hours, percentage of work, or other items, plotted over a horizontal time scale, often used to track cost performance for management. Such curves start slowly, accelerate in the middle, then taper off slowly at the end. The "S" curve is considered to be the normal distribution for such work, and represents essentially one-half of a statistical "bell-shaped" curve.

Schedule: A graphic display of planned work.

Schedule Performance Index (SPI): The baseline schedule efficiency factor representing the relationship between the Earned Value achieved, versus the Planned Value. The formula: Earned Value divided by Planned Value.

Schedule Variance (SV): The numerical difference between the Earned Value less the Planned Value.

Scheduling: The act of preparing and/or implementing schedules.

Scope: A definition of the work to be accomplished on a project or procurement.

Scope Creep: The addition of work as a result of poor or incomplete or vague definition of project scope.

SOW: See "Statement of Work."

SPI: See "Schedule Performance Index."

Standard: A term applied in work measurement to any established or accepted rule, model, or criterion against which comparisons are made.

Standard Cost: The normal expected cost of an operation, process, or product, which typically includes labor, material, and sometimes overhead charges, computed on the basis of past performance costs, estimates, or work measurement.

Standard Time: The amount of time allowed for the performance of a specific unit of work.

Statement of Work (SOW): A description of a product or service to be procured under a project; a statement of requirements.

Subcontract: A contractual document that legally defines the effort of providing services, data, or other hardware, from one firm to another firm.

Summary Level Variance Analysis Reporting (SLVAR): The analysis of performance variances from a plan, done at a summary level by the amalgamation of related control accounts with homogeneous effort, and a description of the common problems causing such variances.

Surveillance: A term used in earned value oversight to mean the monitoring of continued compliance with an approved and validated management control system.

SV: See "Schedule Variance."

Target Cost : *See "Contract Target Cost" and or "Contract Budget Base."*

Task: Also called "an activity," something that takes place over a period of time, generally consuming resources.

TCPI: See "To-Complete Performance Index."

Teams: *See either "Concurrent Engineering" or "Integrated Product Development Team."*

Thresholds: Monetary, temporal, or resource values used as outside parameters, which, if breached, will cause some type of management action to occur.

To-Complete Performance Index (TCPI): The forecast future performance levels, expressed as a CPI, which must be achieved on all remaining work in order to meet some financial goal as set by management. The financial goals are typically two: (1) management's current authorized budget, and (2) the project manager's current estimate at completion.

Total Allocated Budget (TAB): Sometimes also called the "Project Cost Base," it is the sum of all budgets allocated to a project. The TAB consists of the performance measurement baseline (PMB) plus any management or contingency reserves. The TAB will relate directly to the Contract Budget Base.

UB: See "Undistributed Budget."

Undistributed Budget (UB): Temporary budgeted values for authorized work not yet negotiated, or changes in the far term, which cannot at present be identified to specific Control Account Plans, but that must be time-phased and allocated to specific WBS elements in order to maintain a viable performance measurement baseline.

Unit Cost: Total labor, material, and overhead costs for one unit of production; that is, one component, one part, one gallon, one pound, etc.

Unpriced Changes: Authorized, but unpriced, unnegotiated changes to the contract.

Usage: The number of physical units of an inventory item, components, assemblies, consumed over a period of time.

Usage Variance (UV): The numerical difference between the budgeted quantity of materials, and the quantity actually used.

UV: See "Usage Variance."

VAC: See "Variance at Completion."

Validation: A term used in Earned Value to mean the "approval" or compliance with the criteria.

Variable Cost: A cost that changes upward or downward with the production quantity or the performance of services. Variable costs are best contrasted with fixed costs that do not change with a production quantity or services performed.

Variance: The difference between the expected or budgeted or planned values and the actual results.

Variance at Completion (VAC): Any numerical difference between Budget at Completion (BAC) and the latest Estimate at Completion (EAC).

Variance Threshold: The amount of a variance that will require a formal Problem Analysis Report, as agreed to between the performing project and the customer or management. Variance parameters will differ by project, depending on the function, level, and stage of the project.

WBS: See "Work Breakdown Structure."

What-If Analysis: The process of evaluating the impact of alternative strategies.

Work Breakdown Structure (WBS): A deliverable-oriented family tree display of the hardware, software, services and project-unique tasks that completely defines, organizes, and graphically portrays the project.

Work Breakdown Structure Dictionary: A narrative document that describes the effort to accomplish all work contained in each WBS element. The WBS Dictionary will often result in the project or contract statement of work (SOW).

Work Breakdown Structure Element: A discrete portion of a WBS at any level. The single WBS element at Level 1 represents the total project. A WBS element may be an identifiable product, a set of data, a service, or any combination.

Work Package (WP): A detailed short-span task, or purchased item, identified by the project at the lowest level of a Work Breakdown Structure element.

Work Package Budgets: Resources that are formally assigned by the project to accomplish a work package, which can be expressed in dollars, hours, standards or any other definitive unit.

Work Team Control Accounts: *See either "Concurrent Engineering" or "Integrated Product Development Team."*

WP: See "Work Package."

INDEX